B 5-

The AK47 Story

The AK47 Story

Evolution of the Kalashnikov Weapons

Edward Clinton Ezell

Stackpole Books

Published by
STACKPOLE BOOKS
Cameron and Kelker Streets
P.O. Box 1831
Harrisburg, PA 17105

First printing, March 1986
First printing (paperback), January 1988

Printed in the United States of America

10   9   8   7   6   5   4   3   2   1

*Front cover: SSG Larry D. Jarrett, Company C, 203rd Military
Intelligence Battalion (Technical Intelligence), wearing a National
Training Center Opposing Force uniform, demonstrates a Soviet
AK47 rifle. (U.S. Army photo by SFC Armando Carrasco)*

Library of Congress Cataloging-in-Publication Data

Ezell, Edward Clinton
    The AK47 story: evolution of the Kalashnikov weapons/Edward
Clinton Ezell.
        p.   cm.
        Includes index.
        ISBN 0-8117-2247-3 (pbk.)
        1. AK-47 rifle.   I. Title.
[UD395.A16E97   1988]   87-26708
355.8′2435 — dc19   CIP

Contents

Acknowledgments

Books such as this one result from the assistance of many people. While it is impossible to thank everyone who has made a contribution—the list would be several pages long and omissions would be inevitable—these acknowledgments will remind a few of the more important contributors of my debt to them.

First and foremost is a gentleman, now deceased, who translated hundreds of pages of Russian language text, thus freeing the author from that laborious but essential task. I first met Alan W. Cooper in the days immediately before Christmas in 1973 while we were both browsing the book shelves at what was then Collets Russian Book Store on Museum Street in London. I had just discovered L. G. Beskrovniy's very significant book, *Russkaya armiya i flot v XIX veke: Voenno-ekonomichesky potensial Rossi,* which had just been published in Moscow.

As I pondered, in a very struggling manner, Beskrovniy's excellent chapter on Russian small arms developments in the nineteenth century, Alan Cooper started up a conversation by stating that this book was an excellent example of technological history. I muttered that I really wanted to read the small arms chapter, but that my limited ability with the Russian language meant that I was in for some long tiring days of translation. Alan then asked me why I was interested in understanding the contents of this particular chapter, and I replied that I was in the initial phase of writing a book on Imperial and Soviet Russian infantry rifles. At that point he volunteered to translate the materials for me. I thanked him for his offer, but told him that I could not afford to hire a translator. Cooper responded that he did not want to be paid, he just wanted the practice. Having made me an offer I could not refuse, we began a friendship that lasted until his death. A former translator for the World War II British military intelligence service, and a retired interior designer for that famous British institution the public house (pub), Alan Cooper's enthusiasm for this project made me keep my word about writing this book. "Thank you" only begins to record my debt to this gentleman.

Two other men who helped keep me honest and headed toward the final goal are Harold E. Johnson, now retired from the US Army Foreign Science and Technology Center, Charlottesville, Virginia; and Herbert J. Woodend, Custodian (Curator) of the Pattern Room small arms collection at the Royal Small Arms Factory, Enfield (now Royal Ordnance Small Arms Public Limited Corporation). Hal and Herb took turns patiently answering long lists of questions, both provided insights, and either one could have written a book on this same subject. That they continued to help me over a dozen years in writing my book indicates some measure of their generosity and friendship.

Within the limits of their system, the Soviets were reasonably helpful. As a shot in the dark back in 1972, I wrote to Mikhail Timofeyevich Kalashnikov requesting information about his career. About thirteen months passed, and then one day a letter with an autographed photograph appeared in the mail. While playing down his personal importance within the scheme of Soviet military technology, Kalashnikov referred me to two very useful biographical publications—an article about him in the *Great Soviet Encyclopedia* and a book-length biography entitled *Vtoroe rozhdenie* (Second birth) by V. Zhukov, published in 1963 by the Military Publishing House of the Ministry of

Defense as part of its "Soviet Hero" series. The *Great Soviet Encyclopedia* article was short but significant because it identified an extremely important 1967 source by D. N. Bolotin entitled "Sovetskoe strelkovoe oruzhie za 50 let" (50 years of Soviet small arms), a Soviet equivalent of a doctoral dissertation, which not only described in archivally documented fashion the history of Soviet infantry weapons developments since 1917, but which also listed the small arms held in the collection of the Voenno-istoricheskogo muzeya artillerii, inzhenernikh voisk i voisk sbyazi (The Military Historical Museum of Artillery, Engineer, and Communications Troops) in Leningrad. An updated version without the arms catalog, entitled *Sovetskoe strelkovoe oruzhie* (Soviet small arms) was published in 1983 by the Military Publishing House of the Ministry of Defense. Taken together, Beskrovniy and Bolotin constitute a basic foundation for this book.

Other specific individuals who deserve recognition include Professor Richard Danik, Queens College, Belfast, Northern Ireland; Colonel John Weeks (deceased); Major Frank W. A. Hobart (deceased); Thomas B. Nelson, TBN Enterprises, Alexandria, Virginia; Samuel Cummings, Interarms, Inc., Monte Carlo, Monaco; and James Kettrick, US Army Foreign Science and Technology Center. Each helped in his own way to move this project along to completion.

Since photographs and other illustrations are essential to telling a story such as this one, photographic and graphic credits need to be presented up front:

J.-J. Buigne and Frederic Proust, Paris: pp. 26, 27.

Anon. *Istoricheskoe opisane odezhdi i vooruzheniya Rossiskhix voisk,*

1825–1855 (Historical account of uniforms and weapons of the Russian service, 1825–1855) (St. Petersburg, 1902): p. 28.

Tower Armories, HM Tower of London, United Kingdom: p. 29.

V. G. Federov, *Evolyutsiya strelkovogo oruzhiya* (Evolution of infantry weapons) (Moscow, 1938): pp. 35, 36 (top), 38, 39, 41, 48 (right), 75, 77, 232.

J. Lenselink, Armamentarium, Delft, Netherlands: p. 36 (bottom).

National Museum of American History, Smithsonian Institution, Washington, D.C.: pp. 41 (left), 64 (left), 67 (left and center), 92, 129, 136, 137, 146, 147, 149, 150, 151, 156, 157.

Eric Long, Office of Photographic and Printing Services, Smithsonian Institution: pp. 136, 137, 146, 147, 149, 150, 151, 156, 157.

John Merchant, Studio M, London: pp. 48 (left), 51, 52.

US Army: pp. 96, 100, 127, 155, 162, 163, 194 (bottom), 201 (top), 213 (left), 217, 218, 221, 223, 224, 225, 226, 233, 234, 235, 237.

US Army, Aberdeen Proving Ground, Aberdeen, Maryland: pp. 53, 64 (right), 115, 116, 144–45.

US Army, Springfield Armory: p. 162.

F. W. Hobart (deceased): pp. 65, 67, 122, 123, 163, 165, 213 (right), 214.

Voenno-istoricheskogo muzeya artillerii, inzhenernikh voisk i voisk sbyazi (The Military Historical Museum of Artillery, Engineer, and Communications Troops), Leningrad, USSR: pp. 70, 87 (right), 109.

Markku Palokangas, Sotamuseo, Helsinki, Finland: pp. 73, 74, 202, 203, 204.

Istoriia velikoi otechestvennoi voiny Sovetskogo Soyuza, 1941–1945 (Moscow, 1960), Vol. 1, p. 272: p. 80.

V. Pasechinkov, Tsentral'niy ordena krasnoi zvesdy muzei vooruzhennikh sil (The Central Order of the Red Star Armaments Museum) Moscow, USSR: pp. 99, 110.

Mikhail Timofeyevich Kalashnikov, Izhvesk Machine Building Factory, Urdmurt, ASSR, USSR: p. 121.

Masami Tokoi, Dusseldorf, West Germany and Tokyo, Japan: pp. 81, 85, 86, 91, 98 (bottom), 113, 114, 131 (right).

Andre Jandot (deceased): p. 92.

Stephen L. Fuller and Wyant Lamont: pp. 97, 98 (top), 101.

Royal Small Arms Factory, Enfield Lock, Middlesex, United Kingdom: p. 131 (left).

Jerry Lee Elmore, Houston, TX: pp. 132, 139, 152 (bottom).

Voennoe minnsterstvo Soyuza SSR, *7.62-mm avtomat kalashnikova (AK) rukovodstvo sluzhiy* (1952): pp. 133, 134, 135, 140, 141, 142, 143, 148, 152 (top), 153, 168, 169, 170, 171, 172, 173, 174.

Minnisterstvo oborniy SSSR, *Nastavelenie po strelkovomy delu 7.62-mm avtomat kalashnikova (AK)* (1967): p. 176.

Minnisterstvo oborniy SSSR, *Nastavelenie po strelkovomy delu 7.62-mm modernizrovanniy avtomat kalashnikova (AKM i AKMS)* (1970): pp. 158, 159, 160, 176.

Minnisterstvo oborniy SSSR, *Nastavelenie po strelkovomy delu 7.62-mm ruchnoi pulemet avtomat kalashnikova (RPK i RPKS)* (1971): pp. 158, 160, 167.

Minnisterstvo oborniy SSSR, *Nastavelenie po strelkovomy delu 7.62-mm pulemet avtomat kalashnikova (PK, PKS, PKB i PKT)* (1971): pp. 219, 220.

Colonel John Weeks (deceased): pp. 178, 179, 222, 241.

Federal Directorate of Supply and Procurement, Belgrade, Yugoslavia: pp. 195, 196–99, 200 (top), 238, 239, 240.

Richard G. Smith, Belleville, Michigan: p. 200 (bottom).

Valmet Defence Group, Helsinki, Finland: p. 205.

Israeli Military Industries, Tel Aviv, Israel: pp. 206, 207, 208.

Steyr-Daimler-Puch, Steyr, Austria: pp. 209, 210.

China North Industries, Beijing, China: p. 236.

COL Martin Fackler, M.D., Wound Ballistics Lab, Letterman Army Research Center, Presidio of San Francisco, California: pp. 242, 243, 244 (top), 245.

Despite all the help that I have received, I alone am responsible for the interpretations and conclusions contained in this book. I have attempted to discuss a murky topic clearly, but there has been some guesswork involved. Where I have reached for insights and drawn conclusions without a firm documentary footing, I have indicated that fact to the reader. I hope the reader will enjoy the story of the AK47 and of its predecessors and successors.

Woodbridge, Virginia
June 1985

Introduction
Who Is Kalashnikov?

The grey dawn was filtering through the windows, but still sleep would not come. There was a gnawing pain in the shoulder where it had been hit by a shell splinter. Now and then the silence in the hospital ward was broken by a groan or muffled cry. Senior Sergeant Mikhail Kalashnikov thought of the bitter autumn of the war when he and his T34 tank had been part of the forces fighting General Guderian's armored hordes. . . . During one of the battles the sergeant had opened the hatch and looked around. A blinding flame flashed nearby. Something stabbed him in the shoulder and he felt himself losing consciousness.[1]

Who is the Kalashnikov of this tale? His name has become known the world over because of the Kalashnikov assault rifle he created. The AK47 assault rifle, and its many variants, has become the most widely distributed and best known military shoulder weapon of the post–World War II era. Some people might argue that the United States Army's M16 rifle deserves that title. But it is the Kalashnikov that is seen nightly on the evening television news from Beirut, the Iranian desert, the jungles of El Salvador, or the mountains of Afghanistan. Young children and old men are pictured in the daily newspapers carrying these weapons. The Kalashnikov is at once the symbol of Soviet military prowess, and of revolutionary and reactionary ferment. Based upon the frequency with which the AK47-type weapons show up in the daily newspapers and appear in television news broadcasts, I believe that the Soviet rifle's claim to fame is fully justified. A few additional statistics should help make this point.

An estimated thirty million to fifty million Kalashnikov-type rifles and light machine guns have been manufactured since the introduction of this design in 1947. At least a dozen countries have manufactured or are manufacturing versions of this weapon. At least fifty-five nations and an untallied number of guerrilla and terrorist organizations use these guns daily. It is this almost universal presence of the AK47-type assault rifles that prompted the preparation of this investigation into the origins of the Kalashnikov assault rifles and inquiry into the career of the man who created the weapon.

By examining the Kalashnikov story we can tell more about the manner in which the Soviet armed forces shifted from being dependent upon foreign military weapons designs and manufacturing technology to their current position of self-sufficiency. At the same time, the Soviets have become one of the leading exporters of military hardware. The appearance of the Kalashnikov assault rifles on the world scene was just one sign of the technological coming of age in the Soviet Union. The presence of Soviet tanks and aircraft around the globe make the same statement. The story of Kalashnikov and his weapons is thus a case study that should help answer questions relating to other aspects of the Soviet military-industrial complex.

Who is Mikhail Timofeyevich Kalashnikov? That is one of the most basic questions to be answered. His name has become world famous because of his Avtomat Kalashnikova, but what is known of Kalashnikov—both the man and the designer of small-caliber weapons? This query is prompted in part because of a basic western curiosity about men and activities within the secrecy-shrouded military-industrial complex of the Soviet Union. But it is also the result of a desire to know more about an individual who

has become a technological folk hero for the Soviet people.

Until now there has been very little information published in English about the man who is the leading contemporary designer of small arms in the Union of Soviet Socialist Republics. In addition to the 7.62 x 39mm AK47/AKM/RPK family of light automatic weapons, Kalashnikov has also influenced the design of the 7.62 x 54mmR Dragunov sniping rifle, the 7.62 x 54mmR PK general purpose machine gun, and the 5.45 x 39mm AK74 series. Any individual who can have this impact on the infantry-weapon design process of a major military power must be a personality to be reckoned with.

Pulling together the details of his life has been a detective-like task, given the Soviet interest in secrecy. We are not alone in our interest in this man. Kalashnikov has also been something of an elusive character for his Eastern European comrades. They too have a strong interest in him and his work. Take as an example the following excerpt from an article that appeared in an East German Military publication. The author, M. Novikov, introduced Kalashnikov as follows:

> It wasn't easy to find out his address. Still, after several telephone calls I succeeded and we quickly agreed on an appointment. Then I sat across from him; a middle-aged man of medium height with a full head of hair curling back from his forehead in a jaunty wave. His name is on everyone's lips every day of the week in the Armies of the Warsaw Pact: Mikhail Timofeyevich Kalashnikov, father of the submachine gun which under the nomenclature "Avtomat Kalashnikov" is a familiar object for the mechanized infantryman as it is for the border guard; known by the sentry at the navy pier just as well as by the aircraft mechanic.[2]

In the article that followed, the reader

was presented an interesting mixture of fact and fiction. This appears to be the general case with the Kalashnikov-related biographical materials that have been published to date.[3] Mikhail Timofeyevich, born on 10 November 1919 in Kazakhstan, is usually portrayed as a bright and inventive lad who was conscripted into the Red Army on the eve of World War II. His gun-designing career began while he was recovering from wounds received in a tank battle on the western front in the autumn of 1941. But in typical Soviet fashion, this Russian counterpart of the American Horatio-Alger-type self-made man was, however, dependent upon the skills of his colleagues—comrades—to bring his designs to a successful completion. With the assistance of his technical comrades, he was able to design, perfect, and subsequently improve his first major design, the AK47, in the waning months of the 1939–1945 war.

To explore more fully the career of this interesting man and designer, this book has been arranged into seven chapters. Chapter 1 goes back to the beginning of the nineteenth century and describes the manufacture of infantry shoulder weapons in Imperial Russia from Napoleon's 1812 invasion of Russia to the Russian revolution in 1917. Kalashnikov's career has been shaped by the technological, sociological, and financial environments of Russian/Soviet military enterprise system that has evolved during the last century and a half. Thus, in chapter 1 the general themes of the struggle of the Russian army for military hardware self-sufficiency, especially in small-caliber weapons design, and the related work to establish a reliable domestic capability in the manufacture of such weapons, are explored.

Throughout the nineteenth century, the Russian military establishment faced repeated shortages of infantry weapons. These periodic crises culminated in the major small arms disasters of the First World War.

The revolutionary leaders of the new Soviet state realized at the start of their civil war that they needed to establish a reliable production program for military weapons. That rebuilding process is described in chapter 2, as is the search in the 1920s and 1930s for a self-loading rifle to replace the bolt-action Model 1891 Mosin-Nagant rifle. The result of the high priority given to this field of endeavor was small arms factories capable of meeting the large production requirements for weapons that were made during the 1939–1945 war. The Soviet government's support of its military technologists and engineers also made it possible for the men of the ordnance establishment to field the Tokarev self-loading rifles. But of equal importance is the fact that the small arms manufacturing industry was capable of identifying new talent, and of incorporating younger individuals into the small arms design and manufacturing process.

Kalashnikov was one of the newer generation. In the biographical articles about Kalashnikov, he repeatedly thanks his colleagues for their assistance, and he recognizes the master-student relationship that exists between the technological generations of the Soviet Union. He is ever mindful of the need to serve an apprenticeship—both politically and technologically.

Chapter 3 explores the Soviet search for an assault rifle, the manner in which Kalashnikov and the older generation of small arms designers competed and cooperated, and the fielding of the first version of Kalashnikov's AK47. All of the details of the interpersonal relationships are not available, but enough of the story can be pieced together to indicate that the Soviet small arms designing and manufacturing communities are as complicated in their interactions as they are in the rest of the world. There are competing interests and bureaucratic desires to keep the design bureaus at work.

Evolution of the Kalashnikov assault rifle family is described in chapter 4. Different manufacturing techniques have been used, and the design has been changed and modified accordingly. But equally significant, the Soviets have tended to think in terms of weapon designs that can, over time, be improved, and which can be built upon in such a manner as to create a family of small arms. This concept began with V. G. Federov before World War I, and has been perfected in the post–World War II era by Kalashnikov and his colleagues. This chapter brings the story of Kalashnikov weapons down to the development of the 5.45 x 39mm AK74 version of the Kalashnikov weapons family.

Chapter 5 describes the global spread of the Kalashnikov-type weapons, and shows how the Soviet Union has become in the post-1945 era a major exporter both of military weapons and the manufacturing technology with which to manufacture these weapons.

Chapter 6 examines the different weapons that have emerged from the Kalashnikov design bureau, all of which exploit the basic operating mechanism of the AK47: the 7.62 x 39mm RPK light machine gun, the 7.62 x 54mmR series of PK machine guns, and the 7.62 x 54mmR SVD sniper rifle.

The final chapter summarizes technical information regarding the ammunition used in the Kalashnikov family of small arms.

The reader should be cautioned that nearly all of the historical data that follows is based upon translated materials that have been released by Soviet authorities. Historical studies in the Soviet Union are crafted to serve a political purpose, and few unintentional revelations are made. The Soviets are very careful about revealing military and technological secrets. Thus the data they make available is generally politically motivated and is always closely censored. Although I have made every attempt to present a text that is factually correct, in some cases the internal veracity of the Soviet histories cannot be fully verified. I have had to rely upon the work done by professional Soviet historians, who have themselves written their studies from documents in Soviet historical archives.

Given the nature of Soviet historical writing, the source notes of this book take on a special significance. They record the source of the data chosen for inclusion in this book. In those places where I have some concern for the accuracy of Soviet source materials I will clearly call my questions to the reader's attention. Even if some of the historical interpretation and selection of facts by the Soviet historians betray an ideological bias, it is my hope that this book will provide a useful glimpse inside the world of Soviet weapons design, development, and production. I have not tried to see the development of Soviet small arms through Russian eyes. I write from an American perspective on a Russian evolution of events. This perspective shapes the final story—I hope it does not distort the tale.

It should also be noted that actual Imperial Russian and Soviet weapons have been used as a source material. In several instances surviving weapons have given me a better idea of the historical and technological questions that should be asked. In those places where I have speculated about technological developments based upon my use of weapons as source material, I have noted my conjectures and speculations.

The writing of history is never a completely finished process. There are always new insights to be gained and additional data to be examined. One can choose to write now and take the chance that more material will come to light, or one can opt for waiting until a later day, taking the chance that the writing will remain unfinished. I am taking the chance on being a pioneer. I will be pleased if this book inspires others to examine the Soviet military-technology scene more fully. If they do, then perhaps some of the questions raised in the process of writing this book will be answered in subsequent ones.

1

Imperial Russian Arms Manufacture

The Patriotic War to World War I, 1812–1917

The Soviet small arms industry became self-sufficient during the Second World War (1939–1945). In the four decades following that conflict, the USSR became one of the major sources for infantry weapons. Although great strides have been made since 1917, the foundations of the Soviet small arms enterprise were laid well before the Bolshevik revolution. Though the contributions of early military craftsmen and technicians were often overlooked by tsarist bureaucrats, Soviet historians of military technology have begun to examine the roots of their military industries in an effort to evaluate nineteenth century Russia's military-economic potential.[1] A look at the history of nineteenth century Russian small arms development and production will give Western readers a better idea of the context from which the Soviet arms-design and

manufacturing profession emerged. And men like M. T. Kalashnikov will be easier to understand with this background.

Despite time lags, the development of small arms in Imperial Russia followed the same basic progression it had in other European countries. The Russian military moved from flintlock to percussion lock muskets, from smoothbore to rifled muskets, from single-shot breechloaders to magazine repeating rifles. Although many mid-nineteenth-century designs were of foreign origin, international technological borrowing was the rule rather than the exception in Europe at this time.

For example, while the Americans initially relied upon the British and French for weapon designs (the French Mle. 1763 musket was copied directly by the United States small arms makers for their first standard domestically produced small arm, the US Musket Model 1795), American dependence on foreign technology and manufacturing processes was substantially ended by the middle 1800s. It became Europe's turn to borrow. Military officers from all over the Old World toured Colonel Samuel Colt's factory in Hartford, Connecticut, to see the production of his handguns built on the interchangeable-parts concept. And more important, they purchased manufacturing equipment from American tool-makers who had helped to create the machinery that made it possible to fabricate firearms and other products with completely interchangeable parts. This system of machine tools, jigs, fixtures, and inspection gauges was called the "American System" of manufacturing by its nineteenth century observers.

Russia became through indirect means a user of American-type machine tools by the last quarter of the 1800s, with the result that the Russian small arms factories were capable of mass-producing rifles that would match the quality of infantry weapons made elsewhere in Europe. Russia's main problem was the inability of her factories to meet critical deadlines.

If the Tsar's army was inadequately supplied with infantry weapons when the First World War began, Russian arms designers and production engineers were not wholly responsible. In large measure, the blame lay with the inefficiencies of the Imperial government. Throughout the nineteenth century, there had been numerous unsuccessful efforts to develop a suitable scheme by which the arms factories could be adequately managed. Beyond

this, there was the problem of preserving the serviceability of the arms once they left the factories. But the most telling problem was the huge, never-ending demand for small arms. The massive Imperial military establishment seemed to devour the weapons provided to it.*

Russian small-caliber weapon production figures were enormous compared to those of Great Britain and the United States. Equally astounding were the large numbers of workers involved in the process of fabricating those weapons. While the American armories at Springfield, Massachusetts, and Harpers Ferry, Virginia, and the British armory at Enfield in Middlesex were producing infantry small arms in the thousands, Tula, Izhevsk, and Sestroretsk were producing weapons in the tens of thousands during the first decade of the nineteenth century.

Creation of national centers for weapons production in Imperial Russia paralleled the appearance of state-operated factories in France and preceded the establishment of such facilities in the United States and Great Britain. During the reign of Peter the Great (1682–1725) several steps were taken to raise the level of arms making from the status of a craft dominated by a few skilled foreign gunsmiths to that of a state monopoly that employed thousands of serfs. Peter, with his thirst for military adventure, was among the first monarchs to see the value of government-supported factories for the manufacture of small arms and gunpowder.

Peter took the crucial step, creating the first state manufactory at the traditional center for the metalworking crafts, Tula,

---

*The Imperial armed forces grew from three hundred thousand in 1800 to over five hundred thousand in 1812 to more than one million by 1825. The size of the army varied during the remainder of the century, but the number of men under arms posed a significant burden for the factories responsible for keeping them equipped.

in 1712, during the Russo-Swedish Northern War (1700–1721). A gun factory had been established at Tula (248 kilometers south of Moscow) during the time of Boris Godunov (1598–1605). Later, Mikhail Federovich Romanov (1613–1645) took steps to update Russian domestic capacity for weapons production. Spurred by the 1632–1634 war with Poland, the government sponsored renovation of the armory at the Kremlin and the creation of a new foundry at Tula. Both projects were overseen by Dutch experts. On 15 February 1712, Tsar Peter ordered Count Grigorii Ivanovich Volkonskiy, supervisor of arms production in the Tula region, to take steps for improving the method of arms production. The Count was to locate a site at the gunsmith's village where factories could be erected. If workmen other than Russians were required to staff these factories, then such men should be found and employed. An arms factory was to be built where all artisans would work, and the making of guns in the homes of the artisans was to cease.[2]

State control meant new water-powered machinery and the enserfment of peasants working in the weapons shops. A 1721 decree by the Tsar permitted factory owners of non-noble birth to purchase peasants to work in their private weapons manufactories in the Tula region. This labor pattern continued for the next 154 years.

As originally established, the first new factory building, constructed of stone, contained eight grinding and sharpening lathes for finishing knives and broadswords, and eight boring machines for drilling gun barrels. Production capacity of the Tulskiy Oruzheiny Zavod (Tula Weapons Factory) was supplemented in 1724 by the weapons factory in Sestroretsk, near St. Petersburg. Although

officially founded in 1714, the factory buildings, on the bank of the Sestra river, were not actually built until 1721–24. Construction of the factory was supervised by a Dutch engineer named de Gennin who had previously established and operated the Petrovskiy Zavod (two hundred kilometers northeast of St. Petersburg near Lake Ladoga; sometimes called Olonez Zavod).

When production at Sestroretsk began in 1724, the cost of the first 2,218 weapons was so high that work was suspended temporarily. In 1732, the Petrovskiy factory was closed, and its machines and tools were transferred to Sestroretsk. De Gennin was made the new director of that facility. Between the years 1735 and 1741, the Sestroretsk works fabricated 5,253 shoulder weapons and 44,235 swords. Over the next fourteen years weapons production fluctuated between six hundred and two thousand five hundred firearms per year. Manufacture of new weapons ceased during the forty years from 1756 to 1796. During those decades the factory became a weapons-repair center and the place at which experimentation with new small arms was carried out. An unsuccessful attempt to make muskets with interchangeable components was carried out in the 1790s. Sestroretsk renewed shoulder-weapon manufacture in 1796.

During the years 1805-1807, on the eve of the titanic clash between the Russian and Napoleonic armies, Tsar Alexander I (reign 1801–1825) converted one of the metalworking establishments at Izhevsk into an infantry weapons factory. Izhevsk, in the heart of the Ural mountains, had been an important center for the growing iron industry since the early seventeenth century. The new armory began production of infantry weapons in 1810.

Despite the Russian's head start in the establishment of national weapons factories, their arms industry continued to be heavily dependent upon foreign technology and technicians. Significant innovations—in both weapons design and manufacturing technology—generally came from abroad. The national armories of the United States—Springfield and Harpers Ferry—were authorized in 1794, while the British Royal Armory Mills at Enfield were not established until 1804. Springfield began production in 1795, while Harpers Ferry did not begin sustained performance until 1802. Workers at Enfield concentrated on assembling parts manufactured elsewhere for most of the first half of the nineteenth century. The private gun trade in London and Birmingham continued to be the basic source of British Army infantry weapons until the mechanization of the Enfield factory in 1856.[3]

Soviet historians are quick to point out that Imperial small arms centers were at a distinct disadvantage due to the general industrial backwardness of the Russian economy. It would be easy to overplay this point, since we are considering the early days of industrialization everywhere. Still, Russian industrialization did lag behind the other nations which experienced the Industrial Revolution. While other countries moved toward technological development and innovation during the nineteenth century, in the land of the Tsars industrialization was a continuous struggle politically, economically, and socially. In Imperial Russia, the military was both a source for the encouragement of industrialization and the thwarting of same.[4]

The Arkacheev Era: The First Quarter Century

At the outset of the nineteenth century, Russian infantry regiments carried a variety of flintlock muskets, ranging in caliber from 13mm to 19mm (.51 to .75 caliber).* The weapons that made up this potpourri were in large measure war booty from Swedish and allied forces defeated during the Seven Years War (1756–1763). At the turn of the new century, the Imperial War Ministry (Voennoe ministerstvo) faced a monumental task of reequipping the Army with standardized patterns of weapons. Quantities required were large, and their production placed a strain on the manufacturing resources available.

During the years 1800-1806, the Tula factory alone produced between forty thousand and forty-five thousand shoulder weapons annually. By 1810, the single-year total rose to nearly sixty thousand. Even with a drop in production during 1811 to 48,908, the production figures were still impressive. All the more so since the workers at Tula refurbished and repaired some 9,655 older weapons as well. The Birmingham small arms trade delivered 51,828 weapons in 1805, 186,795 in 1810, and 226,871 in 1811. During the years 1804–1817, the Birmingham Trade averaged 130,500 weapons per year, and the London Trade averaged 60,400.

On 17 August 1812, the state-employed gunsmiths at Tula were ordered to produce seven thousand weapons per month. Private producers were expected to deliver three thousand pieces each month. Most of these were the 17.18mm (.70 caliber) Model 1808 infantry musket. In addition, an average of three thousand weapons

---

*At this time, the Russians reckoned bore diameter in the traditional measure—the *lini*—one *lini* being equivalent to 2.54mm or 0.10 inch.

waited for repairs each month. There was some question if these production levels would be enough to meet army needs.

Despite a relatively long period for preparation, the Imperial regime was not ready when the Napoleonic armies crossed the Russian frontiers on 24 June 1812. A badly outnumbered Russian army (260,000 Russians to 600,000 French and allied armies) was forced to retreat in the face of the Napoleonic onslaught. War Minister A. A. Arkacheev (minister from 1808 to 1825, known also for his repressive domestic policies as commander of the internal security forces and for his desire to maintain a pre-Napoleonic status quo in Europe) directed the weapons manufacturing centers during this "Patriotic War." Tula alone made 456,704 new weapons during the period 1810–1816. An additional 153,129 pieces were reconditioned and repaired.[5]

Administrative turmoil at the weapons factories, a condition that was to prevail for most of the nineteenth century, hindered efficient wartime production. On the eve of that conflict, initial steps had been taken to introduce labor-saving processes into the Russian factories. French arms manufactories had already begun using jigs and fixtures to permit a semblance of serial production, thus speeding the fabrication of musket parts and reducing assembly time. In the United States, Eli Whitney was using similar techniques to expedite the manufacture of contract muskets. John H. Hall, developer of the Hall breechloading rifle, was proposing to establish a rifle factory that would assemble rifles made with essentially interchangeable parts. Russian arms manufacturers appreciated the importance of these developments, but were not able to exploit them during the 1812 war.[6]

Luckily, during their war with the French the Russians had resources other than men and materiel to rely upon. The vast territorial expanses of the Empire, the tenacity of the Russian people, and the savage winter of 1812 came to the rescue of Tsar Alexander's forces. Napoleon entered a desolated Moscow in September 1812. Faced with the prospect of spending a winter very deep inside Russia with limited supplies, no local sources of food, and no medical assistance, the French leader decided in October that a strategic retreat was in order. Napoleon lost more than five hundred thousand men to the Russian weather, famine, and constant harassment by Russian military forces. Only thirty thousand survivors reached the Nieman River on 14 December.

Once peace was restored, the War Ministry ordered the state weapons factories to take steps to improve production by adopting measures that would save time and labor in the manufacture of small arms. By 1817, the Russians were turning on lathes the exterior surfaces of their musket barrels. Previously, the exterior dimension of the barrel had been ground on large grindstones; a laborious and dangerous process, because the stones often disintegrated explosively. The worker was usually maimed or killed when this happened. British small arms makers did not adopt this lathe turning of barrels until 1830. More research is needed to determine a technological comparison between the Russian, British, French, and American small arms factories.

Josif Gamel', in his 1826 *Description of the Tula Arms Factory from Historical and Technical View Points,* noted:

> The arms factory of long renown existing in the town of Tula has in the last eight years

(1816–1826) been so improved, that with respect to craftsmanship no arms factory in the world may consider itself its equal. Its artistic qualities have attained a degree of perfection nonexistent in the best arms factories of England.

Gamel' also repeated a story that sounds familiar to persons acquainted with the legend of Eli Whitney. On 20 September 1825, Tsar Nicholas I (reign 1825–1855), accompanied by Prince Karl of Prussia and Prince Philip of Hessen-Homberg, visited the small arms factory at Tula. The Tsar "desired by his own experience to ascertain whether in all reality complete interchangeability of lock components had been achieved in Tula, a feat considered impossible in other countries." Supposedly, Nicholas took a few locks at random and had them disassembled. After the components had been mixed together, the locks were reassembled without any need to file or fit the parts to make them work. Nicholas was impressed.

The Tsar also wanted to know how his workers compared with those of other countries. He put that question to John Jones, an Englishman working under contract at Tula. Jones is reported to have said that in the whole of England there were none that could surpass the workers at Tula. This was of course the answer the Tsar expected. But the foregoing favorable comments could not hide the fact that there were still some basic problems at the Russian arms factories.[7]

Shortages of raw materials and labor problems plagued armory administrators. Although money was allocated to regularize the supply of raw materials and to provide for the upgrading of production facilities, the demands of the Patriotic War had slowed necessary revamping of internal factory organization and planning.

Once the war came to an end, quantity production became less immediately important, and the War Ministry staff could begin again searching for a rational approach to weapons procurement.

One thing was certain. A reliable domestic source of small arms was a necessity, not a luxury. During the 1812 war with France, the Russian government had been forced to purchase small arms from abroad. Dependence on foreign states for military supplies often had undesired side effects — unwanted allies could result from such a dependency, or a nation could find itself seriously short of weapons if its supplier decided to shut off the flow of materiel. On the eve of the Patriotic War, the Russians had purchased some fifty thousand flintlock muskets from the English. This continuing reliance on foreign arms makers was a leading reason that the War Ministry sought to find a better system for producing small arms in Russia.

The Chernyshev Era: 1827–1853

Small arms shortages continued to be a problem for the Russians during the first half of the nineteenth century. Militia units especially were always short of weapons of a reliable type. Imperial commissions sent from St. Petersburg to investigate the weapons factories after the 1812 war found all of them to be in very bad condition. On one occasion a damaged mill dam at Tula had brought all of the water-powered machinery to a standstill. Instead of seeing repair crews at work, the commissioners found the factory managers haggling with one another about the steps required to get production started again. The Imperial commission, in one of two proposals to Nicholas I, recommended the introduction of steam engines to power the machinery at Tula. The Tsar personally decided against this innovation, ordering instead that the dam be repaired. Between 1831 and 1835 Tula functioned reasonably effectively, but this state of affairs was terminated by a major fire in the latter year. The 1835 fire gave the necessary impetus for a modernization of the Tula shops. Changes made at Tula were paralleled by a reconditioning of the facilities at Sestroretsk and Izhevsk. This cleanup, repair, and reorganization process had to precede the successful manufacture of the new family of 18mm (.71 caliber) Model 1828 small arms.[8]

Although the modernization program made it possible for the three weapons centers to increase their production levels, these efforts were apparently not sufficient. The number of small arms made at the three factories never met the barest needs of the basic body of regular troops. An attempt again was made to bridge the gap by means of orders to a number of English factories for a total of one hundred thousand Russian-type muskets. The quality of these weapons was very poor. Of 85,000 received in 1832, 52,025 had to be reworked in the Russian factories.

Clearly, something fundamental had to be done if the Imperial Army was to have the weapons necessary to fight the many wars in which Nicholas I seemed destined to embroil his armed forces. From 1826 to 1828 Russian troops campaigned against Persian (Iranian) forces, and in 1828 the Tsar's soldiers were at war with the Turks. During these conflicts, small arms were consumed in such quantities that the arms makers could not keep enough replacements flowing to the field units.[9]

As a result of these continuing difficulties, War Minister A. I. Chernyshev established a new committee to improve production at the armories. The committee's recommendations led to no perceptible increases in production. During the years 1825–1850, the three arms factories consistently failed to meet their production quotas. As a general rule they only made about half of the weapons ordered. The quotas reflected not only on the inabilities of the factories but also on the unreasonableness of the goals established by the War Ministry.

During this same period, the Russian army continued to search for new and improved weapons through the creation of yet another special committee—the Arms Commission of 1835. Out of these deliberations ultimately came the Model of 1839 flintlock shoulder-weapons family. Since this new series was only a marginal improvement over the earlier patterns, the commission tested various Russian and European schemes for converting flintlocks to a percussion system.

As part of this activity, the Arms Commission sent Colonel Glinka-Mavrin to France to study the work going on there. As the result of Glinka-Mavrin's intelligence reports from Paris and other European capitals, the War Ministry introduced a conversion program for their flintlock muskets. These converted weapons were given the designation "Model of 1844." Starting in 1845, an entirely new family of 7.1 line (18mm) percussion smoothbore weapons were standardized. While experiments continued with a variety of other new types, the Ministry faced the awesome task of organizing production at the three weapons factories. The factories were just getting set up for large-scale production of the Model 1845 weapons when the Crimean War began in 1854.

Earlier in the 1840s War Minister Chernyshev had hired James Nasmyth, an Englishman, to establish at Tula his system of steam hammers for forging small arms components. In 1850 Nasmyth reported to a British Parliamentary commission investigating the small arms production technology in English factories that the Russians were finishing most of their gun parts by machine processes, with the notable exception of the gunstock. He went on to comment that the extent to which machine tools were employed in the Russian small arms factories surpassed any of the manufactories in the Birmingham trade, where, as he put it, work was "done in a ruder manner." Most significant to him was the fact that the Russians, copying the best of foreign-weapons patterns and engineering techniques, were fabricating most of the production jigs and fixtures needed in their shops, thus reducing their dependence on foreign toolmakers.

Nasmyth concluded that the small arms production techniques used by the Russians compared favorably with those used by the Colt Patent Firearms Manufacturing Company in London and the United States, a company which had an international reputation at the time for using the most advanced technological processes for making their handguns. The Russian factories were equal, Nasmyth said, to Colt both in the extent to which machine processes were used and in the resulting quality of their products.[10] While there is the possibility that Nasmyth was overstating his case to get the British government to adopt the "American System" of interchangeable parts manufacture and assembly, it is interesting that he gave the Russian arms factories such high marks.

Nasmyth was commenting on the fabrication of the 1845-year pattern of small arms. These infantry weapons would be the mainstay for the Imperial troops engaged in the Crimean War (September 1854 to March 1856). Russian troops in the field only began to receive the newer Model 1856 rifled muskets at the end of the war in 1856. Attempts to purchase rifled arms from Prussia and the United States were stymied when those countries embargoed further shipments of arms as a result of Russia's war with Turkey, in which the English and French were Turkish allies. Soviet historians have viewed this policy of "neutrality" on the part of the Americans as basically anti-Russian. "And with the start of the war, completion of the arms orders was suspended by both Germany and the USA, both powers declared their neutrality, which meant that they acted in the interests of their allies, and of course, Russia was not one of them."[11]

While the Imperial Army at midcentury still relied predominately upon smoothbore muskets, and while these weapons were in relatively short supply, the Russian situation differed little from that of their allies or their enemies. As of January 1853, eighteen months before the Crimean War began, the Russian army had acquired only 532,835 of an authorized 1,014,959 new-pattern infantry muskets and carbines ready for use by its troops. These shortages would continue to plague the Russian military, but such shortages of shoulder weapons also continued to exist for the forces allied against the Russians. The telling difference on the battlefront was the failure of the Russians to deliver new-pattern rifled weapons rapidly enough so they would be of use to the soldiers in the field.

Soviet historians have been highly critical of the Russian small arms production program during the Crimean War, but a comparison of British and Russian records indicates that the English also had their problems. Large numbers of British troops (seventeen out of forty regiments) landed in the Crimea still armed with the Pattern 1842 smoothbore musket. Prior to 1855, all references to the British Minié rifle referred to the original Minié-type weapon—the 17.8mm (.702 caliber) pattern—adopted in 1851. Only in 1855 did the British arms makers in London, Birmingham, and Enfield begin to deliver the more modern 14.5mm (.577 caliber) Pattern 1853 "Enfield" rifled musket.

British supply of these rifles did not meet the demand. So even the British had to look for foreign sources of additional Pattern 1853 weapons. In October 1854, British Ordnance officials requested twenty thousand Pattern 1853 rifles from Belgian manufacturers in Liège. This was the first of several such orders. The British even ordered Pattern 1853 rifles from the American machine-tool manufacturer Robbins and Lawrence Company in Windsor, Vermont. This factory only delivered sixteen thousand weapons. Still, the contract with the Americans indicated that the British domestic manufacturers had their problems making enough weapons for their troops.

The Royal Small Arms Factory at Enfield was not reequipped with the American-style machinery needed to produce weapons serially with interchangeable parts until 1858. In the year from 1 April 1858 to 31 March 1859, the Royal Small Arms Factory manufactured 57,256 Pattern 1853 rifles. Both Tula and the contractors of the Birmingham Trade delivered about the same number of shoulder weapons each year at this time. Thus the "American System of Manufacturing" was not a simple panacea for solving the weapons-manufacturing problem. Success lay with the efficient marshaling of production capacity, whether it be based on the craftsman's skill or the machine's repetition and precision.[12]

Soviet analysis of the Russians' failure in the Crimea blames the defeat on Imperial Russia's backwardness—social, technological, and economic. These historians remind us that the Industrial Revolution had only just begun in the Russian armament factories. They argue that there was still too much reliance on serf labor and inferior manufacturing techniques. In terms of weapons, victory in battle depended upon three factors: efficient production of adequate numbers of weapons, availability of the right models of weapons, and proper training of the troops who would use the rifles. The smoothbore muskets and cannon used by the Russian army were "absolutely unfit for use when compared with the new and much greater ranged rifled-type weapons."[13]

A correspondent for *The Times* of London, W. H. Russell, made the point of the need for proper weapons quite plainly when he reported on the 26 November 1854 Battle of Inkermann. "The rolling of musketry, the crash of steel, the pounding of the guns were deafening, and the Russians as they charged up the heights yelled like demons. They advanced, halted, advanced again, received and returned a close and deadly fire; but the Minie [rifle] is the king of weapons—Inkerman [*sic*] proved it." The smoothbore musket was not an effective weapon against the enemy armed with such a weapon.

"The fire of the Minie smote [the Russian soldiers] like the hand of the Destroying Angel." Out of 10,729 casualties, one quarter of their troops involved in the battle, the Russians had at least 5,000 men killed. The British, who had only 8,500

A Russian 17.7mm (.70 caliber) flintlock rifle
manufactured by Tula Weapons Factory in 1798,
with a modified hammer affixed in 1805. This
weapon was used by special rifle units, and is
typical of the military rifles used in Europe at
the end of the eighteenth century.

men in the battle, lost only 579 men killed
and 1,860 wounded. French losses were
130 killed and 750 wounded. The effect of
the rifled musket was very telling.

Russell provided the following comments on the Russian infantry weapons.
"Many of the muskets bore the date 1841,
and had been altered into detonators."
These weapons were the percussion Model
1844 conversions of the Model 1839 flintlock smoothbore muskets. "The Imperial
eagle was on the brass heelplate, and on
the lock . . . Tula . . . 1841." Russell noted
that the "Russian musket was a good one
to look at; but must be rather a bad one to
use. The barrel, which was longer than
ours, and was kept polished, was made of
iron, and was secured to the stock by brass
straps, like the French. The lock was,
however, tolerably good. The stock was
of the old narrow oriental pattern, and
the wood of which it was made, white-
grained and something like sycamore,
broke easily."

Some limited numbers of Russian
troops carried Liège double-grooved
short-rifles made by Pierre-Joseph Malherbe. Sometimes called the Luttich carbine, after the German name for Liège,
this second version of the Model 1843
short-rifle was almost an exact copy of the
British percussion Brunswick rifle of 1837.
The only change to these Russian rifles
was their alteration to fire Charles Lan-
caster's "sugar-loaf" banded bullet, which
had been introduced in the middle 1840s.
As so often was the case in the nineteenth
century, the Russian military was relatively quick to pick up on the latest technological innovations from elsewhere in
Europe. Their basic problem was the
acquisition of adequate numbers of weapons. In the case of these Luttich short-
rifles, they had acquired only five thou-

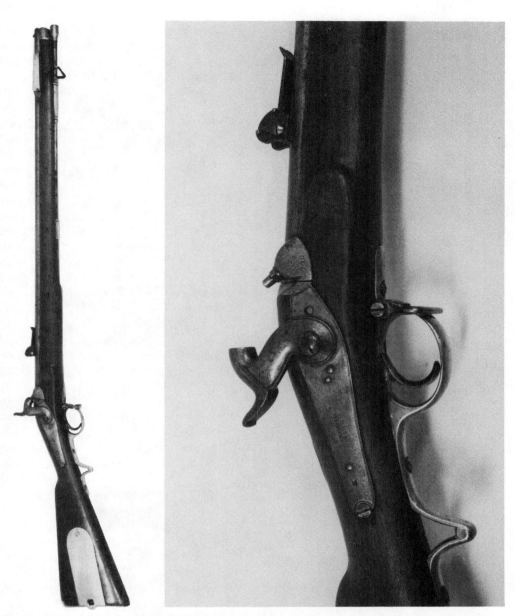

Two views of a 17.78mm (.70 caliber) Russian Model 1843 short-rifle (Luttichkiskiy shtutzer obrazets 1843g), known generally as the "Luttich Carbine" because it was manufactured in Liège ("Luttich" in German). This weapon was the first regulation percussion rifle adopted by the Imperial Russian Army. It was a direct copy of the British Brunswick rifle of 1837. Illustrated here is the second Russian model—ca. 1848—with a quadrant back sight graduated to one thousand two hundred paces, and barrelled to fire the two-groove Lancaster-type bullet. It was manufactured by Pierre-Joseph Malherbe of Liège, who received a contract for five thousand such rifles.

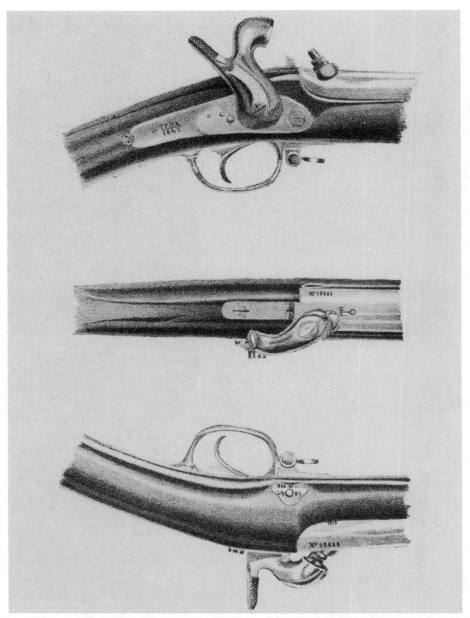

Close-up views of the breech of the 18mm (.71 caliber) Russian Model 1845 smoothbore percussion musket (Udarnoe pechotnoe Ruzh'e obrazets 1845g), which is almost an exact copy of the French Modèle 1842 musket. The major difference was in the use of brass for the buttplate, trigger guard, and barrel bands in the Russian muskets—the French used iron fittings. The stock, made of birch, was stained dark. The musket illustrated here was made at Tula in 1847. Many of these weapons were rifled, beginning in 1854, thus permitting the infantryman to shoot an 18.2mm (.72 caliber) Minié-type projectile.

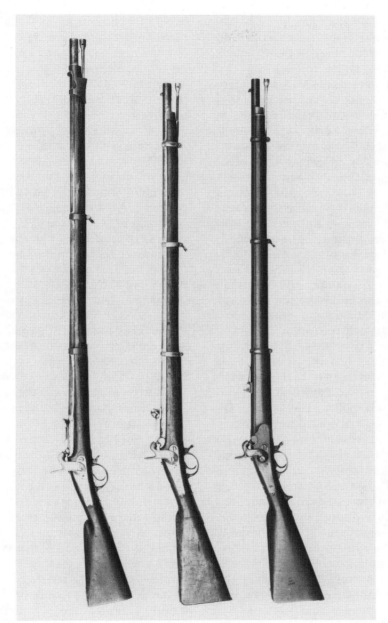

Left to right: **The 18mm (.71 caliber) Russian Model 1845 smoothbore musket converted in 1845 to fire the Minié-type projectile; an 18mm Sestroretsk 1856/57 transitional model Minié rifle; and the 15.2mm (.60 caliber) Russian Model 1856 "6 line" rifle.**

Starting in 1854, the Russian arms factories began converting the 18mm (.71 caliber) smoothbore percussion muskets to a rifled configuration that fired an 18.3mm (.72 caliber) Minié bullet. Something on the order of twenty thousand of these conversions were made. Note the marked change from the Model 1845 with its French-style barrel bands to the Model 1856 with its British Enfield-type clamping bands.

sand from Malherbe. That was hardly enough to make a significant impact on the outcome of the war in the Crimea.[14]

Final defeat of their forces in the Crimea firmly impressed the Russian military of the need to push ahead with the adoption and manufacture of rifled muskets and rifled artillery. Leaders of the Artillery Directorate, which oversaw all weapons development in Russia, reported: "The advantage that the Western Powers have over us by their use of the improved rifled-type armament was aptly demonstrated in the last war and puts responsibility for a serious study of their methods of bullet and shell projection on the Artillery Directorate; [we must] also deal with the question of equipping our armed forces with them in the shortest period of time." This task did not prove to be impossible, just extremely difficult.

On the eve of the 1854–1856 war, updated machinery had been procured for Tula and Izhevsk, and the Model 1856 rifled musket was scheduled to be manufactured on this tooling. The Artillery Directorate coined a new word for the Model 1856 rifled musket—*vintovka*—to clearly differentiate this new class of weapons from the older patterns of smoothbore muskets and rifled weapons.

Earlier, muskets and rifles had been assigned clearly distinct roles in combat. The musket had been used by the main body of infantry to deliver mass volleys of fire at ranges generally less than one hundred fifty meters. Rifles, such as the Model 1843 Luttich carbines, were specialty weapons used by small units of carefully selected and trained shooters to deliver at longer ranges aimed shots at the enemy, especially exposed officers. The new 15.2mm (.60 caliber) *vintovka obrazets 1856g* (Model 1856 rifled musket)

would fill both roles, and would bring the Russians to the same realization that other armies had reached—massed bodies of infantrymen were a thing of the past. Future wars would be fought by more fluid lines of men fighting and maneuvering by fire.

The Russian War Ministry ordered thirty thousand Model 1856 rifled muskets in 1857. A year later, after considerable internal debate, the Ministry decided to arm all infantry of the line with this type weapon. As they evaluated the military potential of this rifle, the Artillery Directorate experts decided to reduce the maximum-range setting on the rear sight from fifteen hundred paces to six hundred paces (*Shag* was the word for pace in Russian, which equalled 1.406 meters or 55.375 inches). As so modified, the rifle was renamed the Model 1858 infantry rifle. "The new infantry and cavalry rifles were far advanced compared with their predecessors, but they had two shortcomings—they were muzzle-loading just like their predecessors, and their effective range of fire was over-rated."[15]

The new Model 1858 weapons were also more difficult to manufacture. Producing the rifled barrel gave the Russians serious headaches. Previously, the factories had been willing to accept a large reject-and-scrap rate in the manufacture of the less expensive smoothbore barrels. At Izhevsk alone, 85 to 90 percent of the rifled barrels produced at the beginning of the switch-over to rifles were rejected. It soon became clear that the traditional reliance on poorly educated and sometimes equally unskilled serf-laborers was unsuitable for a modern steel-oriented barrel-making business. An Artillery Directorate study committee concluded that specially trained technicians would have to replace the poorly educated bonded serfs. As this discussion over the quality of production and the proper type of labor continued, other major changes were taking place.

Many of these management and technology alterations to the small arms factories were brought about by the production goal of 1.2 million Model 1858 rifles established by the War Ministry for the decade 1858–1868. To meet this ambitious target, the Imperial government tried yet another effort at modernizing the weapons factories. Frustrated by the experience with military men as factory managers, the War Ministry sought to contract out for the management of these facilities. Part of this proposal called for emancipation of the serfs so that the best of their numbers could be employed by the contractors as "free" laborers. Elimination of serfdom as the basis of employees for the factories was also expected to allow the civilian managers to recruit workers throughout Russia and Europe.

Among the first group to propose to be contractor/managers was the Liège-based firm of Falisse and Trapmann. These two men had worked together in a partnership since the 1830s, and for nearly a decade they had possessed the Belgian monopoly on the manufacture of nipples for percussion weapons. In 1840 they became the first Belgian manufacturers of percussion caps. Noting the American success with machine manufacture of firearms, the partners established such a factory near Liège at Gravioule in 1851. When this factory was completed in 1853, it was equipped with machine tools of their own fabrication. The success of their new facility and its machinery led to many foreign contracts for their machine tools, including sales to Dutch, Spanish, and Swiss arms factories. In 1857, with the as-

sistance of twenty-four of their workmen from Liège, Falisse and Trapmann installed new barrel-making equipment at Tula and Izhevsk.

Given their familiarity with the Russian small arms factories, Falisse and Trapmann proposed an arrangement whereby they would lease Sestroretsk, reequip the factory, and produce thirty thousand rifles a year. Dimitri Alekseevich Milyutin, War Minister from 1861 to 1881, appointed a special commission to evaluate this proposal. The commission decided against accepting the offer because they did not want foreigners in the position of running such an important military installation. There was considerable opposition to the idea of granting freedom to the state serfs who worked in the arms factories.

Freedom for the arms-factory workers was almost inevitable. The Artillery Study Commission, formed in 1856 under the chairmanship of the Inspector of Factories (General Ignat'ev) drew up a set of "Working Regulations" under which serfs, once emancipated, would work. In spite of their insightfulness in drafting these regulations, several years went by before the guidelines were finally adopted. Delay in emancipating the factory serfs led to much unrest among both unskilled workers and trained craftsman. While Tsar Alexander II (reign 1855–1881) freed most Russian serfs in 1861, three additional years passed before compulsory labor at the state weapons factories ended.[16]

There was far from universal agreement that bonded labor in the weapons and ammunition factories should be abolished. There was a general worry about the danger of unemploying factory serfs. For example, the commanding officer at Tula resisted the adoption of machines to make gunstocks because he believed that "the workmen would clearly be at a loss and in no position to feed themselves and their families." His concern was not altogether out of a worrying about the fate of the serfs. Out of work and unemployable, the freed serfs were a potential source of social unrest. The officer in charge of Sestroretsk had the same fears and he did not want to see the workers placed in a position of "dependence on the public coffers."[17]

Emancipation of the factory serfs ultimately coincided with a change in the management structure of the small arms factories. The government, in an effort to resolve the managerial problems at the weapons factories and at the same time avoid problems associated with the transition from serf to wage-earning laborer, created a system of commercial leaseholds for the factories. First tried at Tula, this new system called for a five-year lease of the facility to a contractual manager. Major General K. K. Standershel'd agreed in 1863 to supply sixty thousand rifles per year at a price established by the government. He would receive a 7 percent commission based on the annual production costs of the weapons. While the government controlled general factory policy — what models and in what quantities — the War Ministry was relieved of the day-to-day supervisory task. In 1865, Standershel'd received another lease to operate the Weapons Factory at Izhevsk. Sestroretsk was turned over to Captain O. F. Lilienfel'd in 1873.[18]

Transfer of the arms factories to "lease-commercial management" provoked complaints from both local business communities and others favoring direct state management of the factories. On several occasions private entrepreneurs petitioned the Ministry of Home Affairs with schemes of their own for managing the factories. A group of Tula industrialists even suggested the creation of a joint-stock company composed of local craftsmen to operate the armories. All of these proposals were rejected.

Proponents of a return to state management had at least one good argument. The leaseholders proved to be poor managers. They had promised to upgrade the manufacturing facilities and maintain a steady rate of production. They did neither because, they complained, they did not have the necessary financial resources to make the required improvements. It does appear that the leaseholders did make substantial commissions, but they simply took the short-run profit-taking view and failed to invest in meaningful capital improvements. It became increasingly apparent to all parties that many changes were still needed in the management of the weapons factories.

War Minister Milyutin appointed a Committee of Investigation, under the direction of General Glinka-Mavrin, to determine a solution to the difficulties. Milyutin was a skillful administrator who was willing to make the sweeping changes necessary to modernize the Russian army. He, most clearly of all of the Tsar's advisors, realized the need for a strong and healthy military-industrial complex. As he noted in one of his official communiques: "Russia is not Egypt or the Papal State to be content to purchase the materiel for her entire army from abroad — we must build our own factories to make our arms in the future."[19] Milyutin also realized that there were just some activities in the Russia of his age that should not be trusted to private entrepreneurs who were often motivated by profits rather than by national security requirements.

During the 1860s and the 1870s, Russians knowledgeable in military affairs debated the best structure for the country's defense industries. Most individuals inside the defense community believed that the weapons factories should be state owned. N. L. Kalakutskiy of the Russian Technical Society and V. L. Chebyshev, editor of the *Oruzheiny Sbornik* (The Armament Review), were the most outspoken on this subject. They argued that the essential feast-or-famine nature of ordnance supply—uncertain fluctuations in the production requirements—made it imperative that the War Ministry not depend upon the uncertain enthusiasm and competence of private sector industrialists. State-managed factories were in theory more reliable.[20]

It was within this context that Glinka-Mavrin's investigative committee delivered its report. The committee confirmed the point that the leaseholders had made very limited efforts to improve the manufacturing process at the factories. In addition, they had not attended to the proper maintenance of the existing buildings and machinery, and working conditions for the workmen had not been improved. Therefore, the Investigating Committee recommended a return of the factories to direct state management. Following that change, the factories could be rehabilitated so as to expedite the production of the Model 1858 rifled musket.[21]

While the factory-management question was being debated, the War Ministry faced another crisis of equal magnitude. The tide of technological change was sweeping the muzzleloading rifle toward obsolesence; throughout the western world breechloaders were rapidly taking its place. Limited use of these new weapons in the latter part of the American Civil War (1861–1865) and the successful employment of the Dreyse *Zundnadelgewehr* (needle-fire rifle) by the Prussians during their war with the Danes in 1864 had opened a new era of small arms and infantry tactics.

One report to War Minister Milyutin noted, "The successful use by the Prussians in the Danish campaign and the use of new model rifles in the North American Civil War have brought to the attention of European governments the need to introduce firearms with a breech-loading mechanism." Milyutin in turn told the Tsar, "Every postponement of a decision in this regard must have fatal consequences."[22]

In typical fashion, the War Ministry appointed a study team in 1866 to consider this subject. Colonel A. P. Gorlov and Lieutenant K. I. Gunius, members of the Artillery Commission, were sent to the United States to study the breechloaders being examined there. They were able to benefit greatly from the data collected by the American officers operating under the direction of Major General Winfield Scott Hancock. The Hancock Board examined and tested forty-seven different types of breechloading rifles and carbines. Gorlov noted that combat reports regarding breechloaders indicated that:

> The quick-firing rifle had enormous advantages; under an almost ceaseless hail of lead from lines of infantrymen armed with quick-firing rifles nothing could stand up, and in the very shortest time, a matter of a few minutes the forward elements of enemy soldiers just disappeared and the rest turned around and fled. All became quiet after a two or three minute rifle fusilade. . . .

Gorlov also pointed out that volunteer troops unfamiliar with weapons demonstrated no difficulty in learning how to handle breechloaders. Equally significant to Gorlov was the American decision to adopt the self-contained metal cartridge (replacing paper, fabric, and rubber cartridges), which made it much easier to load the weapon from the breech, and which eliminated the danger of gas leakage at the breech. "This means, therefore, that the adoption of the quick-firing rifle must be accompanied at the same time with the introduction of the metal cartridge," Gorlov reported home.[23]

While Gorlov and Gunius visited America, the Arms Commission tested a number of foreign and domestic breechloaders, including the Prussian Dreyse, the French Chassepot, and the British Snider. The Duke of Mecklenburg, chairman of the Arms Commission, taking advantage of the confusion at this time, ordered the Terry-Norman percussion-cap breechloading rifle into production. This weapon, designed by William Terry, an Englishman, a decade earlier, was modified for Russian service by I. G. Norman at Tula.* Nearly sixty thousand of these 15.24mm (.60 caliber), 4.5 kilogram rifles were manufactured before the War Ministry scrapped the project in favor of the Model 1867 Karle needle-fire rifle. At best, these Terry Norman rifles can only be considered as a stopgap measure since they were outmoded by the time they were adopted.[24]

The Karle rifle was actually a conversion of the Model 1858 rifle employing a sliding-bolt breechloading mechanism.

An earlier variation of this needle-fire weapon was being used in Sweden, the home of designer J.F.C. Karle.+ As adopted by the Russians, the Karle conversion of the Model 1858 rifle was still far from being satisfactory as a combat weapon and was not well received by the troops in the field. As with other needle-fire weapons of the period, there was a serious problem of gas leakage at the breech when the rifle was fired. This not only tended to unnerve the rifleman but also reduced the initial velocity of the projectile to 305 meters per second (1,000 feet per second), which was less than that of the standard Model 1858 muzzleloader. The Karle conversion's second major shortcoming was associated with difficulty in extracting the fired paper and brass cartridges. After several shots had been fired, it became very difficult to load new cartridges due to powder residue blowing back into the breech area of the weapon. After reading the field reports on these rifles, War Minister Milyutin expressed his total dissatisfaction with this weapon, and in the spring of 1867 two officers, Colonels N. I. Chagin and V. L. Chebuishev, were given the task of reworking it. Their modified version of the Karle was approved in 1868.

While the controversy over the Karle continued, the War Ministry was examining several other designs. The leading alternative conversion concepts to the Karle were the Baronov and the Krnka. The Baronov was promoted as a superior design of Russian origin. Actually, the

---

*Terry received British letters of patent for his weapon on 25 September 1855 (Number 812) and 19 September 1856 (Number 843). Norman was awarded the Order of Stanislav, 3d Class, and given a prize of five hundred rubles for his work on this design.
+ Karle may have been from Hamburg, but his nationality is generally given as being Swedish.

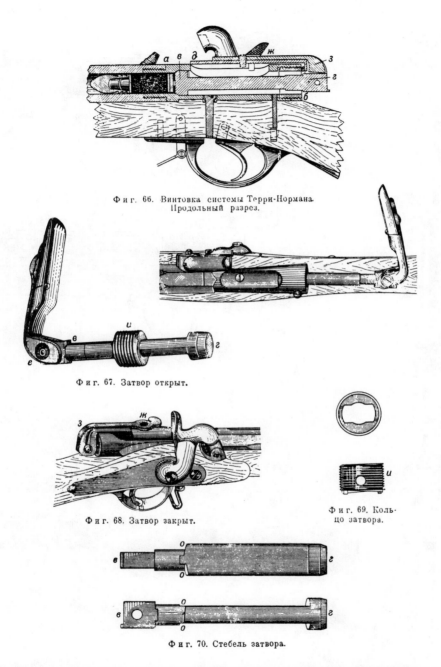

Фиг. 66. Винтовка системы Терри-Нормана.
Продольный разрез.

Фиг. 67. Затвор открыт.

Фиг. 68. Затвор закрыт.

Фиг. 69. Кольцо затвора.

Фиг. 70. Стебель затвора.

The 15.24mm (.60 caliber) Terry-Norman breechloading conversion of the Model 1858 percussion muzzleloading rifle. Nearly sixty thousand of these weapons, which were based upon an idea patented in Britain, were altered before the Ministry of War scrapped the project.

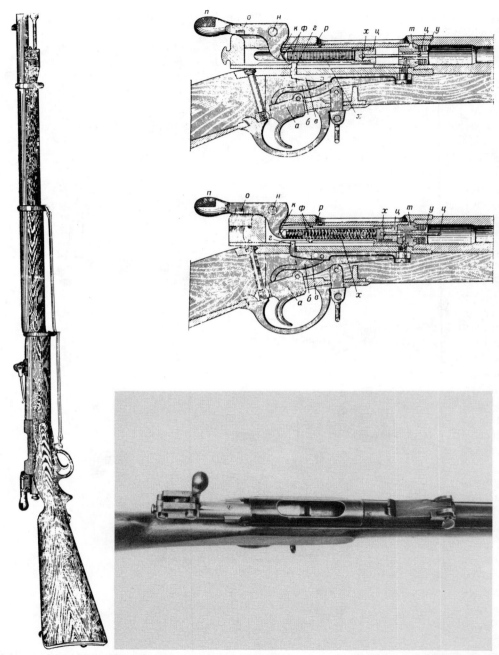

The 15.24mm (.60 caliber) Model 1867 Karle needle-fire conversion of the Model 1858 percussion muzzleloading rifle. Over 213,000 of these conversions were carried out.

rifle was a variant of the Albini-Braendlin, which had been patented in 1866 in England.* It is likely that N. M. Baronov was the Russian agent for the inventors. In 1865, Baronov had submitted this scheme for converting the Model 1858 rifle to the Russian Navy. That service contracted for ten thousand converted rifles through the Pulitov Iron Works in St. Petersburg. The ground forces Arms Commission, chaired by Lieutenant General Rezevyi, did not like the "Russian" Baronov rifle, preferring instead the foreign rifle that had been designed by the Austrian inventor Sylvester Krnka. His system offered a reasonably low-cost method of converting the Model 1858 rifles to a metallic-cartridge breechloader.

In March 1869 the Arms Commission, after War Minister Milyutin's intervention, announced the decision to adopt the Krnka. Overriding a host of complaints, the War Ministry terminated the Karle conversion project and placed large orders for Krnka-converted Model 1858 rifles. Soviet historians have used this decision as an excellent example of bureaucratic favoritism of foreign designs. "The Ministry went through with this decision although it was seen that the Krnka rifle was a significantly poorer weapon than the Baronov rifle."[25]

Krnka's system for converting rifles could be applied to either the standard Model 1858 rifle or to the Model 1858 as modified to the Karle system. The conversion consisted of a bronze breech mechanism with a side-hinging breech block that could be attached to the rear end of a modified Model 1858 barrel. F. V. Greene,

an American military observer in Russia, provided the following description of the Krnka system:

> The breech mechanism consists of a block turning to the left around an axis parallel to that of the barrel; when closed the block rests against two shoulders, on the right and the left, forming part of the breech-piece, which is screwed to the barrel; the recoil is taken up by these shoulders.[26]

To expedite the conversion program, the Arms Commission established a special administrative and executive committee to supervise the work on the Krnka project at the arms factories.

Once again the bugaboo of poor manufacturing facilities and organization at the factories worried the Artillery Department and the War Ministry. A total production budget of 16 million rubles was allocated for conversion of Model 1858 rifles to the Krnka system during 1869–1870. In addition, another 1.2 million rubles were authorized for the leaseholders at Tula, Sestroretsk, and Izhevsk for the purchase and repair of manufacturing equipment. By 1872, the Russian army had in its inventory the following breechloaders:[27]

Karle conversions of the Model 1858 rifle	213,927
Krnka conversions of the Model 1858 rifle	810,000
Krnka conversions of the Model 1859 Cossack rifle	45,500
Terry Norman Model 1866 carbines	30,000
Old and obsolete muzzleloaders	80,840

By the end of 1873, a total of 1,087,364 Krnka-type shoulder weapons were avail-

---

*Augusto Albini, an Italian navy captain, and Francis Augustus Braendlin, a mechanical engineer from Birmingham, received British patents on 20 August 1866 (2243) and 13 October 1866 (2652), following up American William Montgomery Storm's 29 November 1860 (2933) patent. The French converted some of their weapons using this system under the designation Fusil d'Infanterie Mle. 1867.

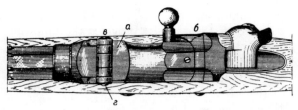

Фиг. 79. Винтовка Альбини-Баранова. Вид сверху.

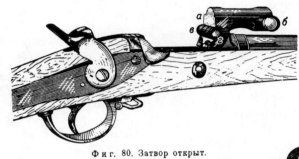

Фиг. 80. Затвор открыт.

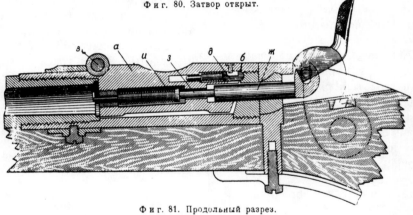

Фиг. 81. Продольный разрез.

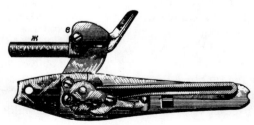

Фиг. 82. Замок.

The short-lived 15.24mm (.60 caliber) Albini-Baronov system used to convert the Model 1858 percussion muzzleloading rifle.

The 15.24mm (.60 caliber) Model 1868 Krnka center-fire conversion of the Model 1858 percussion muzzleloading rifle. More than 850,000 Krnka conversions were issued to Russian troops.

able for distribution to Imperial Army troops. While the newer breechloaders were being issued to the men in the field, the War Ministry was examining the possibility of adopting yet another breechloading rifle.

Before discussing the next generation of breechloaders, it should be noted that the Russian military was following the same progression of patterns as that pursued in other European states. The first step was the adoption of a conversion system that would allow the quick shift to breechloading. The second step was to switch to a better-thought-out breechloader, one that was usually designed from scratch. Thus in England the British army first adopted the Snider conversion, and subsequently adopted the Martini-Henry, which was a "purpose-built" breechloader designed from the start for that role. The only difference between the Russians and the rest of Europe seems to have been the larger number of factions within the Tsar's realm which were promoting a specific design for their own economic benefit.

The First Berdan Rifle

The Russian government was not alone in its indecision and tendency to experiment, and there were literally dozens of inventors, promoters, and arms companies willing to take advantage of this situation. Each had "the best" breechloaders available. One of the most flamboyant inventor-entrepreneurs was General Hiram S. Berdan, late of the US Army. Colonel Gorlov and Lieutenant Gunius had met the former commander of the

United States Sharp Shooters during their tour of the American arms factories. Berdan had resigned his commission as a colonel in the US Army in January 1864 so that he could pursue the development of his various small arms design projects.

The very first Berdan rifle was simply another means for converting the standard Springfield or Enfield .577 caliber (14.7mm) rifled musket to breech loading. This conversion was officially tested in 1866 by the United States Army, and the basic idea (a hinged breech mechanism) was later adopted by the Americans and used throughout the next thirty years in the Springfield trapdoor series of rifles.* But Berdan did not tarry long with this design. He moved on to a new pattern with a reduced bore diameter of 10.6mm (.42 caliber), since he could get greater velocity from the smaller cartridge.

The exact design history of the Berdan No. 1 rifle (Berdan's first system) is unclear, but it would appear that Gorlov and Gunius worked closely with Berdan to rid the weapon of any design faults. Work with the Berdan No. 1 rifle continued throughout 1867 and the first six months of 1868. It is covered by US patent 88436 of 30 March 1869. Gorlov, Gunius, and Berdan all agreed that the 10.6mm (.42 caliber cartridge), with its flatter trajectory, was more lethal than the American .45–70 caliber (11.4mm) ammunition. The early Berdan prototypes were built at the Colt Factory in Hartford, Connecticut. In 1868, the Russian government awarded a contract to Colt for thirty thousand Berdan rifles. A companion contract for 7.5 million .42 caliber (10.6mm) cartridges

---

*Though long credited to E. S. Allin, the "trapdoor" concept appears to have been the simultaneous development of several designers. In 1895, the US government paid Berdan's estate $95,000 for infringement of his US patent No. 52,925 of February 1866.

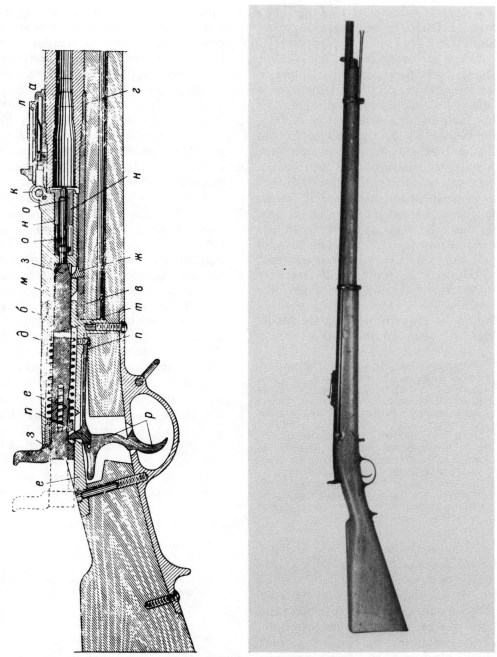

US patent model of the 10.6mm (.42 caliber) Berdan No. 1 rifle patented by General Hiram S. Berdan on 30 March 1869. This model served as the pattern for the Russian Model 1868 rifle. (NMAH 72–4159)

was given at the same time to the Union Metallic Cartridge of Bridgeport, Connecticut.[28]

In the spring of 1869, while Gorlov, Gunius, and their colleagues sought to establish production of the Berdan No. 1 rifle in Russia, Berdan visited St. Petersburg to promote yet another new rifle—the Berdan No. 2. This second Russian Berdan rifle had just been tested by the Artillery Commission, and the preliminary results convinced Minister Milyutin to terminate production of the No. 1 rifle following completion of the Colt contract for thirty thousand guns. (Of 60,000 Berdan I rifles ordered from Russian factories only 16,575 were built.) Deeply offended by this decision, Gorlov, on 26 December 1869, wrote a detailed letter to the War Minister. After recounting the eighteen months of extensive work on the Model 1868 (No. 1 Berdan) rifle, Gorlov stated:

> Berdan's attempts to put forward his new model rifle is understandable, but this model of his with the sliding-breech bolt we [Gorlov and Gunius] never did approve. It was so imperfect in operation that I consider it quite impossible to accept. . . . I consider it a duty to comment on the need to build up a stock of the 1868 model until we decide which is the best model and that the superiority of any other model of rifle over our own 1868 type can be taken for granted only when it is confirmed by thorough testing by officers having the necessary knowledge of quick-firing weapons.[29]

Obviously Gorlov's pride was wounded by the suggestion that the Model 1868 Berdan be dropped. He genuinely believed that it was superior to Berdan's bolt-action model. The No. 1 rifle had combined design elements found in several earlier weapons. Its forward-hinging breech block was an element borrowed from Berdan's 1866 rifled musket conver-

sion system, while the sliding striker—which locked the breech and detonated the primer—was similar in concept to the ones used in the Chassepot and Albini-Baronov rifles. The striker, which moved inside the breech block, had to be pulled to the rear and cocked before the breech block could be hinged opened. This rifle's rate of fire was slower than the later Berdan design, but it had the safety advantage of being positively locked at the moment of firing.

Berdan's No. 2 Russian rifle had a completely different breech mechanism. It looked much more like the sliding-turn-bolt rifle actions that would become the standard pattern in Europe during the next two decades. Unlike its immediate predecessor, the No. 2 rifle was not positively locked at the moment of cartridge discharge, thus raising the possibility that a cartridge could be fired with a partly closed bolt. This circumstance could expose the shooter to the dangers of escaping gas or of a forcefully recoiling bolt. But from a military standpoint, the Berdan No. 2 was desirable because in the hands of an experienced rifleman it could deliver a much higher rate of fire than the first Berdan model.

Milyutin, who was personally upset by Gorlov's repeated complaints against the Berdan No. 2, had the following comments on 21 October 1870:

> [We should] restrict the purchase of arms from abroad [and] in the future set up factories of our own to manufacture our own rifles for our army. The real question is will we meet unsurmountable difficulties when making the 1868 model weapon, even if we agree with Gorlov that these rifles are the best of all those so far known. The so-called Berdan No. 2 model is tempting because it is easy to manufacture, and its bolt action presents no manufacturing problems.
>
> But certainly, if because of considerably

more thorough testing of this rifle we are convinced that there are serious faults with this rifle, as indicated by Gorlov in his report, then let us reject this model and fall back on the 1868 model, even though it is more difficult to manufacture.

In any case it will be of no great misfortune because we will have 30,000 reserve Birmingham-made Berdan No. 2 rifles. But on the other hand, the rest of the army will be equipped with the 1868 model weapon which is already well known to the troops. On such assumption the order to the Colt factory could continue as previously proposed and at the same time give the commission a new impetus to begin [updating] of the Tula factory.

Milyutin's comments on this topic did not stop there. He saw other problems associated with "our unfortunate weapons drama." The key one was a further delay in getting better rifles to the troops. He had thought that this problem had been solved and now more time would be lost while steps were taken to "dispel the doubts brought up by Gorlov." He cast doubts on Gorlov's opinion and some of the tests that the General had conducted. Milyutin found it:

> very regrettable that Gorlov without . . . almost any proof rejects the Berdan No. 2 rifle. He does not detail in full its failings. It is only natural that Gorlov should prefer his own rifle, the one he . . . produced, against all others. All inventors without exception describe all similar inventions as worse than their own.
>
> Therefore it would be desirous that Gorlov gives us as quickly as possible detailed information about the shortcomings of the Berdan No. 2 rifle.[30]

Milyutin simply wanted decent information upon which he could base a decision. After renewed tests of the two rifles,

the Ministry decided to manufacture the Model 1870 Berdan (No. 2) rifle. Yet another commission was created, under General Notbek, to begin preparations at the arms factories.* As the Russians still had not resolved the question of government versus private management of the arms factories, Ministry officials sought technical advice and manufacturing assistance from two English manufacturing companies—the Birmingham Small Arms Company and Greenwood & Batley.

The Birmingham Small Arms Company Rifle Contract

The Birmingham Small Arms Company (BSA) had been involved with the evolution of the Berdan No. 2 rifle from its inception. John Denk Goodman, Chairman of the BSA Board of Directors, had visited St. Petersburg in 1865 in an effort to sell rifled muskets to the Russian military. At that time he had been told that the Imperial government was still undecided about the future course of its small arms program. Later in 1869, on the eve of the Franco-Prussian War (1870), BSA sold twenty thousand Berdan No. 2 rifles to the French government. After a series of trials, the French decided against keeping the Berdan and instead adopted the Mle. 1873 Gras rifle—a product-improved metallic-cartridge version of the Mle. 1866 Chassepot. Meanwhile, Leone Gluckman was retained to act as European sales representative for BSA's version of the Berdan No. 2 rifle.

Gluckman visited St. Petersburg in June 1869, two months after Hiram Ber-

---

*Gorlov continued his opposition to the Berdan No. 2 rifle. In a report of 30 March 1870, he recommended adoption of the British Martini-Henry rifle. "This rifle although not the equal of our 1868 model is nevertheless in many respects a better gun than the Berdan [No. 2]."

dan had been in the Russian capital. Gluckman offered to provide three hundred thousand Berdan No. 2 rifles to the Russian government from the BSA factory in Birmingham, England, over a period of three years. Under Gluckman's proposal, delivery of rifles would begin four months after an agreed-to "sealed pattern" model rifle was delivered by the Russians to the BSA factory. The sealed pattern was the master model against which all production models would be gauged; it was at the same time a specification statement and a quality control guide. Gluckman also proposed that BSA would sell all of the BSA machine tools, jigs, fixtures, and gauges to the Russians once the three hundred thousand rifles were delivered.

On 24 October 1869, the Birmingham Small Arms Company and the Imperial War Ministry signed a contract for the manufacture of thirty thousand Berdan No. 2 rifles; 10 percent of the original number proposed. A preliminary sealed pattern was proposed and accepted on 30 October 1869, but finalization of the pattern was elusive. There was a series of delays on this contract while the War Ministry procrastinated in the establishment of a sealed pattern. Until this pattern was established, work on the contract in Birmingham stood still.

The longer the Russians delayed, the more uneasy the BSA directors became. The company had already expended £20,000 on preparations for this program, and they had an idle work force. On 30 April 1870, the chief officer of the Russian supervisory commission, Captain P. A. de Bildering, arrived in England to oversee the production of the Berdan rifles and to inspect the finished weapons

before shipment to Russia. He was soon joined by Captains Kushakevich and Bouniakoffsky. The English manufacturers did not know about the Gorlov-inspired debate that was keeping the Imperial War Ministry in an uproar. The initial delivery date for Berdan No. 2 rifles was slipped from 1 February to 1 May 1871.

New problems surfaced with the arrival of Captain P. A. de Bildering. In the first weeks of the production program, Inspector de Bildering rejected almost as many rifle parts as he accepted. After a spirited protest by the BSA directors, the Russian inspector loosened his stringent quality requirements. Throughout the life of the contract, the Russians were far tougher in their acceptance inspection standards than were the British inspectors of the period. The first one hundred BSA Berdan No. 2 rifles were delivered at the English factory for shipment to Russia for field tests on 24 July 1870. Nothing had been resolved about the sealed pattern, and the BSA directors were still pressing the Russians for information regarding contracts for the remaining 270,000 Berdan No. 2s. When the War Ministry requested BSA to send finished components and in-process samples of the same parts in various stages of manufacture, the BSA management said absolutely no. The BSA directors were becoming more and more convinced that the major reason the Russians had entered the contract with the company was to receive a tutorial in the mass production of a modern military rifle. Indeed, the Russians seemed to be more interested in the production machinery and technical processes employed in the manufacture of the rifles than they were in the finished rifles themselves.

An inspection room had been established at the BSA factory to house all of the production drawings and inspection gauges. The Russian officers in Birmingham engaged draftsmen to copy all available drawings. Where no drawings existed, the Russians had their own made. They gathered up anything that might have made it easier to manufacture the Berdan No. 2 rifle in Russia. BSA suspicions were confirmed when General Berdan telegraphed from St. Petersburg with a request from the Russian government for a quotation on a price for all of the Berdan No. 2 machinery and tooling, exclusive of the main shafting and motive power. The Russian goal was production equipment that could be used to make two hundred Berdan rifles per ten-hour work day. Seeing the drift of events, the BSA Board replied that the equipment requested would cost £180,000.

Meanwhile, the War Ministry had received the first one hundred Berdan No. 2 rifles from England and upon testing them were very happy with the finished product. After these tests, the War Ministry submitted the sealed pattern on 1 February 1871. This was the fourth version of the Berdan No. 2 to emerge from the BSA–War Ministry negotiations. This definitive design included at least two patented improvements conceived by BSA factory foreman James Smiles.

BSA ultimately completed its contract for 30,000 second-model Berdans, but they never got the contract for the other 270,000 weapons. Desirous of making the Berdan No. 2 in Russia, the War Ministry had been concurrently negotiating with another English firm for a complete factory of equipment and tooling, which would be installed at the Tula Weapons Factory. The War Ministry's second contract was with Greenwood & Batley of Leeds in Yorkshire.[31]

The Greenwood & Batley Machinery Contract

Greenwood & Batley in the 1870s enjoyed an extremely favorable international reputation as manufacturers of machine tools for the production of military equipment. The driving force and mechanical genius behind the firm's success was Thomas Greenwood (1814–1873). After an early career at the Wellington Foundry, during which he had concentrated on improving machinery with which to manufacture textiles, Thomas Greenwood turned to the manufacture of small arms production tooling for both the private gun trade and the Royal Small Arms Factory at Enfield during the Crimean War. In 1856, he joined forces with John Batley to establish a new company at the Albion Foundry, which was dedicated to building a wide selection of machine tools, but they specialized in fabricating equipment for arms factories.

The new company served as consultants and contractors during the reequipment of the Royal Small Arms Factory at Enfield. Much of the American-pattern machinery for that factory ultimately came from Greenwood & Batley. In 1861 Greenwood & Batley provided the major part of the machine tools, jigs, fixtures, and gauges for the newly established Birmingham Small Arms Company. Later, the Leeds company provided similar factory equipment for the London Small Arms Company, the Macon Armory of the Confederate States of America (tooling not delivered), the Oesterreichische Waffenfabrik Gesellschaft at Steyr, the Manufacturer de Armes de le'Etat at Liège, and the Schweizerische Industrie Gesellschaft (SIG) at Neuhausen am Rheinfall. It should have been no surprise then that the Imperial War Ministry decided to bypass the Birmingham Small Arms Company and go directly to the factory that was the source of the manufacturing technology they required for their small arms factories.

On 19 March 1871, Thomas Greenwood wrote to an old American colleague and friend, James Henry Burton,* from St. Petersburg about a contract pending with the Russians. Greenwood and Burton had worked together during the re-outfitting of the Royal Small Arms Factory in 1856–1860; in 1862–1863 when Burton was trying to establish a series of small arms factories in the Confederacy; and again in the immediate post–Civil War period, 1865–1868. Greenwood and his colleagues came to respect Burton's knowledge of production techniques and factory layout, and his general grasp of machine manufacture. Greenwood's letter to Burton was his way of recruiting a skilled engineer with small arms production experience. He was also looking for a man he could trust with a difficult mission:

> I hear from Enfield that you have been thinking of coming once more to the Old Country and trying your hand again with the old trade. Now I am out here negotiating for a Small Arms Factory and should I succeed which I think very probable as I have already signed the preliminary Contract, We shall want some one to superintend the special parts of the work and spend 18 months in Russia to see the place fairly going. . . . Now what do you say to . . . 2 or 3 years employment to do a job like this[?] . . . I will give you a fair amount but I cannot afford to be extravagant. . . . There would be a good chance for a permanent [position] or engagement for a term at a good salary after the factory is at Work by the Russian Gov-[ernment]. There is no reason why you should not live comfortably at Tula. It is a town of some 60,000 inhabitants. The factory most of which will be new will be driven by 2 turbines and 2 steam Engines. And they are to make 300 guns per day producing everything but Barrels . . . and forgings for the show [receiver] which they will get for some time at least from the barrel makers ready bored. The Gun is the "Berdan" puled together by a Committee and what the Birmingham Small Arms Company has done lost. They have a contract for 30,000 guns but have only yet sent in some 200. I think this is all I need to tell you at present to enable you to give me an early answer. If all goes Well and the Contract is completed . . . the sooner you come out the better. Write me as soon as you can to Leeds where I hope to be the first week in April. . . .[32]

Burton agreed to Greenwood's proposition and traveled to England in mid-1871. He found the Greenwood & Batley factory personnel at work on the Russian contract, which had been formalized on 23 March. This contract called for the preparation of factory machinery capable of fabricating three hundred rifles and bayonets per ten-hour work day. This package included boilers to produce steam, steam hammers, forging machines, milling ma-

---

*Burton was born in Shennondale Springs, Virginia, on 17 August 1823. He received a basic education at Westchester Academy in Pennsylvania, and he worked in a Baltimore machine shop at the age of sixteen. In 1840, he went to Harpers Ferry Armory, where he was promoted to foreman in 1845 and acting Master Armorer in 1849. After working at the Ames Manufacturing Company, in Chicopee, Massachusetts, he took in June 1855 a five-year appointment as Chief Engineer at the RSAF, Enfield. There he supervised the installation of the American System of Manufacturing. In 1860 he returned to Virginia where he supervised the State Armory at Richmond. During the Civil War he served as a lieutenant colonel in the Confederate Ordnance Corps and Superintendent of all Confederate Armories. He renewed his acquaintance with Greenwood & Batley personnel while purchasing machinery and tooling for the armory being constructed at Macon, Georgia. After the war, Burton retired to his Leesburg, Virginia, farm to await his pardon for participation in the rebellion. After his sojourn at Tula in 1872–1873, he retired again to his farm where he died on 18 October 1894.

chines, shapers, drill presses, lathes, stock-making machines, all maintenance machinery and related material, and all the jigs, fixtures, cutters, and gauges (production and inspection)—a total of 948 machines. In the 1830s, the Tula shops had incorporated only 182 machines. By 1860, the number of machines had grown to 329. When the revamping of the factory was completed in 1874, the shops had a total of 1,118 machines. Exact improvements in productivity are not known, but the quality of weapons manufactured each year was substantially improved.

When the factory complement of machine tools was completed in Leeds, the Greenwood & Batley team manufactured a small lot of rifles and bayonets to test out the equipment. The whole lot of equipment was then packed up and shipped to Tula. Several technicians, led by James Henry Burton, followed the machinery to Tula where they supervised its installation and the initial operation of the equipment. The Greenwood & Batley field representatives spent most of 1872, all of 1873, and the first months of 1874 in Tula.[33]

While the Greenwood & Batley people were producing the new equipment for Tula, a commission under General Notbek was preparing the physical facilities for the arrival of this material. In the course of their work, the commission called once again for the return of the arms factory to state management. Refitting of the factory was carried out without halting production of the older patterns of rifles. Originally scheduled to have been completed in 1873, the reequipment process dragged on until early 1874 due to the late arrival of machines from England. At the same time as this work was being done at Tula, plans were under way to restructure

the production facilities at Sestroretsk and Izhevsk. A large percentage of those machine tools were also acquired from Greenwood & Batley.

On 29 May 1874, A. Krell, the chief engineer at Tula, wrote a letter of thanks to the Greenwood & Batley management. He wanted to express his "earnest & sincere thanks for the intelligent, energetic & amicable support, which you have afforded me personally during the execution of the task that was entrusted to me, as also for the scrupulous conscientiousness & reliability in the performance of all the work that was entrusted to you."[34] Over the next eighteen years, the Tula factory manufactured 1,227,652 Model 1870 Berdan II–type weapons. The total for the three factories was 3,482,854.

On the eve of the Russo-Turkish War (1877–1878), sixteen divisions out of forty-eight had been equipped with the Berdan No. 1 or Berdan No. 2 rifle. An additional five divisions used the Karle, and twenty-seven were equipped with the Krnka. All dragoon troops had the Krnka, and all Cossack troops carried the Albini-Baronov. By the end of the Russo-Turkish conflict, all combat units and most regular line forces had been issued the Model 1870 Berdan rifle.

Search for a Repeating Rifle

The Imperial Russian military began its search for a small-caliber magazine repeating rifle as a consequence of the Russo-Turkish War. While most Turkish troops carried either Peabody-Martini or Snider single-shot rifles, some were equipped with .44-40 (llmm) Winchester Model 1873 lever action rifles. Although these were short-range weapons, the Russians had been impressed with the rate of

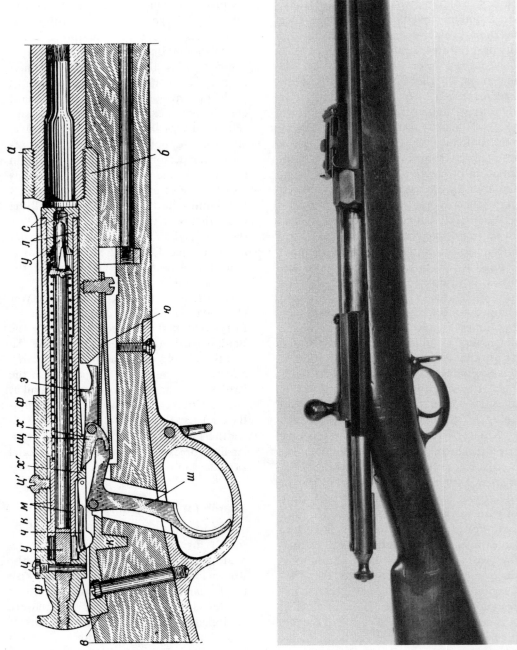

A Greenwood & Batley prototype model of the 10.6mm (.42 caliber) Berdan No. 2 rifle, which was adopted by the Imperial Russian Army as the Model 1870 rifle.

fire that could be produced with a magazine repeater. The task of searching for a magazine repeater was assigned to a small arms section of the Main Artillery Commission (Glavnoe artilleriiskoe upravlenie or GAU). Their work was intensified in 1883 when the GAU established a special magazine-rifle study and testing commission under the direction of Lieutenant General N. I. Chagin.*

General Chagin's committee proceeded slowly at first. Then in 1887 the War Ministry began to receive reports from its military attachés about a variety of foreign magazine-rifle development programs. This gave new impetus to the Russian search because the newer rifles were smaller in caliber and were not using the standard black gunpowder. The new smokeless gunpowder could produce higher velocities for the bullet, and it reduced the mechanism-fouling powder residues that were a continual problem with black powder. When the newer propellants were coupled with the repeating concept, rapidity of fire was added to increased lethality. Reports of the French success with their 8 x 50.5mmR Mle. 1886 Lebel rifle really spurred Russian interest in developing a repeating rifle. The Russian repeating-rifle committee hastily conceived a plan for a repeating-rifle development program in July 1888. Technical tests of candidate rifles were to be conducted at the Infantry Officers Training School at Oranienbaum. The first round, in 1888, included the 10-shot side-mounted magazine Ignatovich, the under-barrel magazine Kvashneveskiy, and other magazine models by Lutkovskiy, Melkov, Mosin,

Mauser, and Gras-Kropatsheck. Two rifles were early favorites: the Lutkovskiy and the Mosin.

Captain Sergei Ivanovich Mosin's (1849–1902) was an evolutionary development of the Model 1870 Berdan (No. 2) rifle. In 1882 he had begun his experimentation with improving the Berdan by placing an 8-shot magazine on the stock of the weapon. Existing descriptions do not indicate if this was a tubular magazine in the butt, or one under the barrel, or a box-type magazine under the bolt in the receiver. In 1885, Chagin's committee had ordered one thousand 12-shot Mosin-Berdans for extended field testing by army troops. During the next four years Mosin continued to experiment with variations on the 10.6mm rifles. In 1889, Chagin's committee recommended adoption of the best of Mosin's designs, but the War Ministry staff was not convinced that this was the best course of action to follow. Therefore, the search continued, with a variety of Russian and foreign rifles being examined.

Meanwhile, Mosin was developing a 3 *lini* (7.62mm) rifle of a more modern type. His turning-bolt 5-shot Model of 1890 demonstrated considerable promise. Almost simultaneously, Leon Nagant (1833–1900) of Liège presented his 3.5 *lini* (8mm) rifle. These two weapons were subjected to field tests by the Pavlovskiy Life Guards, Izmailov Life Guards, the 147th Samara Regiment, and the Sharpshooter Battalion. Three hundred each of the Model 1870 Berdan and Model 1890 Mosin rifles were issued to men from these units, while one hundred Nagant rifles

---

*General Chagin had been involved in small-arms investigations for nearly two decades. In 1868, he had been in charge of resolving the problems encountered with the functioning of the first Karle-converted Model 1858 rifles. He and Konchevskiy had submitted a rifle design for consideration by the GAU in the late 1860s. Thus he had a good background for this project.

were issued. Mosin's rifle, with a Nagant-derived magazine, was selected as the best design.[35]

There has been considerable debate about the extent to which Leon Nagant was involved in the design of the Model 1891 rifle. Nagant had been a frequent visitor to St. Petersburg for many years. In 1888, he was in the Russian capital at the time discussions were continuing regarding the search for a replacement for the Model 1870 Berdan No. 2 rifles. Nagant had also participated in frequent discussions regarding rifles and handguns—Nagant's company was the source of the Model 1895 Russian revolver—with Colonel Mosin, as a consequence of the latter's position as assistant head of the tool-making department at the Tula Weapons Factory.

Most recent research seems to point to Colonel Mosin as the source for the majority of design ideas embodied in the 1891 rifle. These same investigations suggest that Nagant had less influence than previously presumed. Nagant's key contribution appears to have been the magazine follower, the design of which prevents double-feeding. This feature had been incorporated in Nagant's 1888 rifle tested by the Belgian army—that rifle was rejected in favor of the Mauser design that became the Belgian Mle. 1889. Nagant may also have influenced some of the features of the Russian rifle's bolt, and he may have been responsible for the charger clip used to strip cartridges into the receiver of the rifle. Given his influence, it is still appropriate to refer to the Model 1891 weapon as the Mosin-Nagant rifle. The accompanying photographs of the Berdan No. 2, Nagant Mle. 1888, Mosin-Nagant (which is described in a Belgian patent 95370, 22 June 1891) and the Model 1891 Mosin-Nagant help to illustrate the evolution of the new Russian rifle.[36]

War Minister P. S. Vannovskiy noted that design simplicity was one of the major reasons for selecting the Mosin-Nagant rifle. Simplicity of design would contribute to low manufacturing cost. This was important because it meant that "the production of such a rifle could be speedily set up in our factories." With this in mind, the Ministry of War recommended the adoption of the new rifle to Tsar Alexander III (reign 1881–1894) in April 1891. The Tsar quickly approved this proposal, and the weapon was given the official nomenclature *trekhlinneioi vintovki obrazets 1891 goda* (3 line [7.62 x 54mmR] rifle model 1891).

Selection of the rifle was just the first step toward obtaining the new infantry weapon. Once again, the three weapons factories—Tula, Izhevsk, and Sestroretsk—had to be retooled and largely re-equipped to manufacture the Mosin-Nagant. As in 1871, the Russian government turned to Greenwood & Batley to provide most of the new equipment needed for Tula. Subsequently, the other two factories were equipped with Greenwood & Batley, French, Swiss, and domestically built machine tools. A total of 972 new machines were acquired for Tula, 675 for Izhevsk, and 206 for Sestroretsk.

Isolated in the Ural mountains, Izhevsk posed several special problems for the Main Artillery Commission. Labor was more difficult to recruit and it took longer to get new machines delivered and in place. In the late 1880s and the early 1890s, Izhevsk was providing manufacturing and engineering assistance to the builders of the Trans-Siberian railroad. The factory management also continued to have problems with the now-free work-

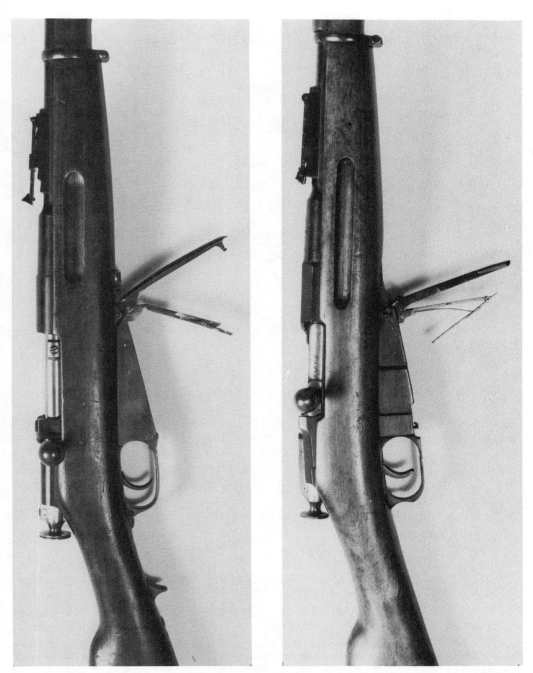

The Nagant Mle. 1888 experimental rifle (*left*) influenced the final design of the 7.62 x 54mmR Model 1891 Mosin-Nagant production rifle (*right*).

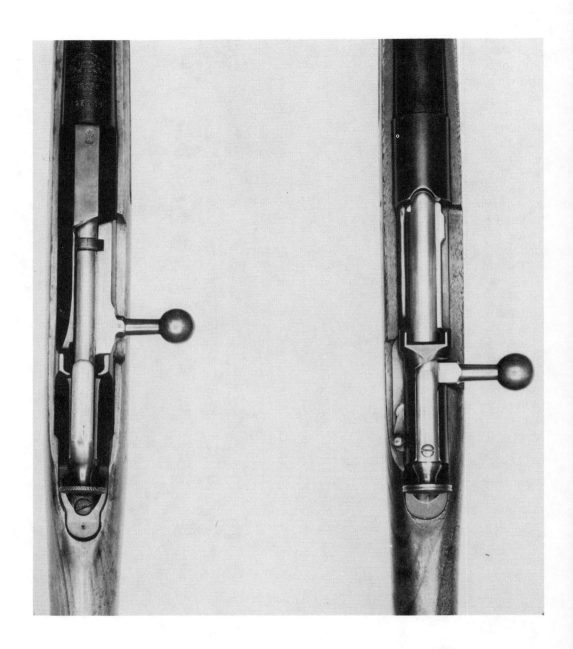

Top view of rifles in preceding photograph. In this photograph the Model 1891 Mosin-Nagant is on the left and the Nagant experimental Mle. 1888 is on the right. The Model 1891 rifle was made at Sestroretsk in 1905. Note the different locations of the bolt handles in relation to the receiver bridge. The bolt of the Mle. 1888 more closely resembles that of the Berdan No. 2 rifle than it does the Model 1891 Mosin-Nagant.

ers, who were drawn away by better-paying jobs at other factories that were springing up in the region east of the Urals.

Given these considerations, the Main Artillery Commission decided to mechanize the Izhevsk works completely, thus eliminating hand finishing and hand fitting of rifle components at that factory center. Despite these activities, Izhevsk never met the expectations of the government. Ultimately, the target of 200,000 rifles per year had to be reduced to 160,000 per annum.

The Main Artillery Commission proposed to build 3,290,000 Mosin-Nagant Model 1891 rifles for the total cost of 80.5 million rubles (approximately 40.25 million dollars). Of this sum, 39.5 million rubles were allocated to reequipping the factories, and 41 million rubles for making the rifles; i.e., 12.46 rubles ($6.13) direct cost per rifle. An additional 69 million rubles were earmarked for reworking the cartridge-making tooling at the ammunition factories, and 5 million rubles were set aside for the establishment of smokeless-powder manufacturing facilities.

Originally, it had been anticipated that rehabilitation of the rifle factories would be completed by mid-1891. Slow delivery of new machine tools, late receipt of the definitive rifle specifications, and a lack of properly trained workers all combined to delay the start of production. Some of the much-needed production machinery did not materialize until the end of 1892. To overcome the anticipated shortfall of rifles and to speed the delivery of the new pattern rifles, the War Ministry contracted with the French small arms factory at Chatellerault for 503,000 rifles. These were to be delivered between 1892 and

Right and left side views of the 7.62 x 54mmR Model 1891 Mosin-Nagant rifle.

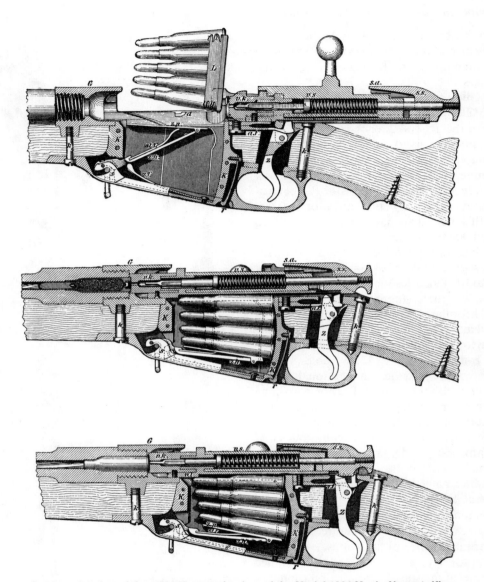

Cutaway drawing of the operating mechanism of the Model 1891 Mosin-Nagant rifle.

This rifle is a variant on the Mannlicher-type of turning bolt action. The bolt handle passes through the top of the bridge with the usual Mannlicher arrangement of mainspring, firing pin, and cocking piece. It has two locking lugs that enter the action vertically and turn into a horizontal position in the receiver ring. This positioning of the locking lugs differs from most other bolt-action rifles. The bolt handle acts as an additional safety lug. The main locking lugs are located on the separate bolt head, and are somewhat weakened by the cuts made to accommodate the ejector and extractor.

In this design, the extractor turns on the rim of the cartridge case. This extractor often rode over the rim, leaving the cartridge case in the chamber. This was one of the basic design weaknesses of the Model 1891 rifle.

The magazine is contained in a special assembly built into the forward part of the trigger guard and is of the single-row type. A special type of follower prevents double feeding of cartridges. The safety is unique, reliable, and reasonably economical to manufacture. To activate the safety it is necessary merely to cock the rifle, then grasp the knob of the cocking piece and pull it slightly to the rear and rotate it a quarter of a turn.

1895 at a price of fifty-nine francs each (approximately $10.38). The Russians shipped the first set of Model 1891 tools, jigs, and fixtures to Chatellerault in November 1892.

Tula began production of the Model 1891 rifle in late 1892, so only 1,439 weapons were manufactured. These were suitable only for training purposes, because proper tools, jigs, and fixtures were not ready until March-April 1893. Serious production did not begin until the second half of 1893, with 193,323 rifles being delivered by the end of the year. During "Phase 1"—initial rearmament with the new rifle, 1892–1896—the three factories manufactured 1,470,470 combat rifles and 32,443 training rifles. An additional 503,539 were produced in France at the Manufacture Nationale d'Armes de Chatellerault.

In 1897, control and management of the second phase of Model 1891 rifle production—1897 to 1903—was assigned to the Main Artillery Commission. The Phase 1 executive and management committee ceased to exist as of 1 January 1897. During the next eight years the three Russian small arms factories produced 1,869,305 additional Model 1891 rifles, a small percentage of which were designated as being suited for training only. Thus by the eve of the Russo-Japanese War (1904–1905), the Imperial government had procured just over 3.8 million of the new rifles.[37]

Post-Russo-Japanese War Rearmament

The war with Japan was the first post-rearmament test of the Imperial army and its new materiel. This was the first of Russia's modern conflicts, and it was in most respects a disaster. The immense distances between European Russia and the battle zone in the Far East caused logistical problems for both the Russian army and navy. While the new Model 1891 rifles performed satisfactorily and were available in sufficient numbers, field-artillery pieces and their ammunition failed on both quantitative and qualitative measures. During the Russo-Japanese War the Russian military learned that modern weapons gobbled up ammunition, and that a modern army had to be quickly resupplied with ammunition as well as food and forage. In 1910, the Imperial Army General Staff created a commission, under General Aleksei Andreevich Polivanov (1855–1920), to study the problems associated with military mobilization and the stockpiling of materiel.

Polivanov's commission delivered its general findings at the end of 1910. They based their conclusions on three factors: First, they believed that any future war would be of short duration—two to six months, and certainly less than one year; second, quantities of supplies and their placement must be based upon experiences derived from the Russo-Japanese War and from an analysis of the geographical location of potential enemies; third, in the initial stages of a new conflict, weapons and ammunition would be drawn from a war reserve of such materiel. After the war was a few months old, weapons and ammunition would be delivered directly from the arms factories. This last point was based on the assumption that materiel held in reserve was only intended to fill a short-term gap while the factories were placed on a war-production footing.

With the advantage of hindsight it is obvious that the Polivanov commission completely missed the mark in their pre-

A soldier of the Regiment of Grenadiers of Foot, ca. 1905, in winter uniform with his 7.62mm Model 1891 rifle, bayonet fixed.

diction about the nature of the next war. But even if one accepts their projection of what the war was to be like, their projections about the levels of weapons/ammunition usage and the ability of the weapons factories to meet the demands for such items quickly also missed the target. In nearly all categories of ordnance, the Tsar's military forces had acquired the numbers of items required for the reserve stockpile. But in nearly all cases the stockpile standards were set too low, and the estimated rates of usage were also too low. The result was early and continuing shortages of materiel that reduced the effectiveness of the Imperial army.[38]

In 1910, the War Ministry established the reserve stockpile for shoulder weapons at 4,272,744 rifles. This number consisted of 3,924,323 7.62mm Model 1891 Mosin-Nagant rifles, and 348,421 10.6mm Model 1870 Berdan rifles. The Mosin-Nagant requirement was essentially the same as the number procured between 1891 and 1904. This was not enough weapons, even if one only looked at the government's own projections. The troop mobilization plan developed in 1910 established the initial mobilization of the army to yield 2,533,847 men above the regular peacetime army of 1,232,738: that is, 3,766,585 troops. That was within 157,738 men of using the total rifle stockpile. But in reality, nearly 4.3 million rifles would be needed to arm the total mobilized strength of 5,432,746 soldiers. This number did not account for wastage and loss of weapons in training and combat, nor did it allow for any reserve stockpile for other emergencies.

By October 1914, when mobilization was only partially completed, the Imperial government found itself short about 870,000 rifles. Commenting on this catastrophe after the war, General G. N. Danilov noted that "the immensity of the requirements surpassed the wildest expectations, and therefore the difficulty of meeting them constantly increased. The rear could not keep up with the front, and, accordingly, both the strength of the army and our supplies of munitions daily decreased." A closer look at the World War I materiel supply problem, as reflected in the supply of rifles, will help to explain the postrevolutionary steps taken by the Soviet government to insure the existence of a self-sufficient armaments industry.

During the years between the rearmament discussions in 1910 and the start of the First World War in 1914, the Russian small arms factories produced the Model 1891 rifle at a very low rate. In 1911, the three factories fabricated rifles totaling about 7 percent of their total production capacity, in 1912 9 percent, and in 1913 12 percent. This substantial cutback in production was a characteristic problem encountered in the manufacture of war materiel. Once the required number of weapons had been built, the Russian government took the natural step of curtailing production. Production machinery at the small arms factories was subsequently run at uneconomical levels required to produce just enough rifles to keep the required number on hand, and to manufacture spare parts. Workmen were likewise diverted to the repair of weapons, or given other manufacturing tasks, or just laid off.

Viewed in the simplest of terms, it would appear that the Imperial government, the War Ministry, and the army were very shortsighted in their failure to produce enough rifles and artillery pieces in the years following the Russo-Japanese War. But there were real financial and political reasons for not running the arms factories at their full capacity. Ordnance manufacture was a drain on the national treasury, and a host of other transportation and industrial development projects needed financing, too. Still, as General Aleksi Aleksyeevich Manikovskiy (1865–1920), who directed the Main Artillery Commission during the 1914–1917 war and War Minister 12–18 May 1917 observed afterwards:

> By curtailing peace-time production in the state plants, the Tsarist government failed to guarantee the factories' equipment, or even reserves of the necessary materials and fuels for use in case of war and the closing of Russia's borders.[39]

But even the stockpiling of raw materials and fuels in a type of strategic reserve was a new and costly concept. Count V. N. Kokovtsov and his subordinates at the Finance Ministry were completely against such ideas. They contended, in a memorandum, that "the state treasury could not agree to the creation of a pool of unprofitable and unemployed capital just to satisfy the needs of some hypothetical and unlikely war." The debate on strategic reserves lasted several years. The end result was a compromise that did not satisfy the Main Artillery Commission. That body had sought twenty-eight million rubles to purchase reserve materials, but only five million were allocated. Furthermore, the reserve stockpile of strategic raw materials was reduced from enough to build military equipment for two years to enough for a single year of production.

The survival of the Imperial regime was to hinge in part on the failure to make adequate plans for a major international conflict. Problems would appear throughout the industrial sector, which would affect the military capabilities of the state.

By the winter of 1916, the economic dislocations caused by inadequate planning would have serious effects on the defense programs. At the end of 1916, coal production was 10 percent lower than it had been in 1914, and iron production was down by 16 percent. This decline in key materials added to the woes of the arms-producing factories.

The problem of keeping state-owned weapons factories operating at useful and economical levels was not unique to Russia. All nations operating their own ordnance factories have had to face this feast-or-famine production scenario at their armories. It remains a problem today for weapons factories around the world. Many nations have resorted to export sales of weapons—past and present—to smooth out the peaks and valleys in their domestic requirements for weapons production. The American System of Manufacturing created the capacity to control the scale of production, and to produce large numbers of a given item, but it did not allow the manufacturer to control the size of the demand for his product.

Thus, while it would have been possible for the three Russian arms factories to have built more Model 1891 rifles, there was no government requirement or money for more rifles. Imperial Army and government officials acquired the number of weapons that they believed they would need. Also, this desired number was balanced against the number that could be afforded by the Imperial Treasury. Although the subsequent small-caliber weapons shortages were devastating for Russia's ability to conduct the war once it did appear, this time the blame could not be laid simply at the doorsteps of the weapons factories. During the interwar years, 1905–1913, the manufacturing capacity had existed. The factories were underused out of consideration of economic and other national concerns.

Rifle Shortages, 1914–1917

Although shortages of all types of weapons would develop during the course of the World War, the rifle crisis was the first to appear, and it remained one of the most serious problems. Government officials had predicted that the three arms factories combined would be capable of fabricating seven hundred thousand Model 1891 rifles per year. Soon they saw that this number was completely inadequate. The Imperial Army was losing in one way or another about 200,000 rifles per month; or 2.4 million rifles a year. It became clear all too quickly that the Russian military needed at least 5.5 million Model 1891 rifles to arm the initial troops placed in the field in 1914, 5 million rifles to equip men subsequently called up, and about 7.2 million more rifles to make good combat losses during a three-to-four-year war. This total of 17.7 million Model 1891 rifles was 11.1 million more than originally anticipated by the Polivanov committee in 1910.[40]

In addition to the 4,652,000 rifles available when the war began, the factories added 278,000 in 1914; 860,000 in 1915; 1,321,000 in 1916; and 1,120,000 in 1917. Another 2,461,000 were acquired from abroad, and 700,000 were taken from enemy soldiers. That yielded a grand total of about 11,392,000 rifles, which was nearly 5.2 million fewer than actually needed. This shortfall delayed recruiting. As General Danilov noted:

> Owing to the shortage of rifles the army units, although greatly reduced, were unable to fill up their gaps, and the reenforcements sent from the rear had to be kept behind in the depot battalions, swelling their number and hindering the training of new contin-
> gents. . . . by the end of November, 1914, there were 800,000 men, mostly trained, in the depot troops, whereas the army in the field suffered from an appalling shortage of men.[41]

In 1915 the situation became worse. Only a part of the men at the front were armed; the remainder had to wait for an armed comrade to be wounded or killed to acquire a rifle. In an attempt to solve this problem, the Imperial High Command made some strange proposals. At one point early in the war, Lieutenant General N. N. Golovine, Quartermaster General of the Ninth Army, received a telegram from the headquarters of the southwestern front that suggested that some of the infantry companies be armed with long-handled axes. Such companies, it was suggested, could protect artillery positions. General Golovine noted that "this project to revive 'halberdiers,' reads like fiction," but is illustrative of the atmosphere of despair in which the Russian army operated during the campaign of 1915.[42]

The rifle shortage problem was compounded by the fact that the Minister of War Vladimir Aleksandr Sukhomlinov (1846–1926; War Minister 1914–1915) refused for many months to acknowledge the reports of weapons shortages coming back from the battle fronts. General Sukhomlinov was the epitome of the incompetence against which both conservative and radical reformers complained. He was known for his boast that he had not read a military manual in twenty-five years. In the age of repeating rifles, machine guns, and rapid firing artillery, this crusty old General still placed his faith in infantry bayonet charges and Cossacks with sabers and lances.

Having acquired a peacetime bureaucratic slowness, Sukhomlinov and his colleagues did not want to accept the reality of the disaster that faced the Imperial government. The result was an entirely inadequately equipped army. Thousands of men had no shoes. Wireless communications equipment, airplanes, and sufficient horse-drawn or gasoline-powered transportation were unrealized dreams. The absence of all of these elements contributed to the catastrophic battle of Tannenberg in August 1914. This overwhelming inability of his Minister of War to adjust to the harsh truths of the war forced the Tsar to dismiss Sukhomlinov from his post on 13 June 1915, and replace him with General Aleksandr Andreevich Polivanov (War Minister 1915–1916), his former deputy.

Among the host of disasters facing the Imperial Army, Polivanov had two immediate problems to solve relating to infantry weapons: Ensure the repair of existing rifles and related ordnance, and the acquisition of additional fighting materiel. Prior to the war, the War Ministry had not developed plans for field workshops to repair or overhaul combat materiel. Their plan had been for the rifle factories to carry out this work, but that course of action would have diverted men and production equipment from the production of additional rifles. General Manikovskiy reported that:

> The factories, of course, protested against such added work . . . but they were forced to do it, although it would have been possible to organize, promptly and on a large scale, the repair of small arms in the workshops of the depots in the interior, and . . . to set up special workshops in the zones of military operations. All this was done later, but unfortunately it was done after a long delay, during which the proper work of the factories, burdened with such repairs, was held up.[43]

Failure of the War Ministry to foresee the rifle shortage had other consequences.

Purchases of supplementary rifles abroad were not started soon enough. As early as September 1914, the Main Artillery Commission, discovering the impossibility of sufficiently expanding the production of the three rifle factories, began to look for rifles overseas. At first, they wanted to purchase foreign-made Model 1891 rifles; later they would become willing to settle for any rifle in any caliber just as long as it could be obtained with sufficient quantities of ammunition. Prior to his dismissal, War Minister Sukhomlinov had for a time discontinued this search because he did not want to introduce different-caliber rifles into the supply system. Under ideal conditions, that would have made sense, but in a crisis situation where millions of rifles were needed, such considerations had to yield to the greater need for weapons. On 15 December 1914, the Chief of Staff ordered the purchase of any rifles no matter what the caliber. Rifles were desperately needed.

When the monarchy fell to the 1917 revolution, Sestroretsk and Tula were in the combat zones between the contending factions of the revolution. Only Izhevsk in the Ural Mountains was relatively free from the turmoil. Still, production at the rifle factories dropped significantly. About 380,000 Model 1891s were built in 1918, and about 557,000 were fabricated in 1919. Once the civil war between the Whites and the Reds ended in the early 1920s, reestablishment of large-scale production of rifles at the three factories was one of the highest priority projects facing the new government of the Soviet Union. The new leadership was determined to succeed in establishing military hardware independence through domestic production. Where the Imperial government failed, the Soviet government was successful.

2

The First Generation of Soviet Infantry Rifles, 1917–1945

The Bolshevik military forces that fought the Russian Revolution, the Civil War, and the Polish border conflicts — basically an irregular collection of troops — used several variants of the 7.62 x 54mmR Model 1891 Mosin-Nagant rifle as their basic small-caliber weapon. Continued shortages of weapons and ammunition made revitalization and reconstruction of the small arms ammunition factories one of the earliest priorities for the new Soviet leadership. The turmoil that preceded and followed the October 1917 revolution disrupted many of Russia's key industrial centers. The weapons factories at Tula, Izhevsk, and Sestroretsk were fully embroiled in this political and military storm.

The ordnance manufacturing centers needed to be brought firmly under the physical and ideological control of the Soviet government so they could be used to manufacture arms and ammunition for the "Worker's and Peasant's Red Army" (Rabochye-Krest'yanskaya Krasnaya Armiya — RKKA), which had been formed on 28 January 1918. Leon Trotsky (1879–1940), as People's Commissar for War, was one of the key individuals responsible for working the Red Army into shape. He also oversaw the revitalization of the military factories so the new army would have the necessary weapons. By the end of 1920 the Red Army had grown to almost five-and-a-half-million men. Most of these individuals were infantrymen who required a weapon.

Steady production of small arms was a continuing problem. Trotsky continuously worried about weapons and ammunition shortages. In a 29 July 1919 letter to the All-Russian Central Executive Committee

(Vserossiyskiy Tsentral'niy Ispolnitel'niy Komitet), Trotsky reported: "The lack of small-arms ammunition and the extreme shortage of rifles is fatal to the front. The Ninth Army has 20,000 men ready for action, but they are all without rifles and expecting to receive half the required number. Ammunition is issued in abysmally small quantities, and this, given even the slightest complications, makes for fatal results." Looking at the total operational readiness of the Red Army on the Southern front, Trotsky warned the Central Committee that the "entire operation may come to grief over the matter of small-arms ammunition."[1] Two weeks later, Trotsky wrote again. "It must be said that everyone in the Ukraine except the soldiers possesses rifles and ammunition. . . . the number of rifles held by the population is such that, when one brigade foraged around in the area where it was quartered, it collected a thousand rifles. The well-fed kulak who has his rifle hidden regards the Red Army man, barefoot and hungry, with contempt; the latter feels uncertain of himself and humiliated."[2] While this sounded similar to the reports from Imperial commanders before the revolution, Trotsky saw no reason why the Red Army or the Soviet State should be as ineffectual in equipping its troops as had its Tsarist predecessors. He and his comrades would take steps to correct this state of affairs.

Clearly, the Soviets needed a strong and healthy domestic military industry. For both political and ideological reasons, the revolutionary leadership could not purchase arms and ammunition from the capitalist manufacturers abroad as had the Imperial government and the Provisional government once headed by Aleksandr Fyodorovich Kerensky (1881–1970). They could not obtain mili-

tary assistance from the European powers as did the armies of the "counter-revolution." At first their problems were complicated by the fact that the Izhevsk Weapons Factory, and the Simbirsk, Votkinsk, Lugansk, and Ivashchenko ammunition factories, and a number of key military depots had been overrun, occupied, and operated by anti-Bolshevik forces. Sestroretsk was only being used for the repair of weapons because many of its workers had been evacuated. As a result, during the first phase of the Civil War the Soviets had only Tula industrial at their disposal. And those weapons shops and ammunition factories were functioning at less than half of their average First-World-War capacity.

Because the new revolutionary government had only this one basic source for new small arms, Trotsky and V. I. Lenin (Vladimir Ilyich Ulianov—1870–1924) paid special attention to the progress of manufacture at Tula. Lenin was of the opinion that "arms and ammunition are more important than all else," and he directed that the Tula factories produce only military equipment. At the beginning of 1918, weapons production at Tula averaged each month ten thousand rifles, two thousand revolvers, and thirty machine guns. The monthly averages in 1916 had been sixty thousand rifles, fifteen thousand revolvers, and one thousand two hundred machine guns. In the fall of 1918, between September 6 and 9, the Red Army captured the small arms factory at Izhevsk and the ammunition factory at Votkinsk. Izhevsk rifle production had dropped from a monthly average in 1916 of fifty-four thousand rifles to fifteen thousand rifles.

By late in the summer of 1919, ammunition and weapons production had been re-

Table 2-1
Small Arms Production 1918–1920

	Tula			Izhevsk	Sestroretsk
	Rifles	**Revolvers**	**Machine Guns**	**Rifles**	**Rifles**
1918	150,803	52,863	4,446	214,891	14,545
1919	290,979	79,060	6,270	171,075	NA
1920	Total for all factories: 429,898 rifles and 4,467 machine guns				

Source: D. N. Bolotin, "Sovetskoe strelkovoe oruzhie za 50 let" (Leningrad, 1967), 12–14.

stored at several of the formerly occupied factories. By the end of 1919, the Izhevsk Weapons Factory had reestablished its World War levels of production. To insure the continued improvement of production activities at the ordnance factories, the All-Russian Central Executive Committee created the Extraordinary Commission for Supplying the Army and the Navy (Chrezvychanyniy upolnomochenniy sovyet oborony po snabzheiyu armii i flota). As a result of the guidance of this commission and the work of the people at the weapons factories, the small arms production levels increased slowly over the period 1919–1920.

Total small arms production for 1918–1920 small arms deliveries were 1,272,191 rifles, 175,115 revolvers, and 15,383 machine guns. Another 920,000 rifles and 5,000 machine guns were repaired during that period. Once production of standardized patterns began to stabilize, the Red Army could begin to look for more modern small arms.

On 3 October 1922, the Republic Revolutionary Military Council (Revolutsionniy voyennyi sovyet respubliki — Revvoyensovet — RVSR) proposed a scheme for the more rapid reequipping of the Red Army. Among the items desired was a more modern rifle. While plans progressed for the development of a successor

to the Mosin-Nagant rifle, the state small arms factories were to produce a single simplified version of the Model 1891 rifle based on the Model 1910 Dragoon rifle. The new rifle would be 1,232mm (48.5 inches) overall with a 730mm (28.75 inch) barrel, whereas the older M1891 rifle had an overall length of 1,305mm (51.375 inches) and a barrel 803mm (31.625) inches long.

This Russian decision to shorten the barrel followed the actions taken elsewhere in Europe; for example, the German shortening of the Gewehr 98 to produce the 98a and later 98k short rifles and the British creation of the Short Magazine Lee-Enfield series of rifles. All of the major powers discovered that satisfactory accuracy could be obtained with shorter barrels. In cutting down the barrels, the arms factories produced rifles that were handier in the close confines of trenches and other obstacles of modern warfare. Production of the longer M1891 rifle would be terminated once all the in-process materials — receivers, barrels, and stocks — were used up.

The Model 1891/30 Rifle

Izhevsk was to be the first factory to manufacture the new version of the Dragoon rifle, and Tula was scheduled to

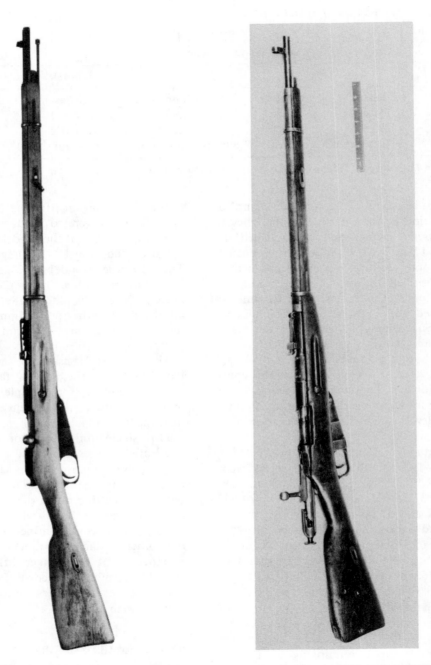

Left, the 7.62mm Model 1910 Dragoon rifle, which, with its shorter barrel, served as the pattern for (*right*) the Model 1891/30 rifle. This somewhat simplified rifle reduced the amount of machine time required to manufacture the basic infantry rifle for the Red Army. (NMAH 77772)

A Soviet sniper from the Second World War period aims his 7.62mm Model 1891/30 sniper rifle. Note that the bolt handle has been altered by being lengthened and turned down so that it could be operated more easily when the telescope is mounted to the rifle.

begin production in 1924 of the modified weapon.[3] During the next seven years, a series of new ideas to improve the performance and reliability and to simplify the production of the Model 1891 rifle were examined and tested. This work led to the creation of the Model 1891/30 rifle (*Vintovka obrazetza 1891/30 goda*), which was standardized on 28 April 1930 by the Revvoyensovyet. In addition to shortening of the barrel, the most important change to the Model 1891/30 was the simplification of the profile of the receiver (the old octagonal shape forward of the bolt was eliminated in favor of a simple cylindrical shape). This one alteration made it much easier to manufacture the receiver, thus

saving time and energy. The rear sight of the Model 1891/30 was graduated in meters as opposed to *arshins* (0.71 meters) on the Model 1891 rear sight. Simplifications were aimed at the more efficient production of the rifle.

On 10 June 1930, Ieronmin Petrovich Uborevich (1896–1937), head of armament production for the RKKA, issued the order for the production of this new rifle equipped with the improved bayonet designed by Ye. K. Kabakov and I. A. Komaritskiy. Between 1930 and 1940, a total of 4,463,388 Model 1891/30 rifles were manufactured by the arms factories. An additional 53,683 sniper versions were also assembled. During 1941 and 1942, the small arms factories produced 3,900,156 Model 1891/30 rifles; 1,106,510 Model 1938 carbines; and 53,195 Model 1891/30 sniper rifles. This accomplishment was all the more amazing since the last three months of 1941 were spent relocating the Sestroretsk and Tula facilities and personnel. Bolt-action rifle production was cut back in 1940–1941 in favor of self-loading rifles; it was never terminated. Still in 1943, the Soviet arms factories produced about 3.4 million more rifles and carbines. The total bolt-action rifle production for the years 1930–1943 exceeded thirteen million weapons.[4]

Combat experience with the Model 1891/30 rifle and the Model 1938 carbine clearly indicated that the shorter weapons were better suited to close-quarter combat. The one shortcoming cited for both weapons was the absence of a bayonet permanently affixed to it. In May 1943, eight different systems for attaching a nonremovable bayonet were tested by Soviet ordnance officials. One of these, the one designed by B. V. Semin, was adopted.

On 17 January 1944, the State Committee for Defense (Gosudarstvenniy komitet oborniy) designated this new weapon the 7.62mm Model 1944 Carbine (7.62mm Karabin obrazetza 1944 goda). Production of this carbine began in February 1944 and continued until at least 1948 in the Soviet Union. Poland, the People's Republic of China, and other countries manufactured this bolt-action rifle until the mid-1950s. Data on the number of Model 1944 carbines manufactured has not yet been encountered.

During the 1939–1945 Great Patriotic War, the Soviet defense factories manufactured more than 2.5 million submachine guns and several million self-loading rifles. Thus by 1945 the Soviets had obtained a much cherished goal—national self-sufficiency in the production of infantry weapons. Development and successful production of the submachine gun and self-loading rifle-type weapons had another effect. It stimulated interest in the assault-rifle class of weapons that had been introduced by the Germans at the end of the Second World War. Although the submachine gun and the self-loading rifle had separate evolutionary paths, many of the same Soviet designers participated in the creation of both. Development of self-actuated rifles had begun back in the Tsarist era.

Self-Loading Rifle Development, 1905–1939

During the latter years of the nineteenth century, the world's arms designers began to explore the possibilities of developing self-actuated rifles. The American designer Hiram S. Maxim was the first to produce experimental self-loading weapon designs, the first two of which appeared in 1881 and 1883. Two years later, Ferdinand Ritter von Mannlicher, the Austrian weapons genius, produced the first of his self-loading designs, a short-recoil rifle. Soon a host of other rifle, handgun, and machine gun designers had joined in the search.

In the decades that followed, the major armies of the world also began to consider the merits of self-operated rifles. In 1902, the American Chief of Ordnance, Brigadier General William B. Crozier, took note of this turn of events in his annual report. He stated for the benefit of the Secretary of War and the American Congress that the only radical improvement in military rifles then under study was the

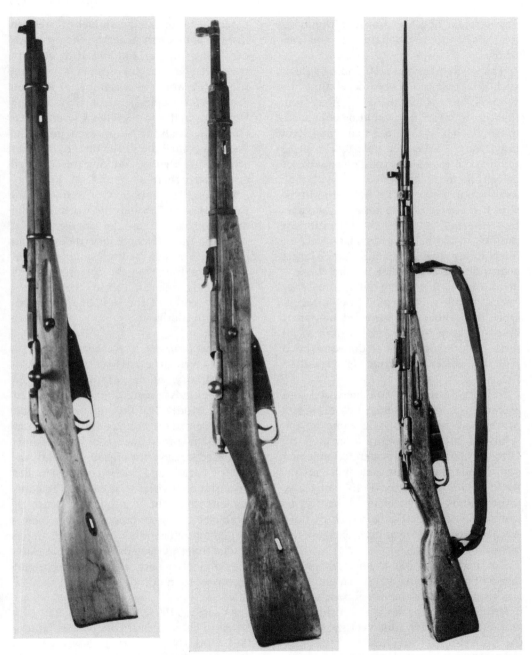

These three photos illustrate the evolution of the Mosin-Nagant carbine. *Left to right:* the Model 1910 Carbine (508mm barrel); the Model 1938 Carbine (508mm barrel); the Model 1944 Carbine (518mm barrel), with folding bayonet extended. (NMAH 72-5398 and 72-5399)

development of a weapon that would re-load itself upon discharge of the car-tridge.[5]

The advantages of a self-loading rifle, if such a weapon could be successfully de-veloped, were obvious. Firepower from the individual soldier would be enhanced, as would that of the troops en masse. Not only would soldiers be able to fire more rapidly, but they also would be capable of delivering more accurate fire. Although the introduction of the bolt-action-type rifle had increased the rapidity of shots from the military rifle, the operation of the bolt itself had the distinct effect of interrupting the rifleman's aim. Target acquisition was essential. In the employ-ment of a self-loading rifle, the jerky operation of the bolt would be eliminated. Once the soldier had acquired his target he could keep his eye on his man at all times. All he would have to do would be to pull the trigger each time he wanted to fire.

Military interest in the increased and accurate firepower promised by designers of the semiautomatic rifle came as the result of another invention created by Hiram Maxim: the self-operated machine gun. While the Maxim machine gun fa-vored the military forces on the defensive, some military officers believed that the in-troduction of the self-actuated rifle would help to shift the advantage back to the troops on the attack.

Despite the obvious theoretical advan-tages of self-loading rifles, suitable de-signs would have to be developed, proper cartridges evolved, and a considerable amount of military conservatism against the introduction of new technologies would have to be overcome.

If these difficulties were significant ones for inventors who were trying to con-vince the ordnance personnel of Western Europe and North America, the problems of selling the self-loading rifle concept were even greater for designers working within the world of the Imperial Russian Army. Nevertheless, there were among Russian small arms designers several crea-tive individuals who appeared upon the scene to contribute to the development of self-actuated rifles. Among these small arms "konstructors" were Y. U. Roshche-pei, V. G. Federov, S. G. Simonov, and F. V. Tokarev. Through the work of these men, one can witness the emergence of a domestic Russian capability to design and manufacture self-loading small arms in Russia. In following the careers of these individuals, one can also see the Russians join the ranks of the best of the world's small arms designers.

Yakov Ustinovich Roshchepei (1879– 1958)—During the early years of the twen-tieth century, numerous proposals were presented advocating the conversion of existing Model 1891 bolt-action rifles into self-loaders. This was a common phenom-ena of the time, since such conversions promised large savings through the utiliza-tion of barrels and other parts assemblies from standard rifles. Use of existing com-ponents could be translated into use of established production equipment, a con-cern of major economic importance. In the United States, Great Britain, France, Aus-tria, and elsewhere, local designers had proposed to modify the existing service rifle.

As early as 1905, V. G. Federov had pro-posed such a conversion of the Model 1891 Mosin-Nagant rifle in a written pre-sentation. But the first firing model of an altered Model 1891 rifle was the handi-work of Yakov Ustinovich Roshchepei.

Styled by Soviet historians as a "soldier-inventor," Roshchepei appears to have been a rather skillful armorer who had an eye for improving the Model 1891 rifle.

Existing ordnance influenced the development of the initial self-loaders. The first designs looked much like existing bolt-action rifles, because the designers did not immediately break with the past. These individuals and their military customers had set ideas about the proper appearance of a military rifle. Early self-loaders were also patterned after older rifles because if they could use components from existing weapons, they might be able to break down technical and economic resistance to a new design.

Roshchepei's design followed this pattern of development. He apparently retained the Mosin-Nagant rifle receiver in essentially unaltered form. He also used the standard barrel and bolt. Details of his design are still sketchy, but he apparently developed a retarded blowback bolt assembly that permitted him to obtain self-actuation from his modified Model 1891 rifle. One Soviet historian has praised this design, while condemning the Tsarist officers who failed to see its merits:[6]

> The rifle of Roshchepei reportedly excelled in its simplicity and compactness, and in this sense evoked great interest. But the incompetent Tsarist officials, bending low before the West without faith in the ability of the Russian people, did not appreciate the talented originality of this simple soldier who worked as a regimental blacksmith. The Russian warriors were not fated to hold the rifle invented by Roshchepei in their hands.

While we lack further details of Roshchepei's design, it is safe to conjecture that this weapon likely suffered from the same failings as similar conversions made in Europe and the United States. These early conversions were generally very heavy, of awkward design, and mechanically complex. They were also fragile and unreliable.[7] Roshchepei, like so many other inventors, pursued his work into the late 1920s, long after other designs had rendered his ideas technologically obsolete. The design ideas of V. G. Federov fared much better.

Vladimir Grigorevich Federov (1874–1966) — This energetic man, who is usually described as the father of the Russian school of automatic-weapons design, was born in St. Petersburg on 16 May 1874. Since his father was the holder of a minor position in the Imperial government, Vladimir Grigorevich was permitted to attend the Gymnasium and the Mikhailovskiy Artillery School. At this time the Gymnasia were open to carefully selected boys who were at least twelve years old. The three-year course of study included mathematics, natural philosophy (physics), history, physical geography, natural history, language (Russian, German, and French), mechanical drawing, military drill, and gymnastics. Distinguished graduates of this program were admitted on a selective basis to the Mikhailovskiy Artillery School and other advanced programs. The artillery course included instruction in advanced mathematics, chemistry, more physics, and other basic courses. In addition there was a curriculum of tactics, fortification, artillery, military law and administration, as well as other subjects suited to the needs of a professional military officer.[8]

Following graduation in 1895, Federov served as platoon commander in the First Guards Artillery Brigade. With two years active duty behind him, he was selected to attend the Mikhailovskiy Artillery Acad-

Vladimir Grigorevich Federov (1874–1966), the father of Soviet self-loading rifles and avtomats.

emy in St. Petersburg in 1897. The three-year course there was a postgraduate ordnance program in which he pursued the study of ballistics and applied mechanics as well as more routine military subjects. He once again proved himself to be a superior student, and he earned the first of many military honors: the right to wear the academy's badge on his uniform.

Upon completion of his course of study at the Artillery Academy in 1900, Federov was assigned to the Weapons Section of the Main Artillery Commission (Glavnoe artilleriiskoe upravlenie—GAU). This was a prized assignment because the Weapons Section was responsible for examining samples of new armaments, domestic and foreign. In effect it performed a function similar to the special committees and ordnance boards that existed in the other European and the United States armies. In this assignment, the young Federov had the opportunity to study and in many cases actually handle new military hardware. This was in effect a practical course in ordnance that complemented his academic training.

At about the same time, Federov had an opportunity to work with S. I. Mosin. The latter was then Director of the Sestroretsk Weapons Factory in the St. Petersburg suburbs. As a consequence of these early studies, Federov decided that the self-loading rifle was the weapon of the future. Working in the tool-making shops of the Sestroretsk Weapons Factory, Federov built his first experimental weapon, a self-loading conversion of the Mosin-Nagant rifle.

While his initial mechanical work was underway, he began a parallel career as a military technical writer. In 1907, he published his first book, entitled *Avtomaticheskogo Oruzhie* (Automatic Weapons).

This work was similar to other books appearing at this time in the West. Federov described the functioning principles of the basic self-actuated weapons designs that had appeared to 1907, together with an analysis of their relative merits. His special focus in this volume was the self-loading rifle.

Avtomaticheskogo Oruzhie and Federov's subsequent books and technical articles assumed great significance in his native land because they were among the very limited number of Russian language technical texts available to his countrymen. As a result, *Avtomaticheskogo Oruzhie* and its 1938–39 successor *Evolyutsiya Strelkovogo Oruzhiya* (Evolution of Small Arms), also by Federov, became the primers for two generations of Soviet small arms designers. Both S. G. Simonov and M. T. Kalashnikov have credited Federov as being a basic inspiration in their careers. This honoring of the "grand old man" goes beyond the basic Soviet tendency to revere technological giants. Federov was not simply a designer or simply a writer—he combined the best of both skills. So as Simonov reported: "Federov was my teacher who gave me the principles for designing and producing small arms systems."[9] The teacher gained the respect from his students because he could translate his textbook ideas into functioning mechanisms made of steel.

By 1906, while working at the Infantry Officers Training School at Oranienbaum, Federov had completed a self-loading rifle that had a rotating bolt. It is still unclear whether this was another version of a self-actuated Model 1891 rifle or a totally new design. Some time during 1906, Federov and Vasily Alekseyevich Degtyarev (1879–1949) began working on a new self-loading rifle, which had a recoiling barrel that carried twin pivoting locks designed to engage lugs on the bolt. This first true Federov rifle is often called the Model 1907 by Soviet historians. It was this operating mechanism which was perfected in Federov's later models.

The 1907 Federov experimental rifle demonstrated failures to extract the fired cartridge case once the barrel became hot. Test shooting also disclosed that when the rifle was fired with the muzzle elevated, the recoil springs did not always have sufficient strength to propel the recoiling parts to the forward-and-locked position. Still, this first version of Federov's rifle demonstrated sufficient promise for the Imperial military authorities to arrange for Federov and Degtyarev to be transferred to Sestroretsk. This change of location gave them access to better workshops.

In 1911, Federov's reworked self-loading rifle was tested again. This time his design was pitted against a rifle developed by his colleague F. V. Tokarev, and rifles submitted from abroad by Karl A. Brauning (made by Fabrique Nationale of Liège), and Carl Axel Theodor Sjogren (made by AB Svenska Vapen och Ammunitionsfabriken of Stockholm). At the end of this comparative trial the Federov rifle was judged to be the best of the weapons submitted. Each of Federov's ten prototypes had been fired thousands of times with only a minimum number of significant problems. As a consequence of this exercise, the government ordered 150 more of the Model 1912 experimental rifle from Sestroretsk. For his work on this rifle design Vladimir Grigorevich was awarded the Great Mikhailovskiy Prize, an honor bestowed once every five years for the most important contribution to improvements in ordnance.

Federov served his government in a variety of capacities in the years before World War I. In the winter of 1913, he was despatched to Germany to scout out information on the latest ordnance developments in the Kaiser's domain. This thirty-nine-year-old colonel did not make a very successful spy. After several close encounters with the German intelligence community, Federov beat a hasty retreat to Switzerland. Once the war began in 1914, he served on several delegations which visited Japan, England, and France in search of additional rifles and related equipment for the Imperial Army. During most of the war, he continued to work on the self-loading rifle and other experimental rifle projects at the Sestroretsk Weapons Factory.[10]

Available evidence suggests that Federov decided around 1912 that the standard 7.62 x 54mmR Model 1891 cartridge was too powerful for use in a self-loading rifle. To have increased parts life, improved feeding, and better firing control when the rifle was used as a fully automatic weapon, Federov decided that he should use a less powerful cartridge, which would have lower recoil forces and a rimless cartridge case. After three years additional work, in 1916 and in the midst of the World War Federov unveiled his new rifle to which he gave the name Avtomat.

This 6.5 x 50.5mmSR caliber weapon was more than just another self-loading rifle. It was the predecessor to the class of weapons that are now called "assault rifles" in the West. Federov oversaw the manufacture of a small sample of his Model 1916 Avtomat, which was issued to a carefully selected company of the 189th Izmail'skiy Regiment so the Army could collect some data about its suitability in

Right and left side views of the 6.5 x 50.5mmSR Model 1916 Federov Avtomat, serial number 643. This extraordinary weapon was the grandfather of the modern assault rifle. It weighed 4.4 kilograms (9.7 pounds), was 1.045 meters (40.9 inches) overall, had a 666 m/s (2,664 f.p.s.) muzzle velocity, and had a cyclic rate of six hundred shots per minute. The magazine contained twenty-five cartridges. The Federov avtomat embodied the short-recoil system of operation, with the bolt being locked to the barrel by a pair of locking blocks.

Disassembled view of the 6.5 x 50.5mmSR Model 1916 Federov Avtomat, serial number 643, shown in the preceding photos.

combat. So it occurred that the first assault rifle (Russian) was tested against the first enemy (German) in December 1916.

The 1917 revolution, as noted in chapter 1, created turmoil in the Russian armaments industry. With the coming of the revolution, Federov decided to cast his fortunes with the revolutionaries, and he placed his design talents at the disposal of the Bolsheviks. Their Soviet of Labor and Defense commissioned Federov, in 1918, to arrange for the manufacture of nine thousand Model 1916 avtomats. It was the hope of Red Army leaders that production of these rifles would enhance the firepower of their troops in the field through the acquisition of more rifles and rifles that had better firepower potential. This

hope was dashed upon the rocks of production difficulties.

The legacy of Tsarist dependence upon foreign manufacturers and the unsettling effect of the revolution on the weapons factories manifested itself when the factory personnel were not able to tool up for the fabrication of Federov's avtomat. The Soviet leadership decided in mid-January 1918 to sponsor the development of a production line at the Sestroretsk Arms Factory for the Federov avtomat. Federov was told that deliveries of his weapons would begin on the first day of February 1919. It was never realistic to expect Federov and his team to meet this schedule. The proper men, machines, and raw materials were all in short supply.

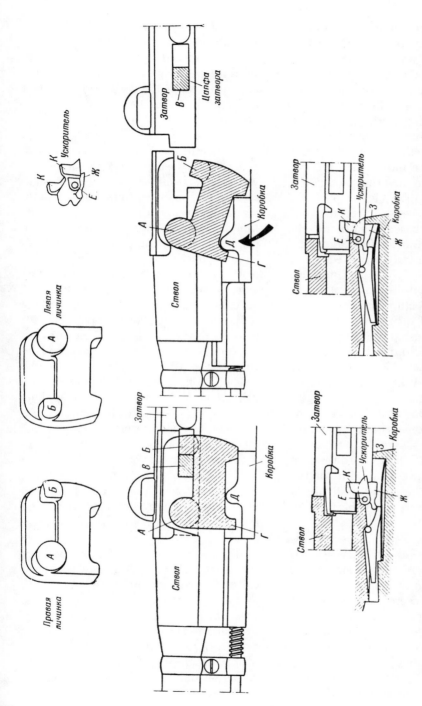

This drawing from Federov's book _Evolyutsiya strelkovogo oruzhiya_ (128) illustrates the operating mechanism of his Model 1916 Avtomat.

When a shot was fired from his weapon, the barrel and the bolt recoiled together for a short distance. During this travel, the barrel return spring (located beneath the barrel) was compressed. Then the lugs on the bolt (_see arrow_) struck the forward end of the locking block ("A"), and forced the locking block to cam downward. The locking block, which was attached to the barrel assembly, no longer held the bolt in check; therefore, the bolt could open and travel to the rear. During this process, a projection on the accelerator ("K") struck an abutment fixed in the receiver, causing the accelerator to pivot suddenly. This action stopped the barrel and speeded the rearward movement of the bolt.

As the bolt continued rearward, extraction, ejection, and cocking took place. During this period, the barrel was kept in the rear position by a latch. Under the action of the return spring, the bolt moved forward, driving a cartridge into the chamber. In its forward movement, the bolt struck the accelerator, thereby causing it to pivot. This motion disengaged the barrel latch, permitting the bolt and barrel to move forward together. As they reached the battery position, the locks were cammed upward, and the weapon was ready to fire again.

Despite the unreasonableness of the government's expectations, Vasily Alekseyevich Degtyarev was assigned the task of selecting qualified teams of production workers and rounding up the necessary machines. Degtyarev's tasks were difficult ones. He had been supervising the workers of the Sestroretsk Arms Factory who had been gathered together to repair small arms. To turn these individuals into the cadre of a real manufacturing production line was virtually impossible.

The partnership between Federov and Degtyarev was one based upon friendship and professional respect. Professionally, Degtyarev was not nearly as well educated as Federov in a strictly formal sense, but Degtyarev had an intuitive understanding of weapons manufacture and design that had been obtained on the factory floor. The personal friendship was very important on several occasions to Federov, especially on the occasion when the Bolsheviks imprisoned him in 1919 on allegations of sabotage and counterrevolution. Degtyarev was able to intercede on his comrade's behalf and convince the revolutionary authorities that he should be released. But neither friendship nor professional competence could overcome some of the problems facing these two individuals when it came time to build the Federov avtomats.

The Revolutionary War Council (Revolutsionniy voenniy sovyet — Revvoyensovyet) and the Main Artillery Commission jointly continued to insist on the expeditious supply of Federov avtomats and Madsen light machine guns to the Red Army. Although full-scale production was not possible due to a shortage of cutters and other tools and a lack of machine operators, Federov suggested the retreat to a production program that would com-

bine machine and hand-work processes. He dubbed this "semi-hand manufacturing." He warned against trying to make rifles totally by hand, because this would have diverted qualified workers from their main work of rehabilitating the small-arms factory.[11]

On 2 March 1919, the Main Artillery Commission told Federov: "According to a decree of the Emergency Commission you are to take all measures to establish as rapidly as possible production of automatic weapons . . . of your system and the Madsen system. Moreover, according to instructions of the head of the Main Artillery Commission you are quickly to begin work on 150 copies of your hand-held system by the semi-hand made method." Federov was not to pursue his "disturbing proposal" for incentive wage payments for his skilled workers. To this idea, officials up and down the Soviet ladder said an emphatic "No!"

The Main Artillery Commission did help Federov and his team by making more workers available. Industrial, management, and engineering personnel at the factory were excused from military service. About one hundred workers from the Yaroslav and Moscow military regions were transferred to the Federov team, and Federov was given the right to request more engineers as the need for them was clearly identified.

To get started with Federov and Madsen production, Federov, Degtyarev, and their colleagues were sent to the former Danish machine gun factory at Korov, near Moscow, where the Danes had previously fabricated the Madsen light machine gun. As work with the rehabilitation of the Korov factory progressed, it became apparent to all parties that it was going to be troublesome to start up production simultaneously for the Federov avtomat and the Madsen light machine gun. Therefore, the Main Artillery Commission decided to pursue only the manufacture of the avtomat. Rifles were of more immediate need than light machine guns.

In a manner of speaking, Federov and his avtomat were victims of their own success. In a 6 February 1920 telegram, S. S. Kamemev of the Extraordinary Commission for Army Supply, commenting on examinations of the first two hundred post-1918 Federov avtomats, stated: "The Central Committee having become acquainted with the hand-held machine gun of the Federov system found it both technically and practically . . . suitable and therefore requests that all measures be taken for increasing production capacity for these guns at the factory so that 300 hand-held machine guns will be manufactured as soon as possible."[19] Desires of the Central Committee could not immediately be translated into higher production levels. In September 1920, the rifle factory delivered fifteen avtomats. By the end of the year a total of one hundred more rifles had been assembled, and monthly production had stabilized at fifty per month.

On 21 April 1921, the Soviet Ministry of Industry reported that mass production of the Federov avtomat had become a reality. This was true in the sense that the rifles were being made by machine production processes. Still, the numbers being fabricated were very small when compared to the production of bolt-action Mosin-Nagant rifles. Between 1 October 1922 and 1 October 1923 only 822 avtomats were delivered. The absolute total for Federov production had reached only 3,200 avtomats when production was terminated on 1 October 1925.

During the five years of its manufacture, a number of modifications had been made to the basic Federov avtomat design. A bolt stop had been added to the top of the bolt to hold the bolt open when the last cartridge had been fired. The shape of the ejector had been changed, and other internal parts such as the firing pin had been redesigned for greater life expectancy. An aluminum forestock had been introduced to facilitate barrel cooling, and an interrupter was incorporated into the trigger assembly to reduce the likelihood of multiple discharges. Other changes included modifications to the sights, front and rear.

Federov's Model 1916 avtomat was ahead of its time both as a weapon and as a

A line drawing from Federov's book *Evolyutsiya strelkovogo oruzhiya* (225) illustrating test shooting of the water-cooled light machine gun version of Federov's avtomat.

military concept. It must be remembered that Federov presented his weapon at a time when most self-loading rifles were relatively clumsy and unreliable. The Soviets thus have a real reason for being proud of their accomplishment. Federov was an accomplished designer, and the success of his weapon was attributable in large part to his own abilities as a mechanical engineer. Selection of a suitable cartridge was a key decision made by Federov. Other self-loading rifle designers met significant difficulties because they selected cartridges that were too powerful or unacceptable for other reasons for use in a self-loading design.

From his earlier studies, Federov understood the relationship between cartridge size (bullet diameter and cartridge overall length) and power in determining the effectiveness and reliability of the resulting rifle. As a result, he designed his avtomat to fire the Japanese Arisaka 6.5 x 50.5mm semi-rimmed rifle cartridge. The Russian military had experienced firsthand the effectiveness of this cartridge in the 1905 Russo-Japanese War and they had purchased substantial numbers of these weapons during the 1914–1917 war.

Federov knew that from the standpoint of recoil, control during automatic fire, and durability of the rifle's mechanism, a more satisfactory weapon could be designed to fire the medium-power 6.5 x 50.5mmSR cartridge than could be designed to fire the fatter, fully rimmed 7.62 x 54mmR Model 1891 cartridge. This cartridge question was not often understood by officers in the field who were wedded to shooting their rifles at ranges out to one thousand two hundred meters. Distance requirements such as these were unrealistic for even most bolt-action magazine re-

peating rifles. In the case of self-loading automatic rifles the larger cartridges were totally incompatible. The Russian officer corps was not alone in refusing to abandon the full-power infantry cartridge when the decision was made to require the small-arms designers to use the 7.62 x 54mmR cartridge in post-Federov avtomat self-loading rifle designs.

European and American designers also encountered this prejudice against a smaller caliber, medium-power rifle cartridge. In fact, one of the major problems before the 1930s on both sides of the Atlantic Ocean was the absence of a standardized cartridge specification within most ordnance establishments. When the cartridge was finally defined in most countries, the one selected was generally too powerful to be best suited for a self-actuated rifle.

Although the Model 1916 Federov avtomat had several attractive features, nearly thirty years would pass before the tactical advantages of this type of weapon were fully appreciated in the Soviet Union or elsewhere. The Soviets were the first to introduce and use an assault rifle, but they would only later learn from the German invaders its full potential in combat. Federov's avtomats remained standard weapons in the Soviet inventory until 1928, at which time they were recalled from service and placed in storage. Combat experience had shown these weapons to be too delicate for the rigors of military service. Dirt tended to jam the mechanism, and full-automatic fire accuracy was rather poor. When the Soviet Union fought the Finns before World War II, some of the Model 1916 Federov avtomats were issued for service once again. Thus this weapon should be considered a first step toward the creation of an automatic assault-type shoulder weapon for the Soviet Union.

Federov also started the Soviet military thinking about families of military small arms. Between the years 1921 and 1926, Federov, Degtyarev, and their colleagues developed a series of experimental guns based upon the Model 1916 Federov avtomat operating mechanism. These included:

6.5mm	Federov-Degtyarev light machine gun test model 1921 with Lewis gun-type cooling jacket.
6.5mm	Federov-Degtyarev light machine gun test model 1922 air cooled.
6.5mm	Federov-Degtyarev light machine gun test model 1922 water cooled.
6.5mm	Federov-Shpagin sniper light machine gun model 1922 (twin air cooled with inverted mechanism).
6.5mm	Federov-Degtyarev single aircraft machine gun.
6.5mm	Federov-Degtyarev aviation machine gun test model 1922 (twin air cooled, each with 50-shot pan type drums). A single trigger fires both guns. There was also a three-gun version of this weapon.
6.5mm	Federov-Ivanov-Shpagin sniper tank machine gun.

Despite the fact that none of these guns were adopted, the Soviets would later pursue the concept of families of weapons built around one basic weapon-operating system. The seeds sown by Federov were later harvested by M. T. Kalashnikov.

Federov retired from active service in 1933 at the age of fifty-nine, after having reached the rank of Lieutenant General in the Artillery Engineering Service (ordnance). He was recalled to duty with the Ministry of Armaments during World War II (1944–1946), and he continued to be listed as a member of the staff of the Artillery Academy until 1953. He was the grand old man of the Soviet small arms community, and from the early experiments started by him grew a whole generation of small arms designers. These designers were dominated by the "big three," V. A. Degtyarev, S. G. Simonov, and F. V. Tokarev. Degtyarev is best known for his contribution to the development of machine guns and submachine guns, and Simonov and Tokarev made their primary contributions in the field of self-loading rifle development. All of these men influenced the later work of M. T. Kalashnikov.

Fedor Vasil'evich Tokarev (1871–1968) was born in a large Don Cossack village of Yegorlykskaya. By the time he had entered primary school at age nine, Tokarev had already demonstrated a keen interest in firearms, stimulated by an itinerant gunsmith from Tula. In 1882, he became apprenticed to the village blacksmith and two years later he went to work with a gunsmith named Krasnov. Because of his technical aptitude, he was accepted as a student at the Novocherkassk Military Vocational School. After four years of study, Tokarev graduated as a Cossack noncommissioned officer and master

In a photograph taken during the 1939–1940 Russo-Finnish Winter War, two of the Soviet soldiers shown here are equipped with the 6.5mm Federov Model 1916 Avtomat. At this point in time the Soviets were employing any infantry weapons they could to provide the needed firepower.

craftsman. He was appointed Master Armorer of the 12th Don Cossack Regiment, which was then stationed on the Austro-Hungarian border.

Four years later, Tokarev returned to the Novocherkassk Military Vocational School as an instructor in the small arms-making course. After several successful years as a teacher, he was selected to attend one of the elite cadet schools and in due course became a Cossack officer. By 1907, he was studying at the Officer's Rifle School at Oranienbaum, an experience which further prepared Tokarev for a career in designing small arms. It

was at Oranienbaum that he began to work out the design details for a self-loading rifle. He continued this work after he was transferred to the Sestroretsk Weapons Factory in 1908. These first rifle prototypes were tested in 1910 and 1914.

The Russian revolution and civil war found Tokarev serving as Assistant Director for Inspection and Manufacture at the weapons factory of Sestroretsk. His popularity with the workers was such that, even though he was an Imperial officer, they elected him as the technical director of the works after the revolution. At all times he continued to tinker with his design, which

Fedor Vasil'evich Tokarev (1871–1968), master gun designer and accomplished technological politician.

had a massive bolt that locked into a barrel collar that was also rather massive. The trigger mechanism was relatively simple and was to remain basically the same throughout his subsequent attempts to design a self-loading rifle.

In 1919, Tokarev was transferred to Izhevsk as the senior engineer for the small arms factory, and two years later he was shifted to Tula. On 4 October 1921, Tokarev's self-loading rifle was discussed by the Main Artillery Committee. "Having become acquainted with the aforementioned model, the Artillery Committee is of the opinion that the proposed Tokarev system is of undoubted interest and its further development for the small-caliber (Japanese) cartridge is desirable; instructions have already been issued by the Chairman of RVSR for manufacture of 10 samples . . . at TOZ" [Tul'skiy oruzheiniy zavod] — five rifles and five carbines.[13]

Once the civil war began to wind down and the demand upon the weapons factories for large-scale production of rifles began to slacken, Tokarev, Federov, and others began to work in earnest once again on self-loading rifle designs. Their basic goal was a 4 kilogram (8.8 pound), selective-fire (semiautomatic and automatic-fire) 7.62 x 54mmR rifle having a 50-shot magazine. Rather quickly this requirement for a 50-shot magazine was reduced to twenty-five cartridges because of the bulk and weight of the larger-type magazine. V. G. Federov, F. V. Tokarev, V. A. Degtyarev, I. M. Kolesnikov, and V. P. Konovalov were soon busy at work on different rifle designs.

In January of 1926 the Artillery Commission arranged for the first competitive testing of self-loading rifles. Because of

their incomplete condition the Kolesnikov and Konovalov rifles were removed from the test schedule early in the trials. Federov's entries were essentially 7.62mm versions of his earlier Model 1916 avtomat capable of selective fire. Degtyarev's prototype rifle was a modification of a design that he had first experimented with in 1916. The locking mechanism was a variant of the side-swinging locking bars that would later become very well known in his light-machine-gun family. Tokarev's design involved a recoiling barrel, the movement of which was used to unlock the bolt from the barrel assembly. All of these rifles could be reloaded, with the magazine in place, by using the standard 5-shot clip of the Mosin-Nagant rifle.

After the trials it was the opinion of the test commission that despite the fact that the three rifles had survived the test program, they did not completely meet the basic design requirements. All three weapons were too complicated mechanically, and their strength and reliability could be improved as well. As a consequence, the test commission recommended that the designers be given six months to prepare two completely identical samples of an improved weapon. These new rifles should have barrels approximately 630mm long, magazines for five and ten cartridges, a standard-type bayonet, and rear sight.

A second large-scale self-loading rifle trial was held in June 1928. A group of inventors led by F. G. Federov* submitted three different models, while F. V. Tokarev submitted his own design. One of the Federov "collective" designs was basically an improvement of the recoil-operated Federov avtomat. The two others reflected

---

*The inventor's collective consisted of F. V. Federov, V. A. Degtyarev, D. V. Uraznov, A. I. Kuznetsov, and I. I. Bezrukov.

Degtyarev's gas operation system, with different approaches taken to locking the bolt. Tokarev's rifle was still of the recoil-operation kind.

The Artillery Committee evaluated the test results on 5 November 1928. The records of the committee note that "although 10,000 shots were fired from the test models, the three models of the inventor's collective and the one Tokarev rifle equally withstood the main [phase] of the testing; however, all of the aforementioned models were not in such form that one could finally establish a model and give a final order." Additional improved prototypes would need to be built and tested. All of the rifles were judged to be too heavy, and the Artillery Committee urged that steps be taken to reduce the weight of these rifles without reducing their basic durability. And although there had been no specific problems encountered with the weapons having recoiling barrels, there was a general feeling that such weapons were liable to be put out of service in combat because of their vulnerability to bending of the barrel assembly.[14]

A third round of self-loading-rifle testing was carried out in March 1930. This time the designs were limited to rifles developed by Degtyarev and Tokarev. The former submitted rifles with permanent 5-shot magazines and models with removable five- and ten-cartridge magazines. Tokarev's guns had removable 5- and 10-shot magazines. Since both designs retained some of their previous shortcomings, the Artillery Committee concluded that neither could be considered suitable for the Red Army (RKKA). A further step was taken by the Artillery Committee at a 4–6 April 1930 conference, where it was decided that rifles with recoiling barrels (e.g., the Tokarev design) were militarily

unsuitable, because they could not be used for launching rifle grenades.

Knowing that this problem was likely to eliminate his rifle from consideration, Tokarev had already begun work on a gas-operated self-loading rifle that had a fixed barrel. This new design was to become the basis of the bolt and bolt-carrier operating system that was incorporated in the Tokarev rifle subsequently adopted by the Red Army. This rifle proved to be more robust than Tokarev's earlier model with the recoiling barrel.

Meanwhile, the Revvoynsovyet ordered production of a test lot of one thousand Degtyarev rifles on 28 April 1930. This number was subsequently reduced to five hundred. Members of this Revolutionary War Council were growing tired of the slow pace of self-loading rifle development because they wanted to get on with the reequipping of the Red Army. This weapon was given the official designation *7.62mm samozaryadnaya vintovka obrazetz 1930g* (7.62mm self-loading rifle, model of 1930) by the Scientific Technical Committee of the Artillery Administration. Troop testing of these Model 1930 Degtyarev rifles was carried out in 1933 by the Moscow Proletarian Rifle Division (Moskovskoi proletarskoi strelkovoi divizii).

Looking back on the events of this period, V. G. Federov commented as follows:

At the end of 1930, the question of the automatic rifle again had the same position as it had in 1916. . . . Namely a position of the necessity of supplying a . . . quantity of automatic rifles to the troops for their broader testing. The difference was only in the system. . . . All of this shows that the . . . developing of an appropriate automatic rifle encounters tremendous difficulties.[15]

Much work lay ahead for the Soviet rifle

designers. It was at this point, late 1930, that a new designer appeared on the scene.

Sergei Gavrilovich Simonov (1894–   ) had been born into a poor peasant family. After studying in his village school for three years, he worked at a number of odd jobs until his sixteenth year when he was apprenticed to a blacksmith for whom he worked until he was twenty-one years old. In 1915 he began to work as a metalworker in a small machine-building plant. After two years of this labor he became part of the team of machinists at the Korov factory that was building the Federov avtomats. In 1922, Simonov was granted the title Master Gunsmith, and late Senior Master. Because of his technical skills he was sent to the Moscow Higher Technical School (Moskva Vysshete Teknicheskoye Uschilische – MVTU) to study mechanical engineering. After graduation he became an ordnance inspector at Tula, and in 1927 he became a full member of the Communist Party of the Soviet Union.

As his career advanced professionally and politically, Simonov still found time to concentrate on his first love – the design of weapons. As early as 1922, Simonov had begun to lay down the ideas for a light machine gun and an automatic rifle. He presented his first model of a self-loading rifle for official consideration at the beginning of 1926, shortly after his return to the Federov design bureau at the Korov arms factory. While praising his efforts, the Ar-

tillery Committee noted in its records for 7 April 1926 that the weapon had serious design faults. The key difficulty resulted from his decision to mount the gas-operating system on the right side of the barrel and receiver. This led to an unacceptably wide stock and a weapon that was difficult to field strip.

This initial rejection did not deter Simonov. After reviewing the outcome of the 1930 rifle trials, he decided that he could devise a rifle that was better than those submitted by either Degtyarev or Tokarev. His second major design was completed in 1931. This weapon was gas operated and had a bolt mechanism that was locked by a vertically sliding wedge. This rifle quickly became the major contender as the Red Army extended its search for a replacement for the Model 1891 Mosin-Nagant rifle.

After a rather quick development program, the Revvoynsovyet decided on 22 March 1934 that the Simonov rifle should be adopted for issue to the Red Army. This weapon was designated the 7.62mm Avtomaticheskaya vintovka Simonova Obrazets 1936g (7.62mm Simonov automatic rifle Model of 1936) or AVS36 for short. Production of the AVS36 is summarized in Table 2-2. On 26 February 1938, the Director of the Izhevsk Weapons Factory, A. I. Bykhovskiy, reported that mass production of the Simonov AVS36 was fully underway.

For reasons that are still not clear, the

Table 2-2
Production of Simonov System Automatic Rifles 1933–1938

Year of manufacture:	1933	1934	1935	1937	1938
Rifles manufactured:	40	106	286	10,280	24,401

Source: Bolotin, "Sovetskoe strelkovoe oruzhie za 50 let" (Leningrad, 1967), 131.

Sergei Gavrilovich Simonov (1894–   ), the creator of the 7.62 x 54mmR AVS36 automatic rifle, the 14.5 x 114mm PTRS antitank rifle, and the 7.62 x 39mm SKS45 carbine.

Two views of the 7.62mm Avtomaticheskaya vintovka sistemi Simonova obrazets 1936g (AVS36).

This gas-operated self-loading rifle had a unique straight-line bolt. The bolt lock was a hollow square steel unit, which moved vertically in slots cut in the receiver ring. The forward end of the bolt moved longitudinally through the hollow square. The top section of the hollow square was provided with cam faces that were engaged by suitable camming surfaces on the underside of the bolt carrier.

As the bolt and carrier moved forward, the bolt head came up against the face of the chamber as in the Tokarev. The carrier continued forward, and the camming lug on its underside engaged the camming surface at the top of the bolt, lifting it in its slots in the receiver ring until the lock engaged the bolt. Thus the head of the bolt was locked to the receiver ring.

When the gun was fired and the operating rod was forced to the rear, the camming surface on the bolt carrier forced the hollow square locking member down in its slots in the receiver, thus disengaging it from the bolt, which then was allowed to move to the rear with its carrier.

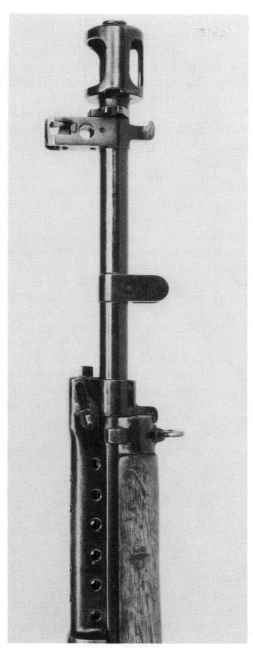

Two close-up views of the 7.62mm AVS36. The left view illustrates the details of the breech section of the rifle, while the right view illustrates muzzle end details such as the recoil brake. Note that the folding bayonet is missing from this weapon.

People's Commissar of Defense and the People's Commissar of Defense Industry announced on 22 May 1935 a new competition for self-loading rifles. Delivery of prototypes was set for 15 June 1938. Soviet historical sources do not explain why, hot on the heels of standardizing the AVS36, it was necessary to continue looking for another rifle. Tokarev gives a clue in a statement he made some years later. Commenting on the Simonov design, Tokarev noted: "His AVS36 was designed for single shot fire and automatic fire in short bursts. However, the experience of manufacture and employment indicated that the design was relatively complicated; malfunctions occurred during firing and the rifleman became fatigued quickly."[16] Western testing of the AVS36 confirms the fact that these rifles were rather sensitive to dirt, propellant residue, and mishandling by the soldier.

Renewed testing of self-loading rifles took place in the fall of 1938 (25 August to 3 September), when F. V. Tokarev, S. G. Simonov, N. V. Rukavishnikov, and others submitted rifles for trial. At the conclusion of these experimental shooting tests, the commission reported that none of the rifles were ready for adoption but that they believed that the Tokarev model could be reworked in a relatively short period of time. As a result, the test commission asked Tokarev to correct the deficiencies in his design and resubmit his prototypes on 20 October. He was specifically asked to eliminate the longitudinal cooling grooves on the exterior of the barrel, which would make the barrel easier to fabricate. He was also asked to provide a bolt hold-open catch that would hold the bolt to the rear after the last shot had been fired, and to add a muzzle brake of the Rukavishnikov type.

On 20 November 1938, the Tokarev, Simonov, and Rukavishnikov designs were tested once again, with the Tokarev clearly out-performing the other two competitors. In the spring of 1939, the Red Army adopted the Tokarev rifle as the Samozaryadnaya vintovka Tokareva, obrazets 1938g (Model 1938 Tokarev self-loading rifle) or SVT38 for short. This action did not end the controversy surrounding self-loading rifles in the USSR.

Problems with Self-Loading Rifles

Having lost out in the technical arena, Simonov turned to the political world in an attempt to save his rifle from oblivion. A member of the Communist Party for a dozen years, Simonov reported to the Central Committee of the Communist Party on 19 January 1939 that he had eliminated all of the technical problems associated with his weapon. This action led B. L. Vannikov, the People's Commissar of Armaments of the USSR, and G. I. Kulik, the Director of Artillery Administration of the Red Army, in May, to create a special commission to compare the Tokarev and Simonov rifles from technical and manufacturing standpoints. Recent Soviet historical studies report that this special study commission discovered that to make the Simonov it took less machine-production and hand-finishing time, less raw materials, and a smaller amount of factory floor space. It was also reported that the Simonov was easier and cheaper to manufacture. Table 2-3 provides comparative data on the manufacturing of the two rifles.

Boris L'vovich Vannikov (1897–1962) in a postwar recollection of this dispute recorded the following:

Table 2-3
Data Describing the Production of the Simonov and Tokarev Rifles

1. For a daily program to produce 1,000 rifles, the production area required for the Tokarev was 4,042 square meters larger than that required for the Simonov.
2. For a daily program to produce 1,000 rifles, 363 more machines were required for the Tokarev than for the Simonov.
3. Each Tokarev took 207 more minutes of machine time and 103 minutes of hand-finishing time than each Simonov. The resulting increase in labor cost was six rubles and seventy-nine kopeks per Tokarev.
4. Each Tokarev required 1.74 kilograms more metal than the Simonov. The resulting increase in raw material cost was one ruble and eighty-five kopeks per Tokarev.
5. The Tokarev had 25 more parts than the Simonov (143 vs. 118), and it weighed .65 kg more (4.825 vs 4.175 kgs).

Source: Bolotin, "Sovetskoe strelkovoe oruzhie za 50 let" (Leningrad, 1967), 136–37.

During the pre-war years, and especially beginning in 1938, I. V. Stalin [1879–1953] devoted much attention to the work involved in creating self-loading rifles. . . . It rarely happened, as I recall, that I. V. Stalin did not touch upon this subject at meetings on defense problems. Expressing dissatisfaction with the slow progress of work on self-loading rifles, he emphasized on more than one occasion the extreme necessity of having such a weapon in our army's arsenal. In speaking of its advantages . . . he loved to repeat that the firepower of a self-loading rifle was the equivalent of ten ordinary rifles. Moreover, Stalin said, the self-loading rifle conserved the strength of the fighting man and enabled him to keep the target in sight.

In commenting on the Simonov-Tokarev dispute, Vannikov reported that:

Simonov had created a lighter model with the best automatic mechanism. But, as a consequence of carelessness by the designer himself in manufacturing the rifle, it showed somewhat poorer results than Tokarev's design. Being a member of the commission, I was in charge of accepting new designs into the arsenal of infantry weapons — an exacting and responsible matter. For example, as opposed to other types of equipment, a rifle is usually accepted for use over many years, since subsequent changes in its design unavoidably require both complicated measures in organizing combat training in the army . . . and also long and expensive technological reequipping of industry. This is especially true as it relates to the self-loading rifle, and it was therefore clear to me that the best of the models represented at the competition was Simonov's. It had not failed because of design failures, but for production reasons . . . which could be eliminated completely.

Vannikov believed that the Tokarev design had been favored because Tokarev was a popular figure and because "he was the senior arms designer and a well-known specialist on automatic weapons. Whereas Simonov was little known, and for that reason alone was somewhat mistrusted."

After reviewing all of the economic, technical, and test data, the Defense Committee (Komitet oboroniy) decided that the Tokarev was the best from the standpoint of combat reliability and projected-life-cycle performance. Vannikov argued against the SVT38 rifle. He reminded Stalin that the Tokarev was heavier than the Simonov, which made the latter better in the field. "Stalin made it possible for everyone to speak as much as he liked during the course of the discussion. He did not express his opinion, limiting himself only to asking questions of those who had spoken." He listened to Vannikov's almost solitary defense of the Simonov AVS36. "How great was my surprise," noted Vannikov, "when I. V. Stalin proposed that Tokarev's rifle be accepted into the arsenal! The question involuntarily exploded from me: 'But why?' I. V. Stalin replied: 'Because everyone wants it that way.'"

Based on Stalin's decision, the Defense Committee, on 17 July 1939, directed that the attempts to develop self-loading rifles for the Red Army be terminated, and that all of the energy of the People's Commissariat of Armament be concentrated on the production of the Tokarev SVT. The following production plan was proposed:

1939	50,000 rifles
1940	600,000 rifles
1941	1,800,000 rifles
1942	2,000,000 rifles

Vannikov recalls that:

we began organizing production of the self-loading Tokarev rifle at one of the arms plants. Since the blueprints had not been fully worked out, on orders from the People's Armament Commissariat, they were refined in the course of mastering production of the rifle. Design shortcomings, and other unfinished work, which hampered the technological process of preparing for mass production of the self-loading rifle were thus eliminated. The volume of this work turned out to be quite considerable, because Tokarev had carried his models only as far as testing, disregarding the aid of design engineers and others in the preparation of the technical documentation.

Since all of this work delayed the production of the SVT38, members of the People's Defense Commissariat complained about Vannikov's armament commissariat to Stalin. Not given a chance to explain his side of the story, Vannikov was

called to a meeting of the Defense Committee at which Stalin dictated the following decree: "It is suggested that Comrade Vannikov stop vascillating and accelerate the release of Tokarev's SVT." After what Vannikov calls "long ordeals," SVT38s began to become available to the troops. On 16 July 1939, the first SVT38 was delivered, and by the twenty-fifth regular assembly of this weapon had been started. Tokarev's self-loader was first tested under wartime conditions during the Winter War of 1939–1940 between the Soviet Union and Finland.[17]

Combat experience indicated that the SVT38 design had some weak points, and steps were taken quickly to eliminate these problem areas. Still there were political repercussions. Vannikov recalled that:

One evening, at I. V. Stalin's request, I saw him in the Kremlin. He was alone and he paced the office gloomily. At a long table standing near the wall were a number of weapons. Leading me to the table, and showing me one of the models, I. V. Stalin asked what kind of rifle this was. I said it was a Federov avtomat and not a recent one. [Presumably a 6.5mm Model 1916 avtomat.] After handling several automatic weapons, he took up Simonov's AVS36, and asked me the same question. I answered. I. V. Stalin . . . immediately asked for comparative data on the Simonov and Tokarev self-loading rifles. When I reported them, he asked sharply: 'Why was the Tokarev rifle and not the Simonov accepted into the arsenal?' When I reminded him of the history of that question, I. V. Stalin flew into an angry rage. He paced the floor: 'You are to blame. You should have proved convincingly which rifle was better and you would have been heeded.' . . . I remained silent. Stalin said: 'We must stop manufacturing the Tokarev rifle and change over to manufacturing of the Simonov rifle.'

As staggered as I was by these accusations, it was inappropriate for me to object and to justify myself. But, at the same time, I immediately imagined the terrible consequences of such a change and considered it necessary to avert it. Ceasing production of the Tokarev rifle, I said, would lead to a situation in which we would not have either the Simonov nor the Tokarev. [Delivery of the Simonov rifles] could only begin in no less than a year to a year and a half. I. V. Stalin thought a while, agreed, and abandoned his plan. Instead of stopping production of the Tokarev, he proposed that its design be improved, basically by lowering its weight and shortening the bayonet. Both of these steps could be taken without a major change in production equipment.[18]

The modified rifle was called the Samozaryadnaya vintovka Tokareva, obrazets 1940g (Model 1940 Tokarev self-loading rifle) or SVT40 for short. Some of the major changes to the SVT38 design included replacement of the two-piece wooden stock with a single-piece stock made of birch. The cleaning rod of the SVT40 was placed beneath the barrel instead of being fitted in a special groove along the right side of the stock. While the SVT was reduced slightly in weight (.68 kg), many of the essential operating parts were strengthened. This weight reduction was made possible by removing extra metal from the receiver and the barrel.

These changes to the Tokarev rifle were carried out by a special commission chaired by Georgi Maksimilianovich Malenkov (1902–?). Vannikov suggests that the haste with which the work was carried out on the SVT40 was the source of the subsequent problems with that rifle. Thus there were still some serious troop complaints about the reliability and performance of the SVT series. First, these weapons were too sensitive to foreign matter such as dust, sand, and excess grease, especially at very high and very low temperatures. Some Red Army soldiers also reported problems with the system for regulating the flow of operating gases,

Two views of the 7.62 x 54mmR Tokarev rifle. On the left, the Samozaryadnya vintovka sistemi Tokareva obrazetz 1940g (SVT40), and on the right the Samozaryadnya vintovka sistemi Tokareva obrazetz 1938g (SVT38). Note the differences in the stocks (two piece vs. one piece) and the location of the cleaning rod (under the barrel vs. alongside the barrel).

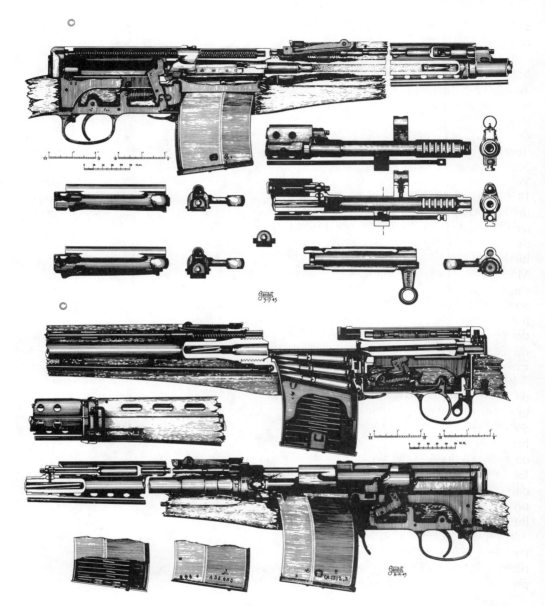

Two cutaway views of the operation of the 7.62 x 54mmR Samozaryadnya vintovka sistemi Tokareva obrazetz 1940g (SVT40).

Unlocking of the Tokarev bolt began with the rearward motion of the operating rod when it struck the forward face of the bolt carrier. The bolt carrier reciprocated in grooves milled into the steel of the receiver. Initially, the bolt remained locked as the bolt carrier started to the rear. Rearward motion of the carrier (after about 7mm) cammed the rear end of the bolt out of its down-and-locked position. The two pieces then continued to the rear, until the cartridge case had been extracted and the recoil spring was compressed to the point where it forced the bolt forward. As it traveled to the battery position, the bolt stripped a new cartridge into the chamber, and the rifle was ready to fire again.

and the fact that the detachable magazine could be easily lost.

Because the war with Germany began before a major redesign project for the Tokarev rifles could be carried out, there was never an adequate opportunity to solve these problems. Thus, despite its drawbacks the SVT40 rifle became an item of large-scale production for the Soviet defense industry during the Second World War, and production of the Model 1891/30 bolt-action rifle could not be terminated, despite the desire of the Malenkov commission to do so. Nor could the production rate for the SVT38 be increased as rapidly as desired by the Malenkov commission. Discussions about the self-loading rifle problem continued to reverberate through the halls of the Kremlin for many months. In the end it was decided that for the duration of the war, the Red Army was saddled with the Tokarev self-loader.

Mass production of the SVT40 began on 1 July 1940. Soviet sources report that in excess of 1,326,000 SVT40s and 51,000 SVT40 sniper rifles were manufactured between 1940 and 1942. Although unclear on the subject, it would appear from inferences in Soviet source documents and dates on surviving SVT40s that production of the Tokarev rifle series continued into 1945.

A January 1945 State Defense Committee study proposed termination of Tokarev rifle production, but for some reason that proposal was never approved by the Defense Committee that Stalin chaired. Data on the number of Tokarev rifles manufactured between 1943 and 1945 has not been encountered. Total production for both the SVT38 and SVT40 probably did not exceed two million rifles. Still, it is important to note that the Soviet small arms factories produced a much better manufacturing record, under some very difficult conditions, than they had when they were under Imperial administration during the First World War. That production record indicated that the Soviets had met their goal of domestic self-sufficiency in the realm of infantry-weapons manufacture.[19]

Still, unhappiness with the combat performance history of Tokarev's rifles was to lead to further experimentation with alternative infantry small arms. One part of that work concentrated on the further development of 7.62 x 54mmR caliber rifles. Another part focused upon the development of submachine guns firing the 7.62 x 25mm Tokarev pistol cartridge. And the final area centered on the evolution of self-loading rifles and avtomats that fired a new intermediate power cartridge, the 7.62 x 39mm M43 cartridge. From this complex environment of new weapons development, which was being carried out as the Second World War raged, M. T. Kalashnikov was able to evolve his very successful assault rifle. That story begins with the development of a new cartridge, and that leads to a new chapter in Soviet weapons-design history.

3

Evolution of the First Kalashnikov Assault Rifles, 1943–1953

Although the Soviet World War II experience with self-loading rifles was not as satisfactory as the military leadership might have wished, there was a strong current of opinion that the Soviet Army needed a self-operated shoulder weapon that would provide increased firepower for the individual soldier. Twin themes pervaded the thinking of the Soviet defense planners—greater firepower in a more compact and lighter package. As Boris L'vovich Vannikov, former People's Commissar for Armaments, recorded in postwar recollections, those goals could only be met if the old 7.62 x 54mmR rifle cartridge was abandoned.

The old 1891-pattern cartridge had been the major source of performance design problems for both S. G. Simonov and F. V. Tokarev while they were developing their self-loading rifles. The difficulties

they encountered can be divided into two basic and familiar categories. First, the old cartridge was too powerful, a fact that led to metallurgical problems with both weapons and ammunition. Second, the cartridge's large base diameter and its wide flanged rim made it unsuitable for use in the double-row box magazines that Simonov and Tokarev had created for their rifles. There were three common malfunctions with the old 7.62 x 54mmR cartridge: failures to extract when the cartridge stuck to the cartridge chamber of the rifle; rim separations from the cartridge case body; failures of the cartridge to feed due to jamming of the cartridges in the magazine.

All of the problems associated with the Model 1891 7.62 x 54mmR cartridge clearly indicated that successful development of new rifles had to be preceded with the creation of a new cartridge. V. G. Federov had made this point before World War I when he selected the 6.5 x 50mmSR cartridge for use in his avtomat. And, Federov had once written that the future "evolution of individual infantry weapons can be directed towards bringing the two types, i.e., machine carbine and submachine gun, closer together on the basis of planning the new cartridge. Rifle equipment of the near future faces the creation of a light caliber automatic carbine, approximating the submachine gun, but developed, needless to say, for use with a more powerful cartridge."[1] But his message was not fully understood by the Soviet military leadership until combat problems with the Tokarev rifles surfaced during World War II.

It is likely that it was the problems with the SVT38 and SVT40 rifles that led Stalin and the other members of the Defense Committee to authorize the search for a new intermediate-power cartridge suitable for a light automatic rifle. The new cartridge, the 7.62 x 39mm round introduced in 1943, helped to guarantee the success of the Simonov and Kalashnikov weapons introduced after the Second World War.

Origins of the 7.62 x 39mm M43 Cartridge

The mythical history of technological developments in the world of small arms are most often more enduring than fact. This is an issue of special magnitude when the "facts" are unavailable to refute the myth. The story behind the development of the 7.62 x 39mm cartridge is a case in point. In the absence of documentary evidence to the contrary, most Western writers have concluded that the Soviet Model

1943 cartridge *(patrona obrazets 1943g, kalibr 7.62mm)* evolved directly from the Pistole patrone 7.92 x 33mm developed by the Germans for their Sturmgewehr weapons series.[2]

That new type of assault weapon had been first introduced into combat late in 1942 when an encircled German unit known as the Kampfgruppe Scherer was airdropped Haenel-made 7.92 x 33mm Maschinekarabiner 42 *(Mkb 42)* assault rifles. These selective-fire weapons replaced the old 7.92 x 57mm Mauser 98k rifles and 9 x 19mm Parabellum submachine guns. The Kampfgruppe Scherer used the additional firepower provided by their Mkb 42s to assist their breakout through the ring of Red Army units. Incidents such as this one are supposed to have exposed the Soviets to the virtues of the assault-rifle-type weapons, and to have encouraged the Soviets to begin investigation of the possibility of adopting intermediate-power cartridges for their own armed forces.[3]

Until recently, this has been the plausible and logically conjectured history of the origins for the Soviet 7.62 x 39mm M43 cartridge. The timing appeared to be correct and the Soviets were relatively silent on the origin of their 7.62 x 39mm cartridge. Recent East Bloc publications have provided an alternative history of the Soviet-assault-rifle cartridge. These sources report that the Soviet small arms design community began to consider the development of a new infantry cartridge in 1939, about one year after similar official work had started in Germany. It is not unreasonable to speculate that some limited Soviet research and development into this subject probably began earlier, as it had in Germany, Switzerland, Finland, and elsewhere. And it is not out of the

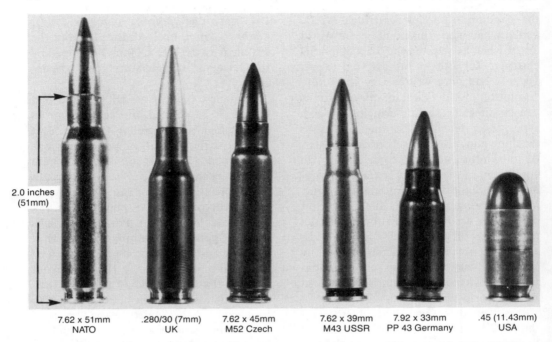

2.0 inches
(51mm)

| 7.62 x 51mm
NATO | .280/30 (7mm)
UK | 7.62 x 45mm
M52 Czech | 7.62 x 39mm
M43 USSR | 7.92 x 33mm
PP 43 Germany | .45 (11.43mm)
USA |

Post–World War II rifle cartridges compared with the German 7.92 x 33mm Kurz and US M1911 .45 (11.43 x 23mm) cartridges.

realm of possibility that the Soviet intelligence agents active in Western Europe "borrowed" ideas from the concurrent research projects of others. For example, Heinrich Vollmer in Germany had developed an automatic rifle for the 7.75 x 38mm cartridge created by the Waffen- und Munitionsfabrik Genschow in the mid-1930s.

Whatever the source of their inspiration, the Soviet ammunition developers were soon involved in the search for their own "intermediate" power automatic-weapon cartridge. Work on an unspecified 5.45mm caliber cartridge for a self-loading carbine had been started in the Soviet Union in 1939. This project soon was delayed by the more pressing nature of war work. At this same time, work was also

terminated on a 7.62 x 25mm Tokarev pistol-cartridge-caliber lightweight carbine, despite the fact that considerable success had been experienced with designs developed by S. G. Simonov, S. A. Korovin, and V. A. Degtyarev. Still, it had become clear that an alternative to existing full-power types of infantry ammunition was required.

The Soviets discovered, as did the Germans and the Western Allies during World War II, that both the pistol-cartridge-caliber submachine gun and the full-power rifle had distinct limitations in mobile warfare. The submachine gun possessed a high rate of fire, which was its most desirable feature, but it fired relatively low-powered pistol cartridges. Such ammunition had very limited striking power and was gener-

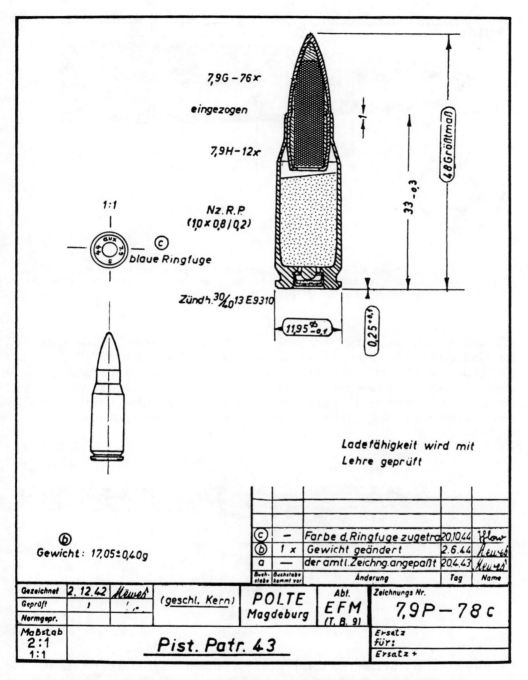

7,9G – 76x

eingezogen

7,9H – 12x

1:1

blaue Ringfuge

Nz.R.P.
(1,0 × 0,8 / 0,2)

Zündh. 30/40 13 E9310

1

48 Größtmaß

33 –0,3

11,95 –0,1

0,25 –0,1

Ladefähigkeit wird mit
Lehre geprüft

Gewicht: 17,05 ± 0,40g

		Änderung	Tag	Name
c	–	Farbe d. Ringfuge zugetra	20.10.44	Flow
b	1 x	Gewicht geändert	2.6.44	Heu 44
a	–	der amtl. Zeichng. angepaßt	20.4.43	Heu 43
Buch- stabe	Buchstabe kommt vor			

Gezeichnet	2.12.42	Mäwes	(geschl. Kern)	POLTE Magdeburg	Abt. EFM (T. B. 91)	Zeichnungs Nr. 7,9 P – 78 c
Geprüft	1					
Normgepr.						
Maßstab 2:1 1:1			Pist. Patr. 43			Ersatz für: Ersatz +

The German 7.92 x 33mm assault-rifle cartridge as made by Polte of Magdeburg.

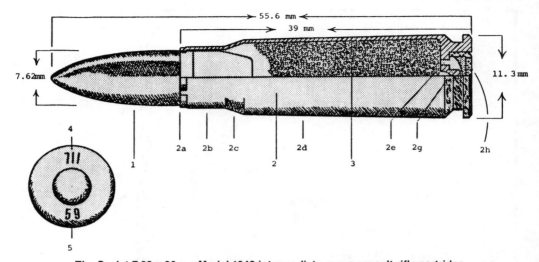

The Soviet 7.62 x 39mm Model 1943 intermediate-range assault rifle cartridge.
1, projectile; *2*, cartridge case; *2a*, case mouth with crimp; *2b*, neck; *2c*, shoulder; *2d*, body; *2e*, primer vent; *2g*, anvil; *2h*, Berdan primer; *3*, propellant; *4*, factory code; *5*, production date.

ally good only for very close-quarter combat. On the other hand, most of the rifles used by the World War II combatants fired cartridges designed for the extreme ranges of fixed-position warfare. That ammunition reflected the tactical realities of the previous great war. Thus most standard infantry rifles of the 1939–1945 era were capable of delivering a lethal projectile to ranges greater than twelve hundred meters. In order to obtain such ranges, relatively heavy charges of propellant were used, and

It is still not clear to what extent the Soviet assault-rifle program was inspired by the appearance of German Sturmgewehr such as the Haenel 7.92 x 33mm Maschinenkarabiner 42 (MKb42) illustrated here.

the recoil forces ("kick") from such weapon/ammunition combinations were generally heavy.

Self-loading rifles chambered to fire these standard full-power cartridges were usually unmanageable when fired rapidly. Thus one of the advantages of the self-loader — improved target acquisition through elimination of the operation of the bolt-type mechanism — was negated. This problem was even more severe when steps were taken to convert self-loading rifles to full-automatic fire. Both the Tokarev AVT40 and the Simonov AVS36 were totally uncontrollable when fired as full-automatic weapons. Equally troublesome was the difficulty of obtaining satisfactory life expectancy for rifle parts when one tried to obtain a lightweight weapon that shot the full-power cartridge.

Creation of the "intermediate" cartridge was a technological attempt to strike a compromise between the manageable automatic fire of the submachine gun and the lethality of the infantry rifle. Such a cartridge made the twin goals of light weight and greater firepower a reasonable goal. It was logical then for the Soviets to perceive the wisdom of developing such cartridges and weapons. S. G. Simonov was among the first to exploit the Soviet "intermediate" 7.62 x 39mm cartridge in the SKS45, but he was soon followed by M. T. Kalashnikov and other Soviet designers in the search for weapons that would exploit this new type of ammunition.

Simonov Semiautomatic Carbine (SKS45)

Sergei Gavrilovich Simonov's weapon that became the SKS45 had a long design evolution. For this 7.62 x 39mm carbine,

Early in the Second World War, S. G. Simonov and other Soviet designers sought alternatives to the 7.62 x 54mmR rifles and the 7.62 x 25mm submachine guns. This experimental 7.62 x 25mm Avtomaticheskiy karabin sistemi Simonova created in 1941 represents one of the attempts that was thwarted by the escalation of the war.

S. G. Simonov's 7.62 x 39mm Samozaryadnya karabin Simonova obrazets 1945g (SKS45), with its folding bayonet extended.

Simonov used the basic design features incorporated into two earlier weapons—the 14.5 x 114mm PTRS self-loading antitank rifle, and the 7.62 x 54mmR SKS41 semi-automatic carbine. Simonov's lack of success in having his AVS36 manufactured by the Soviet defense industries did not dampen his inventiveness. A brief look at both the 14.5mm PTRS and the 7.62mm SKS41 will provide a useful background for understanding the SKS45.

With the appearance of large numbers of enemy armored fighting vehicles, the Soviet military commanders expressed the need for a shoulder-fired infantry weapon that could be used to defeat the armor plate of such machines. V. A. Degtyarev and S. G. Simonov were among the Soviet small arms designers who developed successful antitank rifles for shooting at enemy tanks. They employed the powerful 14.5 x 114mm cartridge, which had been developed specifically for this task. On 29 August 1941, the State Defense Committee accepted both the bolt-action Degtyarev (PTRD) and self-loading Simonov (PTRS) antitank rifles for services.

When problems with the Tokarev SVT40 rifles began to be reported from the battle fronts, Simonov, ever ready to compete with his old rival, reduced the operating mechanism of the 14.5mm PTRS to the scale of the 7.62mm x 54mmR cartridge to produce a shortened self-loading infantry carbine. This new weapon, called the SKS41, was praised because of its simplicity of design, the ease with which it could be disassembled and reassembled, and the incorporation of a permanent magazine that was charged with stripper clips. There were two versions of the prototype SKS41: one had a 10-shot magazine capacity, the other had a

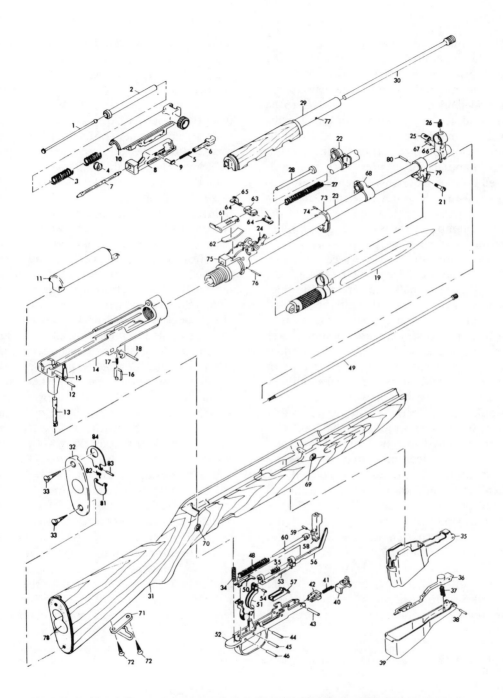

An exploded view of the 7.62 x 39mm Samozaryadnya karabin Simonova obrazets 1945g.

5-shot magazine capacity.

The increasing grip of the war and the disruption of the small arms factories by the German military advances caused proposed field testing of fifty SKS41s to be delayed for three years. All small arms factory manpower was diverted either to relocation of production facilities or to the manufacture of previously standardized infantry weapons. When the test program for the Simonov rifle came about, it was conducted with a new version of the SKS chambered for the 7.62 x 39mm "intermediate" power cartridge.

Development of "intermediate" cartridges had been given new life in 1943. At that time the small arms ammunition designers were presented with the task of creating a 7.62mm caliber cartridge that would still possess moderate killing power at ranges of one thousand meters when fired from a 500mm to 520mm barrel.* In more practical terms, the Soviet military planners sought a new cartridge that would kill effectively in an automatic weapon at a maximum combat range of three hundred to four hundred meters. + Of the cartridges submitted, the one developed by N. M. Elizarov and B. V. Semin was judged to be the best technical solution. It was adopted as the 7.62 x 39mm Model 1943 cartridge.[4] Additional technical discussion of this cartridge is presented in chapter 7.

Simonov's carbine for the 1943 cartridge differed in only minor ways from his SKS41. In addition to reducing its size so that it was tailored to the size and power of the new cartridge, Simonov removed the muzzle brake assembly and improved the latching mechanism for the nondetachable folding bayonet. The clip guides for the stripper clip were shifted from the upper part of the receiver to the bolt carrier. This new 7.62 x 39mm carbine was a direct design descendant of the PTRS and the SKS41.

In the summer of 1944, a number of these Simonov carbines were sent to forces fighting on the first Byelorussian front, and to other test sites for examination. After glowing reports and only a few modifications, this weapon was adopted as the 7.62mm samozaryadnyi karabin sistemi Simonova obrazets 1945g (7.62 x 39mm Simonov system self-loading carbine Model 1945) or SKS45. Despite the very favorable reception that this rifle received, it was destined to be just an interim weapon. Combat experience with the submachine gun, especially when used by infantrymen fighting in cooperation with tanks, and the experience with the Sturmgewehr, demonstrated the effectiveness of massed-automatic-weapon fire when employed by advancing troops.

It is interesting to ponder just why the Soviets adopted a semiautomatic self-loading rifle. Clearly this type of weapon, within their tactical doctrine, was obsolete. Adoption of the SKS45 may have been a technocratic way of apologizing to Simonov. More likely it was a means of establishing a production base for the 7.62 x 39mm cartridge. Still, the day of the semiautomatic rifle was approaching its

---

*The Soviets defined the killing power they wanted to be on the order of 20 kilogram meters² seconds (i.e., 200 joules), which is equivalent to 271.1 foot pounds of kinetic energy. At one thousand meters the 7.62 x 51mm still has about 385 foot pounds of kinetic energy.

+ A fuller discussion of the practical ranges at which combat rifles are used can be found in Edward C. Ezell, *The Great Rifle Controversy: Search for the Ultimate Infantry Weapon from World War II Through Vietnam and Beyond* (Harrisburg, Pa.: Stackpole Books, 1984).

end. The era of the high-rate-of-fire assault rifle was about to begin. And the man to start the era in the Soviet Union was M. T. Kalashnikov.

Kalashnikov's Early Years

Mikhail Timofeyevich Kalashnikov (1919–) — Mikhail Timofeyevich was born to a peasant family in Alma-Ata in southeastern Kazakhstan on 10 November 1919. At the age of seven, he entered the ten year school, the Soviet equivalent of the American primary and secondary educational system. He graduated from that program in 1936, and took employment with the Turkestan-Siberian Railroad system, where he rose to the position of technical secretary prior to his conscription or enlistment in the Red Army in 1938.[5]* In the Soviet Union, as in other industrializing nations in the twentieth century, the railroad system was one of the earliest continuing repositories of technological knowledge. As such it nurtured the mechanical talents of many young men like Kalashnikov.

During his early months in the army, Kalashnikov became increasingly interested in machines of all kinds, with small arms of special fascination. According to a 1968 interview given by Kalashnikov, as a young soldier he constantly got on his company commander's nerves because he kept asking questions about the manner in which small arms and other pieces of equipment operated. Although such inquisitiveness was not always encouraged in the Soviet military, Kalashnikov's commander saw that his young charge had real mechanical talent, and as a result he recommended Kalashnikov for a technical

course that would train him as an armorer once he completed his basic military training.[6] Subsequently, Kalashnikov attended the training school for tank drivers, and while there he designed and built his first piece of new equipment — a device to measure fuel consumption for tanks. Within a short while he had also devised an improved track assembly for tanks.

Kalashnikov's mechanical talents won him promotions. In the latter part of 1939, Sergeant Kalashnikov was sent to Leningrad where he served as a technical advisor to the factory manufacturing his fuel meter and his tank-track assembly. This pleasant interlude, which combined the best aspects of military and civilian life, soon ended when the German Wehrmacht invaded the Soviet Union in June 1941.

Recalling his years as an armorer and tanker, Kalashnikov said that the armorer's "inclination for being fussy stems from the fact that in refitting weapons, they must always put two and two together, and while trouble-shooting, they must think through the weapon's mechanism over and over again." But not all armorers are creative individuals; Kalashnikov was obviously a person with an inventive streak and, as he put it, more than a little audacity. His constant work with small arms and armored vehicles led him to consider bold projects. For example, at one point he considered entering the 1938–1939 search for an improvement over the standard Tokarev TT1930–33 pistol. But, "the war came," and as Kalashnikov put it, "an armorer had other things to do instead of inventing new pistols."[7]

When Senior Sergeant Kalashnikov rejoined the active army, he served in a

---

*As the source notes indicate, it is not clear which is the actual case. All that is important is the fact that he did serve.

front-line combat unit and not as a rear-echelon armorer. During the dark autumn days of 1941, when the Red Army was reeling under the onslaught of the advancing German panzer divisions, the Soviet Union needed fighters more than repairmen. Kalashnikov served as a tank commander in Marshal Katukov's First Tank Army. In September, 1941, during the battle for Bryansk, his T34 tank was hit by a German shell, a splinter of which tore a very bad wound in his shoulder. Unlike many of his wounded comrades, Kalashnikov had a strong constitution that survived the rigors of the battlefield first aid station, the secondary field hospital, and the subsequent evacuation to a hospital in the rear.

As he lay in the hospital, his wounds healing ever so slowly, Kalashnikov exchanged war stories with his wardmates. Their endless tales of superior German infantry and armored firepower left a lasting impression on him. Later he was to recall the remarks of a junior sergeant whose legs had been smashed in combat. "We had only rifles against the Fascists' submachine guns." Another of his wounded comrades remarked: "We've got submachine guns too, but the trouble is that there are so few of them."[8]

These and other conversations in the hospital led Kalashnikov to think that perhaps he could contribute something more to the war effort by designing weapons for the Red Army. He asked the hospital librarian to bring him all the books she could find on small arms so he could begin study on existing small arms design. Along with several thin pamphlets, the librarian Marusya loaned him V. G. Federov's basic weapons textbook *Evolyutsiya Strelkovogo Oruzhiya* (Evolution of Small Arms), which had been pub-

lished in 1939.

"That was my lucky day," Mikhail Timofeyevich recalled. "The book by Vladimir Federov proved to be invaluable. It gave me my first insight into the principles of developing automatic firearms, and put me straight on the positive and negative aspects of each class of firearms. But while he was getting these new insights into the world of gun design and the functioning aspects of different small arms mechanisms, his wounds were still bothering him and giving him considerable pain.

One day, Kalashnikov was summoned to see the head doctor of the hospital in which he was recovering. *"The head doctor of the hospital sat behind his desk sorting papers. As he worked he chatted quietly with the hospital commissar. Seeing Kalashnikov enter the anteroom, they both stood up and smiled as he entered the doctor's office.*

"'Sit down over here please,' the doctors said pointing to an arm chair. 'We have called you in so we may congratulate you on your government award. . . .' As the doctor spoke these words, Kalashnikov automatically stood to attention. The doctor continued: 'For exemplary fulfillment of your command mission, for courage and bravery by Order of the Presidium of the Supreme Soviet you are awarded the Order of the Red Star.' The doctor stood up and extended his hand. 'I congratulate you from the bottom of my heart.'

"The commissar also shook Kalashnikov's hand and said: 'Allow me to congratulate you too.' The three men stood there in silence for several seconds. The head doctor broke the silence: 'How are you feeling?'

"'Very well. I feel fine. It is time for me to be released.'

"'We too have been thinking that it is time that you were released from the hospital, but you will not be returning to combat duty. Instead you will be sent on convalescent leave for at least six months. Your arm needs time to heal completely.'

"'Half a year?' Kalashnikov was surprised. 'The war continues and I will not be able to do anything for half a year?'

"'Do nothing, but get well,' the head doctor said sternly looking at Kalashnikov, making him understand that the decision would not be changed. 'Our task is to return only completely healed soldiers to combat. Recover and you'll be welcome again on the tank. You will fight. But now it is impossible.'" *

The seriousness of his wounds can be judged by the fact that during this critical period of the war, the Red Army gave him six months of convalescence leave. After journeying home to Alma-Ata and settling into a small single-story log house, he alternated visits to a local hospital for treatment with thoughts about designing small arms.[9]

After many hours of consideration, Kalashnikov decided to try his hand at designing a submachine gun. Soviet small arms designers had experimented throughout the 1920s and 1930s with pistol-caliber submachine guns. All of these recoil-operated weapons had in common the simple blow-back (slam-fire) method of operation. In this type of weapon the bolt is not locked, and firing occurs when the bolt drives a cartridge into the chamber. The mass of the bolt delays opening of the breech long enough for the gas pressure in the barrel to drop to a safe level. Blow-back weapons have the virtue of being simple mechanically and generally reliable in combat.

Soviet historians credit F. V. Tokarev with being the first Soviet designer to complete a submachine gun. His 1926 experimental design employed the Model 1895 7.62mm Nagant revolver rimmed cartridge. This weapon gave the Soviet military establishment experience with a domestic submachine gun, and while it was never destined for greatness it did stimulate considerable thinking among Russian small arms designers. In the 1930s, V. A. Degtyarev, S. A. Korovin, F. V. Tokarev, S. A. Prilutskiy, I. N. Kolesnikov, and others also began to experiment with submachine guns, but these weapons were chambered to fire the 7.62 x 25mm cartridge adopted for the first Tokarev self-loading pistol (the TT-1930).

The first standard submachine gun to emerge from this process was the 7.62mm Pistolet Pulemet Degtyareva (Degtyarev Machine Pistol) or PPD34, which after some modification became the PPD34/38. This weapon was too difficult to manufacture to make it a really practical submachine gun. As a result, a much simpler weapon designed by Georgi Semyenovich Shpagin (1897–1952) was adopted in 1941 as the PPSh41. This weapon proved to be much easier to manufacture (less than half the machine time was required for the PPSh41) and was much more reliable in combat. One of the most important innovations in the design of the PPSh41 was the utilization of stamped/pressed sheet metal

---

*The italicized text is taken from a Soviet biography of Kalashnikov by Major Vladimir Nikolayevich Zhukov entitled *Vtoroye rozhdeniye* [Second birth] (Moscow: Voyenizdat, 1963). This book is a curious combination of fact and fiction. Excerpts are presented to give a Russian flavor to the Kalashnikov story. This book was translated by the US Army Foreign Science and Technology Center in 1974 as their document FSTC-HT-23-0751-74.

assemblies produced from mild steel. By the end of the war more than five million PPSh41s had been manufactured for the Red Army. Still, there was room for improvement, especially by reducing the weight of the weapon, and by increasing its killing power.[10]

Thus in 1942, the Red Army established a project to create a lighter and still easier to manufacture submachine gun. G. S. Shpagin and V. A. Degtyarev were joined by a host of other designers, including a heretofore unknown sergeant by the name of Kalashnikov. From his remote location in Alma-Ata, Kalashnikov was in no real position to compete in the trials that occurred in 1942. While he labored away, Aleksei Ivanovich Sudayev (1912–1946) was winning the competition with his PPS43.

Kalashnikov's first submachine gun assumes importance because it was the beginning of a career of gun design. In 1942, the Red Army needed to find young technical talent. Thus it was not overly presumptuous for the twenty-three-year-old Kalashnikov to try his hand at weapons design. His first attempt was relatively primitive and made totally with hand tools. Still, when he finished his work he had a firing model. Described as having a semi-blow-back mechanism, Kalashnikov's first weapon appears to have fired from a closed bolt when a striker struck the firing pin. Its other features appear to have been borrowed from other known designs but combined in a reasonably clever fashion.

After his return to Alma-Ata, Kalashnikov went to visit his old friends in the railroad technical section. One of the first people he talked with was Zhenya Kravchenko, a train driver who worked as a machinist in his spare time. Mishenka

Kravchenko *"opened the door of the shed. He couldn't believe his eyes. Before him in full military uniform stood Kalashnikov— Misha Kalashnikov from his political section of the railway, with whom he'd not been close, but whom he had accepted as a good friend. He somehow looked very independent standing in his overcoat and hat with the red star. . . .*

"Kalashnikov smiling walked forward to meet him and the two men embraced. As happens in these cases they began asking all sorts of questions. . . . Kravchenko climbed up on his workbench, continuing to look at his friend. 'Well, you, you're a tankman! Overcoat, insignia—everything in place. Well tell me about yourself.'

"Kalashnikov waved his hands: 'I was in the army as a driver. But about that later. Right now there's work I have for you to do.'

"'Work for you? Interesting!'

"'You understand,' Kalashnikov rolled his gloves in his hands as he looked for the proper words. 'I'm only just out of the hospital. I'm on leave—sick from a wound. I decided to return to Alma-Ata in order not to waste my time to make a new type of machine pistol. It is badly needed at the front, I've already devised something. But on paper it is not all clear, so I need to build a model. That's where you come in.'

"Kravchenko jumped-down from the work bench. 'A machine pistol? A new system? That's great! Of course I've no time or space but I'm ready to help you all the same. And here's my factory at your disposal. Look the furnishings are great.'"

After a brief tour of the "shed factory" and a discussion about use of the machine tools there with the railroad depot director and the local party organizer, an agreement was reached whereby Kalashnikov could call upon the metalworking skills of Kravchenko and others in the shop.

After three months of work, mostly in the evenings and on the weekends, so as not to interfere with the regular work of the "factory," Kalashnikov and his friends had a complete model of his first weapon. His next task was to find someone in a position of authority to sponsor his work. After much investigating and many bureaucratic rebuffs, with his weapon in hand, Kalashnikov sought out an audience with the Secretary of the Central Committee of the Communist Party of Kazakhstan. Although the Secretary was not a technical expert, he saw that there might be some potential to the weapon's design. *"The Party Secretary smiled and ran his hand over his dark smoothly combed hair. 'Well now it's clear, Comrade Kalashnikov that you want to do something great and important for the motherland. . . . I will be your partner. How do you think it would be to do the work in a Moscow Aviation Institute* [Moskovsky Aviatsionniy Institut] *shop? Its been evacuated right here to Alma-Ata. It's a good industrial base and there are sensible specialists. Do you agree?'"* Therefore, the Party Secretary exercised his political influence and arranged for Kalashnikov to work in the model shops of the Moscow Aviation Institute.

At the MAI, under much-improved working conditions, Kalashnikov was soon busy building an operating model of his weapon. The young man, a genuine war hero, was warmly received by A. I. Kazakov, Dean of the Faculty of Rifle and Cannon Armament, and the aviation institute's other personnel, who gave him much encouragement. When Kalashnikov's model submachine gun was finished, it was sent off to the Dzerzhinskiy Artillery Academy for testing and evaluation.

After examining his submachine gun, the testing commission concluded that the Kalashnikov weapon did not offer any advantages over the recently standardized PPS. But this exercise proved to be an important breakthrough because it brought Kalashnikov to the attention of General Anatoliy Arkadaevich Blagonravov, a key person in the Soviet armaments program who occupied the Chair of Infantry Weapons at the Artilleriskoi Akademii RKKA im Dzerzhinskogo (Dzershinskiy Artillery Academy), who noted:

> Although the model itself, because of its complexity and digression from the accepted tactical and technical requirements, is not a design which we could recommend adopting for troop service, at the same time the exceptional ingenuity, the great energy and labor invested in the invention, and the originality shown in solving a series of technical problems forces us to take a close look at Comrade Kalashnikov as a talented self-educated individual to whom it is desirable to give the opportunity of a technical education. Undoubtedly, he can be developed into an excellent designer if he receives proper guidance and is put on the right path.[11]

Although Kalashnikov was naturally disappointed by the testing commission's report, this attention from one of the foremost men in the Soviet field of weapons design made it possible for him to obtain additional formal engineering education and to have access to people and resources that would otherwise not have been available. As a result, he did not rejoin the armored forces, but became a technician at the military small arms proving ground at Ensk.

While at Ensk, Kalashnikov had drawn further attention to his talents through his work on modifications to P. M. Goryunov's machine guns. This activity brought him two "author's certificates," the closest thing the Soviets have to patents for recognizing inventiveness. It was also at Ensk that he first came into contact with designers like V. A. Degtyarev, S. G. Simonov, A. I. Sudayev, and others.

Kalashnikov continued to work on both 7.62mm and 9mm submachine guns as late as 1948, but he began a new and more significant course of experimentation when in early 1944 Kalashnikov was given some Model 1943 7.62 x 39mm cartridges for examination. Some of his colleagues told him: "Listen, Mikhail, many designers are now working on avtomats for the 1943 cartridge. Why shouldn't you give it a try?" He accepted this advice.

As he examined the new cartridge, Kalashnikov realized that its short length and its rimless case made it the answer to a small arms designer's dreams. He immediately began work on a selective-fire self-loading carbine that had a rotating bolt that was operated by a cam lug that moved in a corresponding groove in a bolt carrier. This fixed-magazine carbine was in the same class as the 7.62 x 39mm Simonov carbine (SKS), but it contained design elements that he would later use in his avtomats. The operating rod was located above the barrel as was common in most Soviet self-loading rifles and carbines.

Kalashnikov's First Avtomat

Kalashnikov's 7.62mm self-loading carbine was tested in 1944 and 1945, and despite good marks was terminated as a research and development project after the standardization of the SKS45. Again this design exercise was important because it gave Kalashnikov experience and exposure. It also taught him that a failure in developing a successful small-caliber weapon was

just a first step. A review of the careers of V. G. Federov, S. G. Simonov, F. V. Tokarev, and a number of less successful designers within his own country clearly indicated the value of trying over and over again. History indicated that perseverance was a virtue. At twenty-five Kalashnikov was one of the youngest men to occupy a position of importance in the competitive world of small arms design within the Soviet Union. While other individuals were approaching the age of retirement, Mikhail Timofeyevich was just getting started.

Although he was destined to have his assault rifle design adopted by the Soviet Army, Kalashnikov was not to be the first individual to develop an avtomat to fire the 7.62 x 39mm Model 1943 cartridge. A. I. Sudayev created the first such weapon at the beginning of 1944. Sudayev's avtomat was a blow-back weapon with a massive bolt assembly. While such an operating mechanism might work with a pistol-type cartridge, it quickly became apparent that a slam-fire mechanism was not suited for the new "intermediate"-type cartridge. Proving-ground tests of the Sudayev avtomat, in May 1944, indicated that its operating parts would not withstand the heavy recoil associated with the blow-back-type operation. Still, the test officers recommended that the gun be developed further.

The second Sudayev avtomat was a radically different design. Sudayev reworked his first avtomat to incorporate what is believed to have been a rotating-bolt mechanism. He increased the magazine capacity from thirty to thirty-five cartridges, and he employed a folding buttstock in place of the wooden one of his avtomat. In 1945, a small lot of Sudayev system avtomats were produced for prov-

A twenty-three- or twenty-four-year-old Senior-Sergeant Mikhail Timofeyevich Kalashnikov at the drawing board.

As M. T. Kalashnikov did, A. I. Sudayev and S. G. Simonov developed avtomats to shoot the Model 1943 7.62 x 39mm cartridge. Illustrated here is one of Simonov's experimental avtomats called the 7.62mm Avtomat sistemi Simonova pod patron obr. 1943g., on'tniy obrazets 1948g.

ing ground and troop tests. Experience with this weapon indicated that it was too heavy, and the Artillery Committee of the Main Artillery Commission (Glavnoe artilleriiskoe upravlenie—GAU) issued instructions for decreasing its weight.

Meanwhile, S. G. Simonov and M. T. Kalashnikov were working on their own avtomat designs. Recalling the early history of his avtomat, Kalashnikov wrote:

> In spite of my carbine having successfully passed its tests, I had long been undecided about engaging in work on a new avtomat. It still seemed [presumptuous in my mind, and I asked myself:] "experienced designers and gunsmiths are already working on this, will you be able to say a new word, to make a better system?" But the knowledge that many of my "threatening rivals" had sometimes felt the same way, let me begin on my path. And my audacity increased . . . again on sheets of drawing paper more and more new variants of new designs appeared.[12]

Design elements for his avtomat came to mind only to be discarded. Slowly, a workable design began to take shape, first in his mind and then on paper. He saw his main problem was to develop an operating system that could be used in a variety of automatic weapons. "The new avtomat had to be made reliable in operation, compact, light in weight, and simple in design. But what design path should I follow?" He could have chosen the recoil operation employed in blow-back-type submachine guns. "This would have permitted creation of a simple design. However, the new cartridge for which the avtomat was to be chambered, required a massive bolt, which correspondingly increased the weight and dimensions of the weapon." Reviewing the problems encountered with this type of weapon by Sudayev, Kalashnikov quickly dismissed this concept.

Kalashnikov reports, " . . . therefore I

decided to establish a system of gas operated automatic weapons. . . . Gradually, the shape of the future avtomat began to appear on the [drafting] paper. Even an insignificant change in the shape of the dimensions of one part made it necessary to make changes in all of the drawings previously made. But finally a rough design of my avtomat was ready." After his proposal package of drawings was sent off to Moscow to the Main Artillery Commission (GAU) for evaluation, enthusiasm turned to concern. "But what will the specialists think about it?"

Reaction to the technical data package sent off in early 1946 was received in a relatively short time. A letter received from Moscow advised Kalashnikov that his design had been selected for development as an experimental weapon. Before work was begun on the test models of his gas-operated rotating-bolt assault rifle, Kalashnikov had to create a small "collective" of designers and engineers to assist him in the preparation of a more refined package of engineering drawings. "Days passed filled with stress and hard work. We looked at each new part with excitement, carefully fitting each one to the others. Finally, after the passage of much time, we held in our hands the avtomat glistening with lacquer and grease." Kalashnikov noted that his project was immensely aided by the people and resources assigned to his project.* This first-rate help speeded up my work," said Kalashnikov, "cutting the time in half. What had once been just lines in a drawing was now reality. But how would it behave on the firing range?"

"Testing is a very important moment in the life of a designer, and in the life of the weapon created by him." And Kalashnikov knew that "not everything that is good on paper is right in the testing. And so it was with our avtomat. In spite of the fact that the initial shots demonstrated the positive qualities of our new weapon, a number of design flaws appeared." These problems were resolved without having to stop the test program, and the ultimate result of the proving-ground and troop-testing activities was a recommendation that the avtomat be adopted for the Soviet Army.[13]

Only one photograph of an experimental Kalashnikov avtomat of the 1946 or earlier period has been examined. Appearing on page 233 of D. N. Bolotin's "Sovetskoe strelkovoe oruzhie za 50 let" [Fifty years of Soviet infantry weapons], this weapon appears to be different in many details from the weapon actually placed into production. The receiver body had a slightly different profile, the gas-piston housing was lower (i.e., closer to the barrel), and the receiver cover was of a different shape. The wooden buttstock of this 7.62mm avtomat sistemi Kalashnikova, op'tniy obrazets 1946g (7.62mm Kalashnikov avtomat, test model of 1946) was attached to the receiver by two metal extensions that slid over the butt end of the receiver. It appears that the safety/fire selector lever was mounted just behind the trigger on the left side of the receiver instead of on the right side in the production model AK47s. From the illustration in Bolotin's book it is not possible to determine with certainty the fabrication

---

*A. A. Zaytsev assisted with the reworking of the drawing package for the AK. Engineer-Colonel V. S. Demin contributed to the development of the trigger mechanism, which he reworked ten times. Other design help was received from V. V. Krupin, V. A. Khar'kov, and A. D. Kryakushkin. N. N. Afanas'yev and V. N. Punshin aided Kalashnikov in the testing phase.

techniques used in building the receiver, but it has features that suggest sheet-metal rather than machined-steel construction.

This photograph in Bolotin is significant because it suggests that Kalashnikov's assault rifle evolved considerably during the years 1945–1948. This same photograph also suggests that there is still much to be learned about the research and development process that yielded the AK47. It is inferred from several sources that this further evolution of the Kalashnikov assault rifle took place in the experimental shops of the Tula Weapons Factory, which was once again operational after the war.

One day as Kalashnikov worked in his design bureau, an Engineer-Colonel Vladimir Sergeyevich Demin burst into his study and exclaimed: "Today you must dance Mikhail Timofeyevich. The 'Avtomat Kalashnikova' has been accepted as a standard weapon." And henceforth, Kalashnikov would hear a new form of address. People would call him "Comrade Designer."[14]

Thus in 1949, after slightly more than four years of design and engineering work, the exact extent of which is still a mystery, the Soviet Army adopted the 7.62mm Avtomat Kalashnikova obrazets 1947g (7.62mm Kalashnikov assault rifle model 1947). Although Soviet historical sources are not specific on the subject, it would appear that large-scale production of the AK47 did not begin until 1949–1950. From knowledge of more thoroughly documented small arms projects conducted in Europe and the United States, it is reasonable to project a period during which the Kalashnikov team continued to perfect the

weapon. One should not make the mistake of assuming there were no engineering problems just because Soviet historical sources are mute on this subject. Getting a new rifle into production has always been a long, involved, and tedious process inside or outside of the Soviet Union.*

Further clues to the history of Kalashnikov's weapon can be taken from the Kalashnikov avtomats held in the weapons collection of the Military History Museum of Artillery, Engineer and Signal Troops in Leningrad. The inventory of that collection seems to indicate that small numbers of test models of that weapon were constructed at (probably) Tula between 1946 and 1948. The design of the AK47 continued to evolve during this period as well. Limited serial machine production of the Kalashnikov avtomat appears to have been made in 1948 and 1949, again probably at the Tula Weapons Factory. These latter weapons are likely the ones used for more extended proving-ground trials and troop tests, of which Kalashnikov spoke in the text quoted earlier. It was this pattern of avtomat, with a receiver housing fabricated from sheet metal, that was the first series introduced to the field. Soviet documents refer to undated AK47s of this type as having been made between 1948 and 1951.

Sometime about 1951, the Main Artillery Administration approved a major change in the manufacturing processes used in the production of the Kalashnikov avtomat. For reasons we attempt to describe in the next chapter, the decision was made to abandon the sheet-metal-receiver-type AK47 and change to machining the

---

*For a detailed discussion of United States postwar infantry rifle research, development, and production see: Edward C. Ezell, *The Great Rifle Controversy: Search for the Ultimate Infantry Weapon from World War II through Vietnam and Beyond* (Harrisburg, Pa.: Stackpole Books, 1984), which will give a better understanding of the difficulties involved in creating a new infantry rifle. Many of the problems discussed are generic to all nations and not just limited to the United States.

receiver of the AK47 from either a forging or a solid block of steel. This type of AK began to replace the first type with its sheet-metal receiver in 1951. After a very short time in production this second model AK47 with its machined-steel receiver was modified slightly. This third variant became the basic model that was manufactured from about 1953–1954 until the AKM (7.62mm Modernizirovanniy avtomat sistemi Kalashnikova) was introduced in 1959. This final version in the Soviet 7.62mm series of AKs embodied a new type of stamped-sheet-metal receiver that overcame the shortcomings experienced with the very first model AK47. (A discussion of additional design details for all Soviet models of the AK47/AKM is presented in the next chapter.)

First examination of the production model of the AK47 indicates that Kalashnikov and his design bureau were attempting to continue the manufacturing tradition of using sheet-metal stampings started by Shpagin and Sudayev in their PPSh41 and PPS43 submachine gun designs. As we shall see this first attempt did not work out, but it was one more indication of the Soviet desire to find methods for improving their weapons-production capacity. Unlike their older infantry weapons, where detailed information has been released regarding the numbers manufactured, the Soviets have not yet provided statistical data on the numbers of Kalashnikov avtomats produced by the three weapons factories.

Although there is no hard official data for the numbers of Kalashnikov assault rifles manufactured by the Soviet Union since the weapon's introduction, it is possible to make some reasonable estimates. Extrapolating from Soviet production experience with the Model 1891, Model

The first model 7.62 x 39mm Avtomat Kalashnikova obrazets 1947g, with a sheet-metal receiver. This model was manufactured between 1948 and 1951.

Table 3-1
Selected Annual Soviet Production Rates for Infantry Rifles

1920	423,000[1]
1930–1931	174,000[2]
1932–1934	256,000[2]
1935–1937	397,000[2]
1940	1,461,000[2]
1943	3,400,000 +[1]
1976	250,000 (all infantry weapons)[3]
1980	400,000 (all infantry weapons)[3]

Sources: 1. D. N. Bolotin entitled "Sovetskoe strelkovoe oruzhie za 50 let" (50 years of Soviet small arms) (Leningrad, 1967), 12–14 and 100-103. 2. Julian Cooper, *Defence Production and the Soviet Economy, 1929-1941.* CREES Discussion Paper, (University of Birmingham: Birmingham, UK, 1976), 46–50, quoting Soviet sources. 3. US Congress, Joint Economic Committee, "Statement of Major General Richard X. Larkin, Deputy Director and Edward M. Collins, Vice Director for Foreign Intelligence, Defense Intelligence Agency, before the Subcommittee on International Trade, Finance and Security Economics" (Washington, D.C., 8 July 1981), 86–87.

The second model 7.62 x 39mm Avtomat Kalashnikova, obrazets 1947g, with a machined-steel receiver. Note the method of attaching the stock. This model was manufactured between 1951 and 1954.

The third model 7.62 x 39mm Avtomat Kalashnikova, obrazets 1947g, with a machined-steel receiver. Note the method of attaching the stock. This model was manufactured between 1954 and 1959. This particular weapon was the first AK47 to be obtained by US Army intelligence, in 1956, and was the first time the US Army had a chance to see this new type of avtomat up close.

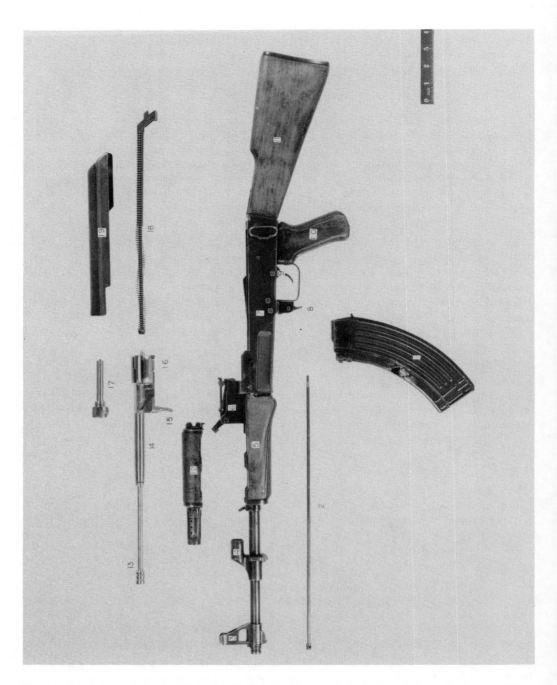

Disassembled view of the third model 7.62 x 39mm Avtomat Kalashnikova, shown in the preceding photo.

1891/31, and SVT40 rifles, it is estimated that between five hundred thousand and one million AK47s were built between 1948 and 1951. After the first model change perhaps a few hundred thousand to one million more were manufactured (1952–1954) before the changeover to the third and "standard" model occurred. Once that third model was issued, it is likely that production stabilized somewhere between five hundred thousand and one million AK47s per year. Thus by 1959, when the AKM was introduced, the total production of AK47s probably totaled between 3.0 million and 7.8 million, with the latter number being an educated guess. Subsequent AKM production likely equaled or exceeded that 7.8 million number.

The reasonableness of this estimate of 15.6 million Kalashnikov assault rifles having been manufactured between 1949 and 1974 can be judged from the fact that the Imperial Russian Army had had 4.65 million Model 1891–type rifles available in 1914, and the Red Army had 8.0 million Model 1891 and Model 1891/30 rifles at the start of the Second World War. The Tsarist military had required 17.7 million rifles, although they never met that goal. During World War II, the Red Army had acquired approximately 14 million Mosin-Nagant and Tokarev rifles and more than 5.0 million submachine guns. Thus the estimated total wartime requirement of shoulder weapons for the Soviet Army during the 1939–1945 war was nearly 30 million weapons. When one considers export sales, the 15.6 million figure actually may be low. Whatever the final total, the Kalashnikov avtomat has probably been produced in larger numbers than any other military rifle in history.

By comparison, between 1957 and 1985,

just over seven million M16-type rifles were manufactured by Colt Industries and its licensees. Heckler & Koch GmbH reports that it and its licensed producers have built over seven million Gewehr 3 assault rifles since 1959. So the number projected for the Soviets' production of the AK series is not unreasonable.

Initially, key cadre units of the Warsaw Pact armies probably received AK47s, and later AKMs, prior to the establishment of domestic production of those weapons in those countries. Today the AKM is the standard Warsaw Pact assault rifle, with most older AK47s having been withdrawn from active units. These older weapons can be found in the hands of reserve units and militia units. Hundreds of thousands of AK47s have also been distributed abroad by the Soviet military assistance program. (Chapter 5 provides more data on non-Soviet versions of the Kalashnikov weapons.)

Although it is believed that the Soviets have terminated production of the AKM in favor of the 5.45mm AK74 series, several countries, including Poland, Hungary, and the People's Republic of China, still continue to manufacture the 7.62mm version for export sales. It is anticipated that at least the elite units of the Soviet Army and the Warsaw Pact armies will be issued the various versions of the AK74. In that event many more AKMs are likely to become available for release to reserve military organizations. Thus more AK47s and some more AKMs will also be introduced into the international arms trade by the Soviet Union and its Warsaw Pact allies.

Mikhail Timofeyevich Kalashnikov's weapon was a success, both as a military weapon and as a commodity that has kept Soviet factories busy and Soviet workers

ГЕРОИ-СОВРЕМЕННИКИ

В. ЖУКОВ

Второе рождение

ВОЕННОЕ ИЗДАТЕЛЬСТВО МИНИСТЕРСТВА ОБОРОНЫ СССР

МОСКВА — 1963

The title page from V. N. Zhukov's biography of Mikhail Timofeyevich Kalashnikov entitled *Vtoroe rozhdenie* (Second birth), published in 1963 as part of a series on Soviet heroes.

ТВОРЕЦ АВТОМАТА АК

Советский юноша, призванный на действительную военную службу в пехоту или артиллерию, авиацию или военно-морской флот, уже в начале своей военной службы с большим интересом знакомится с поблескивающим свежей смазкой, вороненым автоматом АК.

АК — это начальные буквы двух слов: автомат Калашникова.

«Талантливый конструктор-самородок» — так назвал создателя этого автомата Михаила Тимофеевича Калашникова старейший советский оружейник, Герой Социалистического Труда, доктор технических наук Ф. В. Токарев.

Автомат АК — плод многолетней творческой работы конструктора.

Еще в армии, куда он был призван девятнадцатилетним юношей, М. Калашников заинтересовался устройством стрелкового оружия и пытался усовершенствовать пистолет ТТ.

Начавшаяся Великая Отечественная война нарушила все планы молодого изобретателя. В одном из жестоких танковых боев старший сержант Калашников был ранен. В госпитале, когда дело пошло на поправку, Калашников задумал создать совершенный пистолет-пулемет. Получив отпуск по ранению, Калашников с помощью товарищей изготовил стреляющий макет пистолета-пулемета. Затем ему была предоставлена возможность сделать и опытный образец.

Состоялись испытания. Вывод специальной комиссии гласил: представленный образец никаких существенных преимуществ перед известными не имеет. Однако способности к конструкторской работе у старшего сержанта были отмечены, и ему посоветовали учиться и работать дальше.

Неудача не остановила Калашникова. Он занялся изучением теории и стал работать над созданием самозарядного карабина под 7,62-миллиметровый патрон, имеющий меньший вес и габариты, чем обычный.

Конструкция карабина, который успешно прошел испытания, была положена в основу автомата, к созданию которого затем приступил Калашников.

Работая над новым образцом оружия, конструктор особое внимание обращал на простоту конструкции и

надежность в работе. Трудностей у конструктора было много, но с помощью коллектива инженеров, конструкторов и рабочих все они были преодолены. Наконец, на стрельбище была испытана первая опытная партия автоматов. После устранения обнаруженных недостатков автомат был принят на вооружение Советской Армии. За его создание М. Калашников был удостоен Сталинской премии.

Бывший старший сержант танкист, а ныне прославленный конструктор-оружейник, Герой Социалистического Труда М. Т. Калашников получает много писем от советских воинов. Солдаты благодарят его за создание автомата, заслужившего всеобщее признание и любовь.

На снимке: Герой Социалистического Труда М. Т. Калашников.

Текст и фото М. НОВИКОВА

An article entitled "Tvorets Avtomata AK" (Creator of the AK Avtomat), by M. Novikov, which presented details on the life of M. T. Kalashnikov in a 1959 issue of *Voenniy Znaniya* (9), p. 26. This article was an early attempt to introduce Kalashnikov to the Soviet military; it represented the first lifting of the secrecy surrounding the inventor's work.

employed. And as a consequence of that military and economic success, Kalashnikov's career has been a prosperous one. As a young man, this designer—self-educated and lucky—had broken into the elite ranks of the Soviet military technocracy. Following his demobilization from the Soviet Army in 1949, he was assigned to work at the Izhevsk Mashinostroitel'ny Zavod (Izhevsk Machine Factory) as a civilian engineer. This probably meant a transfer from the Tula Weapons Factory. Although the name had been changed from Izhevsk Weapons Factory, the industrial combine still functioned as an arsenal and producer of infantry weapons. While at Izhevsk,* Kalashnikov's professional and political fortunes continued to prosper. There, he worked first as a construction and industrial engineer. From that position he rose rapidly to become one of the senior managers in the production engineering and design operations of the factory.

As he rose in the system, Kalashnikov ceased to be the member of a design team. He became the director of one of the most important weapons-design bureaus in the Soviet Union. After considerable design study and reevaluation of stamped-metal assembly manufacture, Kalashnikov and his bureau were able to perfect a sheet-metal receiver for his assault rifle. This type assembly, as mentioned above, was incorporated into the design of the AKM. Subsequent to that development, the Kalashnikov design bureau produced a squad automatic weapon version of the AKM, which had a longer barrel and larger magazine capacity. This weapon, the Ruchnoi Pulemet Kalashnikova—RPK—

or Kalashnikov light machine gun, was changed little, and of course still fired the 7.62 x 39mm cartridge. The RPK squad automatic replaced the belt-fed RPD (Ruchnoi Pulemet Degtyareva), which also fired the Model-1943 cartridge. Subsequently, Kalashnikov's design bureau created a medium weight, general purpose machine gun, the PK (Pulemet Kalashnikova), which still uses the Model 1891 7.62 x 54mmR cartridge. This weapon has been produced in infantry and flexible and co-axial vehicle models, and it has replaced earlier machine guns designed by V. A. Degtyarev and P. M. Goryunov. The 7.62mm Dragunov sniper rifle (SVD) also bears the stamp of design concepts emerging from Kalashnikov's design bureau. All of these Kalashnikov-related weapons are discussed in more detail in chapter 6.

The Soviet government has honored M. T. Kalashnikov with many awards. In 1948, he was given the Stalin (now the State) prize for industrial methods, which was probably in recognition of his work on the AK47. He became a Hero of Socialist Work in 1949, was granted membership in the Communist Party of the Soviet Union in 1953, and subsequently was selected to serve on the budgetary planning commission of the Soviet Union. In 1966, he was elected to serve as a Deputy of the Supreme Soviet. And in 1971, the government bestowed upon him the title Doctor of Technical Sciences, a Soviet variant on the European concept of knighthood. All of these rewards led one of his biographers to comment:

The Communist Party and the Soviet Government hold M. T. Kalashnikov's great services in increasing our country's defense

---

*The town name of Izhevsk was renamed Ustinov in 1984 in honor of the late Defense Minister Dmitry Fedorovich Ustinov (1908–1984), who had been Minister for Defense Industry between 1955 and 1957. It is not known if the name of the Izhevsk Machine Factory has been changed as well.

A vintage 1973 photograph of Mikhail Timofeyevich Kalashnikov sent by the inventor to the author of this book when Kalashnikov was asked to provide information for this publication.

A 1958 photograph celebrating the fortieth anniversary of the armed forces shows Sergeant Vladimir Maximov with a third model AK47 in front of his unit's banner.

A 1963 photograph illustrating two Soviet frontier guards armed with third model AK47s.

strength in great esteem. He was awarded the title of Hero of Socialist Labor, the Lenin Prize Laureate, and State Prize, and he was decorated with orders and medals of the Soviet Union for his outstanding achievements in creating new types of military equipment.[15]

Kalashnikov today stands supreme as the foremost designer of infantry weapons in the Soviet Union and Warsaw Pact. His weapons form the basis for a complete infantry-weapons system for the Soviet Army. It is not unreasonable to project that the Kalashnikov design bureau will continue to hold sway for many years, and that its influence over Soviet infantry-weapon design may well continue long after Kalashnikov's death.

4

Design Evolution of the Kalashnikov Avtomat, 1948–1959

The production model of M. T. Kalashnikov's AK47 assault rifle went through three distinctive models. This chapter will describe as much of the complex production history of these weapons as our limited information in the West allows us to present.* It will also review the history of the final versions of the 7.62 x 39mm Kalashnikov, the AKM, and the RPK. (Chapter 6 provides details on other more recent Kalashnikov-type weapons, including the AK74 and the RPKS74.) The differences between each of the several models of this weapon are more fully explained through the illustrations that ac-

company this chapter. There are a number of insights that can be derived from examining these weapons, but such an examination also leaves many questions unanswered. It is hoped the Soviets will ultimately record in detail the history of their Kalashnikov-type weapons as thoroughly as they have presented the story of their pre-1945 infantry weapons.

First Model AK47

As noted in chapter 3, the first model AK47 had its receiver assembly built up from a combination of stamped-sheet

---

*Since the mid-1930s, for national security reasons, the Soviets have not indicated the names of their factories on their military rifles and ammunition. Instead they have used a symbol code on weapons and a numerical code on ammunition. Their small arms carry one of the following marks: a triangle with a vertical arrow, a star with a vertical arrow, or a stylized bullet or oval with a horizontal arrow. Identification of the facilities denoted by these codes and symbols is also generally classified by Western intelligence agencies as well.

steel and machined-steel components. The machined-steel insert at the front of the receiver (into which the barrel was screwed) and the stamped-sheet-metal back-plate assembly (there were different versions for both the wooden fixed butt-stock and the metal folding stock) were attached to the stamped-sheet-metal housing by a combination of rivets and welds. At the bottom of the receiver was welded a pistol-grip base and the trigger guard. In this first model AK47, the upper edges of the sheet-metal receiver were bent inward to form the guide surfaces for the operating rod/bolt carrier assembly.

Kalashnikov and his colleagues deliberately designed the AK47 so that it could be manufactured on sheet-metal punch-press-type machinery. The Soviets, like the Germans and other nations fighting the Second World War, had been confronted with shortages of raw material, machinery, and skilled workmen during that war. One of their major efforts to overcome these handicaps was the intensive application of the sheet-metal-stamping production processes — a technology long applied to the manufacture of automotive components in Europe and the United States — to the manufacture of weapons. By making this shift from machined assemblies worked from solid-steel stock to ones stamped out in large presses, the Soviets were able (as had been the Germans and the Americans) to shift much of their skilled work force from the manufacture of the finished components to the creation of the dies used to stamp out the parts.

While there is very little available documentary information regarding the history of the use of sheet-metal production technology in the Soviet small arms factories, the experiences of the German infantry-weapons manufacturers during World War II with this fabrication technique are illustrative of the advantages of stamped-metal assemblies. For example, in manufacturing the 20mm Flak 38 automatic-cannon receiver housing, the German production engineers at the Deutches Waffen- und Munitionsfabriken A. G. discovered that they could reduce their raw material requirements from 45 kilograms (99 pounds) to 8.5 kilograms (18.7 pounds). Man-hour savings amounted to 70 percent, and nearly two hundred pieces of machinery dedicated to fabricating this component were freed up for application to other critical manufacturing requirements.

Although the Soviet arms industry, which was engaged in the manufacture of infantry and artillery weapons, was the best prepared segment of the Soviet economy when the war came, other industrial segments were in trouble. Soviet planners had not nurtured the armored fighting vehicle and aircraft industries in the same fashion that they had attended to the needs of the arms factories. As it turned out, the Second World War, like its predecessor, was a conflict between industrial production capacity as well as military forces. Therefore, the 1939–1945 war required the maximum results and improved efficiency from the Soviet defense industrial combine. While production of rifles and machine guns hit their stride at the weapons factories in 1942, and as a result the delivery of rifles continued at a steady pace through 1943 and 1944, throughout other areas of the Soviet defense industries there was a desperate shortage of machine tools and related production equipment at the start of the war. Skilled workers were also in short supply. Many of the problems were reminiscent of the troubles that had faced the tsarist officers during the First World War.

Machine tools ordered abroad between 1939 and 1941 under a special two hundred million gold ruble allocation and additional machine tools acquired through the American Lend-Lease Program significantly increased Soviet production capacity during the war. Unfortunately, many of these machine tools were not available until very late in the war. As a result the Soviet industrial leadership looked for technological means at hand that would permit them to offset the shortage of critical production equip-ment. Sheet-metal-stamping technology, as applied to small arms, made it possible to reduce the need for some critical machine tools, and at the same time it may have allowed the redistribution of some existing production equipment.

German industrial engineers had discovered that stamped-steel assemblies worked best when they were applied to new weapon designs intended to be manufactured in this manner. Components of older weapons often could be adapted to the punch-press stamping technique, but this often led to problems when inter-

Private Henry P. Riggan of the 9th Army cleans a 7.92 x 33mm Sturmgewehr 44 captured by US Army forces in the fall of 1944. The Stg. 44, and the 7.92 x 57mm MG42 in the foreground, were fabricated with many assemblies made from stamped-steel metal. (SC197095)

changeability with older machined components was required. While it was possible to obtain parts interchangeability, there was also often a prejudice on the part of the military customer against these new-style components because they were not machined in the traditional manner. Stamped and welded weapon assemblies were often more durable than machined ones, but the new process seldom produced components that were as aesthetically pleasing as the previous ones. Nevertheless, stamped-metal parts were not inherently lower in quality or less reliable.

Performance records of the 9 x 19mm Maschinenpistole 40 (MP40), 7.92 x 57mm Maschinengewehr 42 (MG42), and 7.92 x 33mm Sturmgewher 44 (Stg44, also called MP43 for a time), all of which made extensive use of stamped-sheet-metal components, attested to the suitability of this technology for the manufacture of infantry weapons. Although the Stg44 may have influenced Soviet automatic-rifle design thinking somewhat, the Soviets also had developed a strong industrial technology base for fabricating small arms using stamped-sheet-metal components.*

The most well known of Soviet weapons using stamped hot-rolled sheet-metal riveted and welded assemblies were the 7.62 x 25mm Pistolet pulemet Shpagina (PPSh41) and Pistolet Pulemet Sudayeva (PPS43) submachine guns, but the design of the 7.62 x 54mmR Degtyarev light machine guns and a number of other infantry weapons also embodied major assemblies fabricated with similar production techniques. Most of these Soviet weapons provided a reliable service record despite the fact that they were manufactured with extreme speed and with little attention for aesthetic considerations such as the quality of the external finish. The major concern of the Soviet defense industry was the creation of reasonably inexpensive weapons that would shoot.

Of the World War II Soviet weapons it is instructive to compare the manufacture of the 7.62mm PPSh41 and the PPS43, because they show the progress made in the use of sheet-metal components. Georgi Semyenovich Shpagin's submachine gun represented a significant improvement over Vasily Alekseyevich Degtyarev's PPD34/38 and PPD40 submachine guns from a manufacturing standpoint. The PPSh41 consisted of eighty-seven parts as compared to the ninety-five parts of the PPDs. But the real difference lay in the fact that the PPSh41 required only 7.3 hours of machine time versus 13.7 hours for the PPD. In the PPSh41 the receiver, barrel-jacket assembly, and other critical parts were stamped from cold rolled steel that were subsequently either spot or arc welded. While the PPD had seventy-two components machined by traditional methods, sixteen stamped from cold rolled steel, and eight from hot rolled steel, the PPSh41 had fifty-eight machined parts, twenty-four cold stampings, and eight hot stampings.

Aleksei Ivanovich Sudayev's PPS43 more than halved the machine hours required to fabricate each gun: 2.7 hours for each PPS43 and 7.3 hours for each

---

*All of the German Sturmgewher were designed to be manufactured from stamped low-carbon sheet-steel components, and the inspirational relationship of the Stg44 to the first sheet-metal receiver model of the AK47 may be similiar to the relationship between the 7.92 x 33mm cartridge to the 7.62 x 39mm round. It may never be possible to determine the extent to which the production technology incorporated into the Kalashnikov weapon was influenced by German thinking as opposed to its being an independent Soviet creation.

Two Soviet 7.62 x 25mm submachine guns manufactured from stamped-sheet-metal components. On the left, the Pistolet-pulemet Shpagina obrazets 1941g (PPSh41), and on the right the Pistolet-pulemet Sudayeva obrazets 1943g (PPS43). The latter weapon used a much thinner sheet-metal material, and was thus much lighter than its predecessor; 3.0 versus 3.5 kilograms (6.61 vs. 7.72 pounds). (NMAH 72–5402 and 72–5412)

PPSh41. The PPS43 required much less raw steel to start with (6.2 versus 13.9 kilograms) and produced less scrap during the manufacturing process. Sudayev's submachine gun saved nearly one thousand tons of steel each month, and decreased the number of workers dedicated to submachine gun production by 55 percent. By going to a design that was almost entirely stampings, the Armament Commissariat was able to increase monthly submachine gun production from 135,000 to 350,000 guns.

Soviet historical sources are not clear on just how the use of sheet metal components came to be incorporated into the AK47 production plan. It is likely that the production engineers, with whom the young designer Kalashnikov worked, were the source of the decision to build assault rifles using this production concept, because they knew just how much raw material, manpower, and machinery resources could be conserved. Soviet industrialists trying to reorganize and rebuild their factories in the wake of the Second World War were looking for technological shortcuts that would allow the rapid production of new infantry weapons, tanks, and aircraft without embarking upon major machine-tool building programs. Not only would new machine-tool building projects have taken time and required the services of the most skilled workers in the Soviet industrial complex, but they would have cost millions of rubles that the war-torn economy could ill afford to divert to such projects.

It is apparent that considerable energy was expended to develop an assault rifle that could take advantage of the stamped-metal production lessons learned during the war. There is still much to be learned here about the production engineering

phase of the Kalashnikov saga. Nor is it clear just why the stamped-sheet-metal-receiver-type AK47 was abandoned, after only three years of production, in favor of one that had a machined-steel receiver. There are some hypotheses that have been advanced to explain this change, but there is very little data to back up any of these theories.

One reason suggested in the Western technical intelligence community for shifting from the built-up sheet-metal receiver AK47 to a weapon with a machined-steel receiver was the lack of durability of the built-up receiver. It has been theorized that the riveted and welded joints weakened after extended shooting. This might be true, but the first model AK47 illustrated at the top of the photo on page 146 (this weapon was captured from the Palestinians by the Israelis in 1982) evidences considerable use and abuse, yet there are no indications that there has been major wear or loosening of the rivets or welds. Thus, acceptance of this possible explanation of the production technology changeover requires much more additional information about the life-cycle performance of the first stamped-steel receiver Kalashnikovs.

Another reason suggested by technical intelligence specialists for the shift from sheet-metal pressings stems from the nature of the Soviet defense industry's technology base. It has been postulated that in the immediate post-1945 years many sectors of the Soviet defense industry were placing heavy work demands upon key professions such as the tool and die makers who made the stamping dies for the manufacture of small arm, motor vehicle, and aircraft assemblies. During the postwar rearmament (it is further suggested), the sectors of the defense industry that were mak-

First model Avtomat Kalashnikova obrazetza 1947g (AK47), with stamped-sheet-metal receiver assembly. This weapon, from the Pattern Room Collection, RSAF, Enfield, is dated 1951, with the transliterated serial number "Yu P 4911." Note that the magazine is the early flat-side nonribbed type, and that the stock has an arsenal/depot repair.

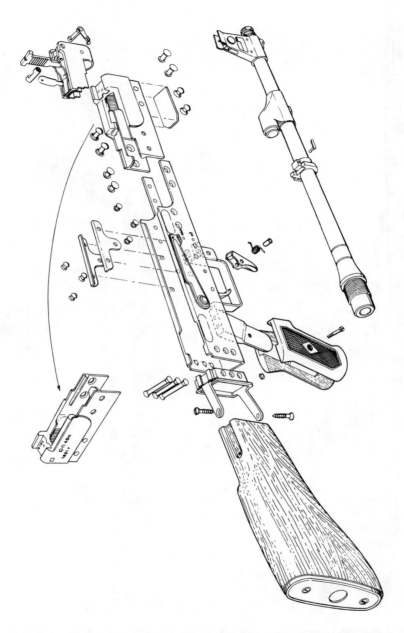

Exploded view of the first model Avtomat Kalashnikova obrazetza 1947g (AK47), with stamped-sheet-metal receiver assembly. This weapon, from the Pattern Room Collection, RSAF, Enfield, is dated 1951, with the transliterated serial number "Yu P 4911."

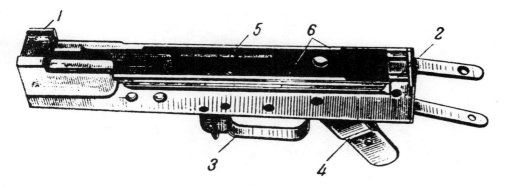

Рис. 14. Штампованная ствольная коробка (сб. 1-1):

1 — вкладыш (сб. 1-7); *2* — затыльник (1-3); *3* — предохранительная (спусковая) скоба; *4* — основание пистолетной рукоятки; *5* — правый угольник; *6* — полочки

Receiver assembly drawing of the first model Avtomat Kalashnikova obrazetza 1947g (AK47), with stamped-sheet-metal receiver assembly from a 1952 Soviet service manual entitled *7,62mm Avtomat Kalashnikova (AK) Rukovodstvo Sluzh'yi.*

1, machined-steel insert for mounting barrel and gas-system assemblies; 2, stamped back-plate assembly; 3, trigger guard; 4, pistol-grip base; 5, bolt guide rails riveted and welded in place; 6, guide rails for the operating rod/bolt carrier assembly.

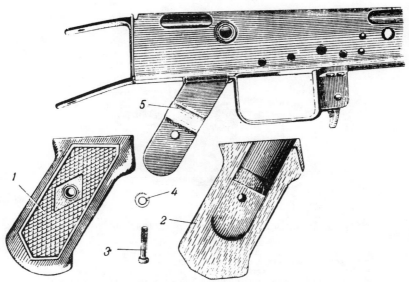

Рис. 46. Пистолетная рукоятка автомата со штампованной ствольной коробкой:

1 — правая щечка (0-17); *2* — левая щечка (0-18); *3* — винт (0-19); *4* — гайка винта (0-20); *5* — основание пистолетной рукоятки

Pistol-grip assembly of the first model Avtomat Kalashnikova obrazetza 1947g (AK47), with stamped-sheet-metal receiver assembly.

1, right grip plate; 2, left grip plate; 3, screw; 4, nut; 5, base of pistol grip.

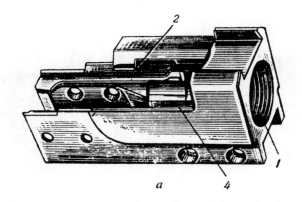

а

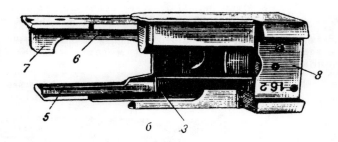

б

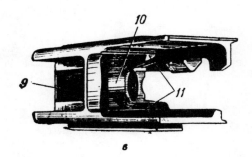

в

Рис. 15. Вкладыш штампованной ствольной коробки
(сб. 1-7):

а — вид справа; *б* — вид сверху; *в* — вид снизу; *1* — резьба
для ввинчивания ствола; *2* и *3* — боевые уступы; *4* — сухарь
(1-9); *5* и *6* — направляющие планки; *7* — отражатель;
8 — паз для основания прицела; *9* — вырез для крепления
цевья; *10* — вырез; *11* — уступы

Steel insert for mounting the barrel to the receiver assembly of the first model Avtomat Kalashnikova obrazetza 1947g (AK47), with stamped-sheet-metal receiver.

1, threaded socket for mounting barrel; *2-3*, locking shoulders for the bolt; *4*, cam cut to turn the bolt to the locked position; *5-6*, forward portion of the bolt guides; *7*, extractor; *8*, groove into which the rear-sight assembly fits; *9*, notch for attaching the forestock; *10*, recess; *11*, shoulders to position the mouth of the magazine.

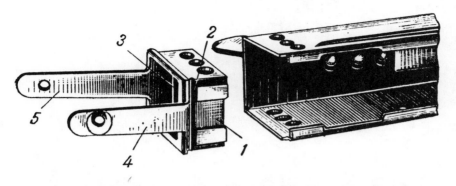

Рис. 16. Затыльник (1-3) штампованной ствольной коробки:

1 — паз для крепления пятки направляющей трубки; *2* — паз для заднего ребра крышки ствольной коробки; *3* — гнездо для крепления переднего конца приклада; *4* и *5* — хвосты затыльника с отверстиями

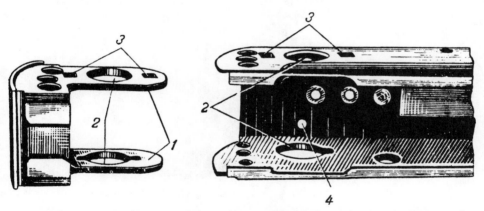

Рис. 17. Затыльник (1-49) автомата со штампованной ствольной коробкой с откидным металлическим прикладом:

1 — ушки; *2* — отверстия для оси приклада; *3* — квадратные прорези для защелки приклада; *4* — отверстие для удобства вынимания штифта защелки приклада

Back-plate assemblies for the first model Avtomat Kalashnikova obrazetza 1947g (AK47), with stamped-sheet-metal receiver. With the folding metal stock the weapon was called the Avtomat Kalashnikova skladyvayushchimsya prikladom obrazets 1947g.

Top: Back-plate assembly for wooden stock; *1*, groove for retaining bolt-guide assembly; *2*, groove for retaining rear end of receiver cover; *3*, recess for forward end of the buttstock; *4-5*, tangs to hold the stock in place.

Bottom: Back-plate assembly for folding metal stock; *1*, back-plate assembly; *2*, stock pin holes; *3*, stock catch-locking holes; *4*, stock catch-pin disassembly hole.

Opposite page and above: **Second model Avtomat Kalashnikova obrazetza 1947g (AK47), the first with a machined-steel receiver. This battlefield relic, from the Smithsonian National Firearms Collection, is missing its forestock. Undated, this AK47 bears the transliterated serial number "RG6905." Note that it does not have any selector-setting markings. (NMAH 85–1298; 85–1301; 85–1302)**

ing major pieces of military equipment—for example, armored fighting vehicles and aircraft—had more political clout than did the small arms factories.

Since many of the major infantry weapons factories still had substantial quantities of the more traditional metal-working machinery (milling, broaching, turning, and drilling tools), it was easier to modify the manufacturing processes for making AK47s than it was to muster the necessary political muscle to get tool and die makers for the sheet-metal presses in those factories. It has been argued that this decision was not a step backward but a lateral movement to use an equivalent technology to produce the same basic product. While there is little hard data to support this argument, it is certainly a speculation provocative enough to warrant further investigation once additional Soviet historical sources become available.

Second and Third Model AK47s

It is clear from examining existing AK47s that the Soviets, after making the first-type AK47 from 1948, did make the shift from built-up sheet-metal and machined components to machined-steel receivers in 1951. Since both types of Kalashnikov avtomats dated 1951 have been observed, it is believed that both types of receivers were produced concurrently for a time. The second model AK47, with its unsatisfactory method of attaching the buttstock, gave way some time in 1953 or 1954 to the basic type of Kalashnikov avtomat that is generally recognized around the world as the AK47. That third model of Kalashnikov's AK47 was manufactured until about 1959, when the Soviets introduced the AKM, which was in effect a reintroduction of the first model of

the AK47, only this time it had an "improved" type of sheet-metal receiver assembly.

The changes in the Kalashnikov weapons reflected changes in the Soviet defense industrial complex. In the decade following the Second World War that combination of manufacturing and military organizations had received large infusions of capital and had grown much stronger in terms of its technological base. By the mid-1950s it appears that an experimental design construction bureau (*opytno-konstruktorskoe byuro*—OKB) focused on the talents of Kalashnikov and his team had been established. Within the Soviet military establishment, the OKBs were responsible for the development and initial testing of new weapons, vehicles, and aircraft. It was the Kalashnikov OKB that was to spawn the AKM and the other derivative design weapons.

It should also be noted that by the mid-1950s Kalashnikov was able to draw on the manufacturing resources of factories beyond the traditional "big three" small arms manufacturers. Soviet military industry had matured considerably since the 1920–1940 period, and as a result many components for military products such as the Kalashnikov assault rifles could be subcontracted to smaller enterprises by large combines such as the Izhevsk Machine Building Factory. Under these circumstances, Kalashnikov and the members of his *opytno-konstruktorskoe byuro* had a stronger industrial base upon which to rely. It is likely that it was this stronger industrial environment that allowed Kalashnikov and his OKB team to create the AKM.

Modernized Kalashnikov

Introduction of the 7.62 x 39mm

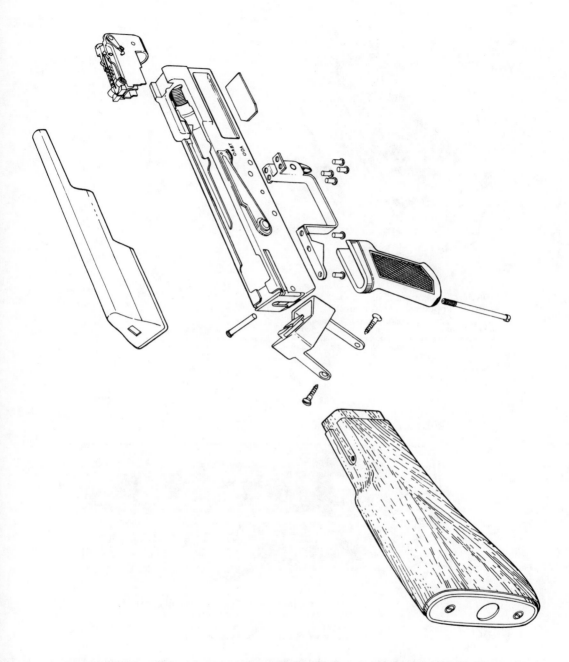

Exploded view of the second model Avtomat Kalashnikova obrazetza 1947g (AK47), the first with a machined-steel receiver. All the bolt and bolt-carrier guides were machined from the block of steel used for the receiver. Note the new method of attaching the buttstock, the pistol grip, and the trigger guard.

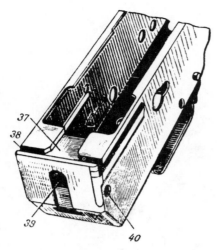

Рис. 11. Задний конец ствольной коробки (затыльник):

37 — паз для крепления пятки направляющей трубки; *38* — паз для заднего ребра крышки ствольной коробки; *39* — паз для крепления приклада; *40* — отверстие для штифта приклада

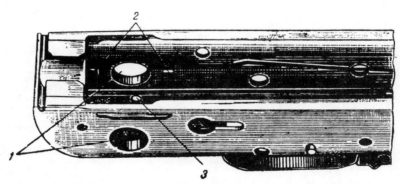

Рис. 12. Задняя часть ствольной коробки автомата с откидным металлическим прикладом:

1 — отверстия для оси приклада; *2* — отверстия для защелки приклада; *3* — отверстие для удобства отделения штифта защелки

Receiver details for the second model Avtomat Kalashnikova obrazetza 1947g (AK47).

Top: Butt end of receiver for wood stock; *37*, groove for retaining bolt-guide assembly; *38*, groove for retaining rear end of receiver cover; *39*, groove for buttstock dovetail retainer; *40*, pin for retaining buttstock dovetail.

Bottom: Butt end of receiver for folding metal stock; *1*, stock pin holes; *2*, stock catch holes; *3*, stock catch-pin disassembly hole.

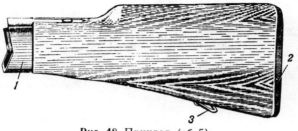

Рис. 48. Приклад (сб. 5):

1 — обойма (5-13); *2* — затылок (5-2); *3* — антабка (сб. 5-1)

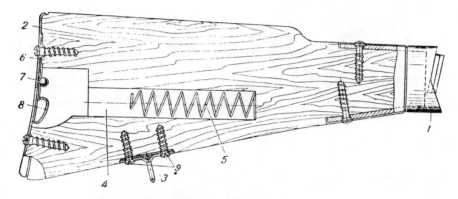

Рис. 49. Приклад (сб. 5):

1 — обойма (5-13); *2* — затылок (5-2); *3* — антабка (сб. 5 1); *4* — гнездо для пенала и пружины пенала; *5* — пружина пенала (5-5); *6* — основание крышки; *7* — ось крышки затылка; *8* — отогнутая часть крышки; *9* — винты

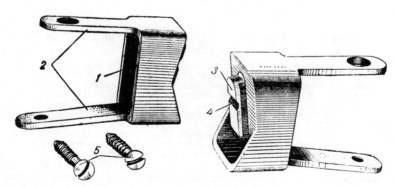

Рис. 50. Обойма (5-13) (левый — вид справа, правый — вид слева):

1 — гнездо для помещения переднего конца приклада; *2* — хвосты с отверстиями для шурупов; *3* — выступ для крепления приклада; *4* — выемка; *5* — шурупы

Buttstock assembly details for the second model Avtomat Kalashnikova obrazetza 1947g (AK47).

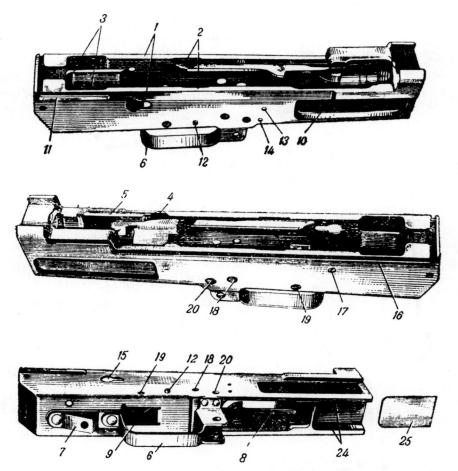

Рис. 9. Ствольная коробка (сб. 1-1) (верхний — вид справа, средний — слева и нижний — снизу):

1 — направляющие полочки; *2* — вырезы для прохода боевых выступов затвора; *3* — вырезы для прохода направляющих выступов затворной рамы; *4* — полукруглый вырез; *5* — скос; *6* — предохранительная (спусковая) скоба; *7* — основание пистолетной рукоятки; *8* — окно для магазина; *9* — окно для спускового крючка; *10* и *11* — выступы для упрочения стенки ствольной коробки; *12* — выступ для ограничения поворота флажка (1-20); *13* и *14* — выемки для фиксации положений переводчика; *15* — фигурное окно для постановки рычага переводчика; *16* — выступ для упрочения верхней части ствольной коробки; *17* — отверстие для левой цапфы рычага переводчика; *18* — отверстие для оси курка; *19* — отверстие для оси спускового крючка; *20* — отверстие для оси автоспуска; *24* — продольный вырез для цевья; *25* — щиток (1-7)

Three views of the second model Avtomat Kalashnikova obrazetza 1947g (AK47).

1, guide for the bolt carrier assembly; 2, recess for inserting/removing bolt lugs during assembly/disassembly; 3, recess for inserting/removing bolt carrier assembly; 4-5, recess and bevel to prevent fired cartridge case from striking the receiver during the extraction process; 6, trigger guard; 7, pistol-grip mounting stud; 8, magazine well opening; 9, trigger opening; 10-11, receiver wall reinforcements; 12, safety/selector limiting lug; 13-14, selector stop recesses; 15, selector opening; 16, reinforcement on exterior of receiver; 17, left trunnion for selector; 18, hammer-pin hole; 19, trigger-pin hole; 20, full-auto sear pin hole; 24, recess for forestock; 25, cover plate.

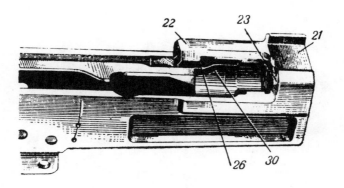

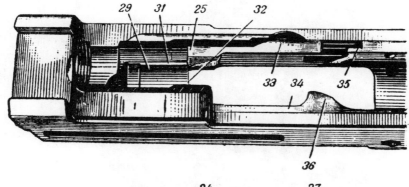

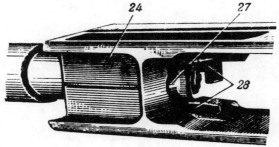

Рис. 10. Передняя часть ствольной коробки (верхний — вид справа, средний — слева, нижний — снизу):

21 — паз для помещения основания прицела; *22* — выступ; *23* — уступ для ограничения движения затворной рамы; *24* — вырез с пазами для щитика; *25* — правый боевой уступ; *26* — левый боевой уступ; *27* — вырез для крепления передней части магазина; *28* — уступы для ограничения продвижения магазина вверх; *29* — сухарь (1-9); *30* — винтовой скос сухаря; *31* — правое ребро сухаря; *32* — направляющая фаска сухаря; *33* — правая направляющая планка; *34* — левая направляющая планка; *35* — паз для рычага автоспуска; *36* — отражатель

Forward portion of the second model Avtomat Kalashnikova obrazetza 1947g (AK47).

21, groove for rear-sight base; *22*, locking shoulder for bolt; *23*, shoulder for limiting the motion of the operating rod; *24*, recess for the forestock; *25-26*, locking lug recesses; *27*, magazine-locking recess; *28*, shoulder-limiting position of the magazine; *29*, cam surface for rotating the bolt; *30*, cam surface bevel; *31*, right edge of the cam surface; *32*, cam surface guide end; *33-34*, right and left guides; *35*, groove for automatic sear; *36*, extractor.

Comparative disassembled views of the second model Avtomat Kalashnikova obrazetza 1947g (AK47), first with a machined-steel receiver, and the third model Avtomat Kalashnikova obrazetza 1947g (AK47), second with a machined-steel receiver, illustrating the design differences between the two weapons.

1, method of attaching buttstock altered; *2*, rear sling swivel repositioned; *3*, Stock attachment piece on the second model only; *4*, selector lever strengthened; *5*, weight-reducing groove altered; *6*, Forestock band altered; *7*, gas pistol housing altered; *8*, front sling attachment point altered; *9*, receiver cover altered; *10*, Magazine strengthened by the addition of stamped ribs.

Photographic comparison of typical 7.62 x 39mm Kalashnikov receivers. *From top to bottom:* undated Soviet first model Avtomat Kalashnikova obrazetza 1947g (AK47), transliterated serial number "3T7599," with stamped-sheet-metal receiver assembly; undated Soviet second model Avtomat Kalashnikova obrazetza 1947g (AK47), transliterated serial number "RS6905," first with a machined-steel receiver; Chinese Type 56 Export version of third model Avtomat Kalashnikova obrazetza 1947g (AK47), second with a machined-steel receiver, serial number 13064828; Soviet Modernizirovanniyi Avtomat Kalashnikova (AKM), dated 1972, with improved-type stamped-sheet-metal receiver, transliterated serial number "FA 0780M." Compare this weapon with the one at the top of the page. Note location of rivets and the means of attaching the buttstock. All rifles from the National Firearms Collection, SI. (NMAH 85–1292)

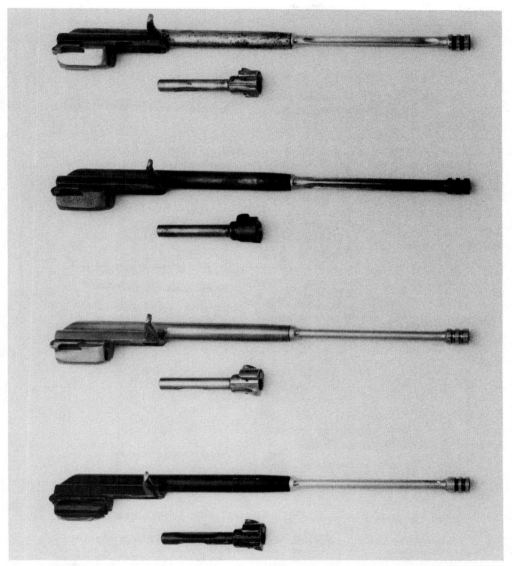

Photographic comparison of typical 7.62 x 39mm Kalashnikov operating rod/bolt carrier/bolt assemblies. *From top to bottom:* undated Soviet first model Avtomat Kalashnikova obrazetza 1947g (AK47), with stamped-sheet-metal receiver assembly. Note the flutes on the operating rod; undated Soviet second model Avtomat Kalashnikova obrazetza 1947g (AK47), first with a machined-steel receiver. Note the flutes on the operating rod; Chinese Type 56 Export version of third model Avtomat Kalashnikova obrazetza 1947g (AK47), second with a machined steel receiver. Note the absence of flutes on the operating rod; Soviet Modernizirovanniyi Avtomat Kalashnikova (AKM), dated 1972, with improved-type stamped-sheet-metal receiver, transliterated serial number "FA 0780M." Note the lightened bolt and the modified bolt carrier. All rifles from the National Firearms Collection, SI. (NMAH 85-1291)

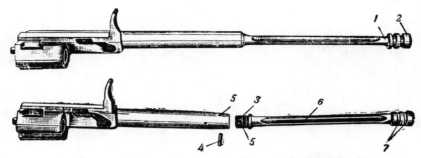

Рис. 27. Затворная рама в собранном и разобранном виде:

1 — шток (3-2); *2* — поршень; *3* — резьба для соединения с затворной рамой; *4* — штифт для соединения штока с рамой (3-3); *5* — отверстие для штифта; *6* — продольные выемы; *7* — кольцевые выточки

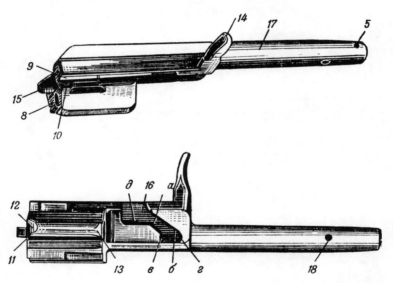

Рис. 28. Затворная рама (3-1) (верхний — вид справа, нижний — вид снизу):

5 — отверстие для штифта; *8* — цилиндрический канал для хвостовой части затвора; *9* — правый паз; *10* — выступ, называемый выключателем автоспуска; *11* — продольная прорезь для отражателя; *12* — задний скос прилива; *13* — передний скос прилива; *14* — рукоятка перезаряжания; *15* — выступ для взведения курка; *16* — фигурный паз; *17* — цилиндрическая часть затворной рамы; *18* — отверстие для выхода воздуха и излишней смазки; *а* — запирающий винтовой скос; *б* — отпирающий винтовой скос; *в* — задняя прямая стенка; *г* — передняя закругленная стенка фигурного паза; *д* — продольная стенка

Two views of the Kalashnikov operating rod/bolt carrier assembly.

1, operating rod; *2*, piston; *3*, threads; *4*, retaining pin; *5*, retaining-pin hole; *6*, flutes; *7*, grooves to prevent carbon buildup; *8*, bolt-guide hole; *9*, right guide groove; *10*, automatic trigger-disconnector lugs; *11*, ejector notch; *12*, hammer bevel—rear; *13*, hammer bevel—front; *14*, cocking handle; *15*, hammer cocking cam; *16*, bolt operating cam groove; *17*, body of operating rid; *18*, bleed hole for excess gas or lubricants.

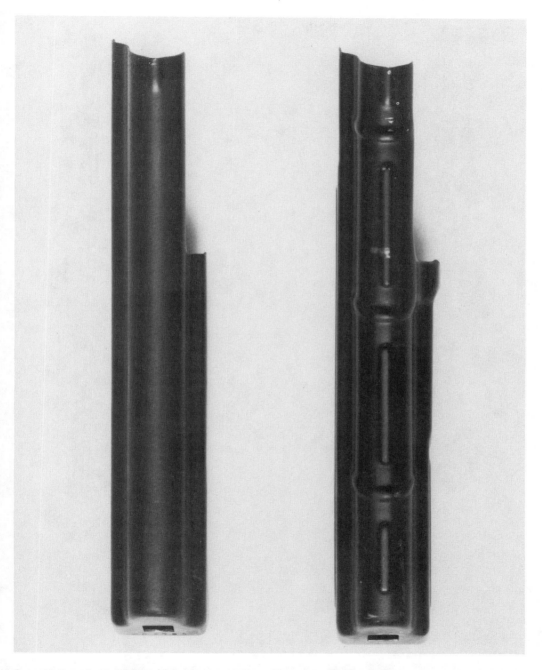

Comparative photograph of (left) AK47 and (right) AKM receiver covers. Note the strengthening ribs added to the AKM receiver cover. (NMAH 85–1290)

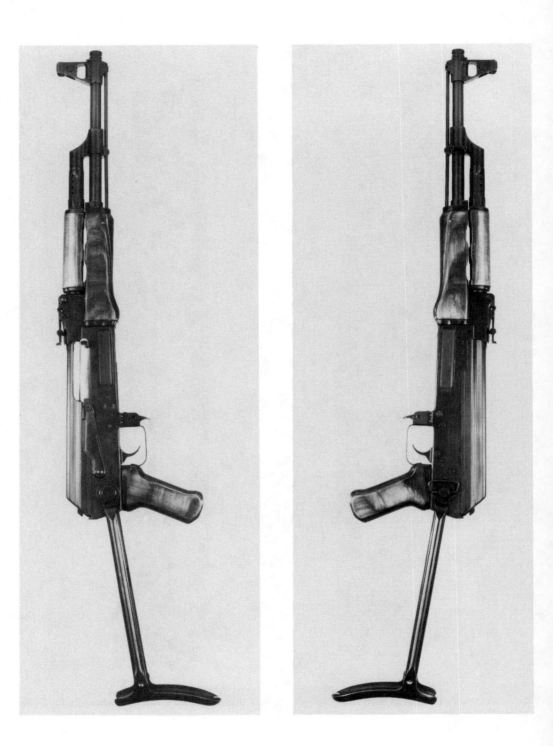

Opposite page and above: Third model Avtomat Kalashnikova skladyvayushchimsya prikladom obrazets 1947g, with transliterated serial number "FA 0780M." Note that the stock bars are machined from steel stock. From the National Firearms Collection, SI. (NMAH 85–1297; 85–1296; 85–1295)

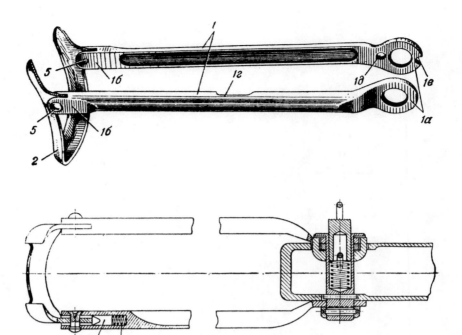

Рис. 53. Откидной металлический приклад (общий вид и разрез):

1 — тяги (1-50, 1-51); *1а* — ушки для оси приклада; *1б* — проушины для осей плечевого упора; *1г* — вырез для прохода загиба флажка переводчика; *1д* — отверстие для защелки приклада; *1е* — выемка для защелки приклада; *2* — плечевой упор (1-52); *3* — фиксатор (1-53) плечевого упора; *4* — пружина (1-54) фиксатора; *5* — оси плечевого упора (1-55)

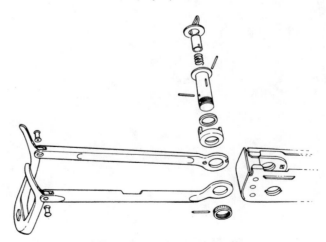

General views of the AK47 metal folding stock.
1, stock bars; *2*, buttplate; *3*, buttplate lock; *4*, buttplate lock spring; *5*, buttplate hinge pins.

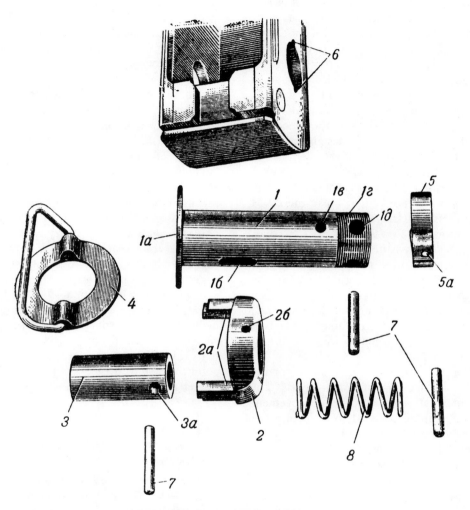

Рис. 54. Защелка приклада:

1 — ось приклада (1-56); *1а* — бурт; *1б* — овальная прорезь для шгифта защелки; *1в* — отверстие для стопорного штифта; *1г* — резьба для гайки; *1д* — отверстие для штифта; *2* — защелка (1-58); *2а* — зубья защелки для фиксации левой тяги; *2б* — отверстие для крепления защелки на оси штифтом; *3* — гнеток защелки (1-57); *3а* — отверстие для штифта; *4* — антабка (сб. 1-10); *5* — гайка для крепления тяг приклада к ствольной коробке (1-60); *5а* — отверстие для штифта; *6* — выемки для стопорного штифта; *7* — штифты (1-6-1); *8* — пружина защелки

AK47 metal-folding-stock latch assembly.
1, stock pin assembly; *2*, stock locking-catch assembly; *3*, stock catch-plunger assembly; *4*, sling swivel; *5*, stock-bar attaching nut; *6*, stock-pin hole; *7*, pins; *8*, stock catch pin.

Modernizirovanniy avtomat Kalashnikova (AKM) is also surrounded by questions. As with the case of the original shift from the sheet-metal receiver AK47 to the machined-steel receiver AK47, there is still no adequate explanation for this change in manufacturing technique. But upon examination of the AKM, it is clear that this version of Kalashnikov's weapon incorporated some significant design improvements.

First and foremost, by reverting to sheet-metal fabrication production techniques it was possible to make the AKM weigh less than the AK47 — 3.14 versus 4.3 kilograms (6.92 vs. 9.48 pounds). Second, the AKM had a new cluster of components added to the trigger assembly that have been described both as having the function of a rate-of-fire reducer and as a mechanism to prevent bolt bounce (i.e., prevent misfires due to a failure of the bolt to lock during automatic fire). The Soviet service manual for the AKM describes this cluster of components as a "hammer delay," and the manual states that: "The hammer delay serves to delay movement of the hammer forward so as to improve the accuracy of fire during the conduct of automatic fire." Since the AKM is supposedly more accurate than the AK47, the Soviet engineers recalibrated the rear sight to have a maximum range setting of one thousand meters instead of the maximum range setting of eight hundred meters on AK47 rear sights.

Quick recognition points for identifying the AKM include the sheet-metal receiver with a small indentation (dimple) on either side in the middle of the magazine opening — these dimples serve as guides for the magazine when it is inserted into the weapon. Other recognizable features include the grasping rails on the wooden forestock (i.e., raised portions to give a better hand grip); the strengthening ribs stamped into the receiver cover (the AKM receiver cover is made of lighter material than the covers used on AK47s); the absence of gas vent holes in the gas tube assembly (the AK47 has gas vent holes); and a small muzzle compensator (to control the rise of the barrel during automatic fire) on the later model AKMs.

In the folding-stock model, the Modernizirovanniy avtomat Kalashnikova skladyvayushchimsya prikladom (AKMS), the stock bars were built up from several stamped-steel pieces instead of being machined from bar stock as they were in the AK47. Over the years several types of materials have been used for AKM buttstocks, forestocks, and pistol grips. Thus, AKMs can be found with laminated wood (plywood), plastic, or nylon stock components. It is not unusual to find a mixture of such parts, especially on Kalashnikov avtomats distributed outside the East Bloc countries. All of these assemblies are fully interchangeable.

The Light Machine Gun Version of the Kalashnikov

In 1961 the Soviet Army adopted the 7.62 x 39mm Ruchnoi Pulemet Kalashnikova (RPK) as a squad automatic weapon. Lighter than its predecessor, the 7.62 x 39mm belt-fed Ruchnoi Pulemet Degtyareva obrazets 1944g (4.99 versus 7.11 kg [11 vs. 15.6 pounds]), the RPK was intended to be the squad-level assault support weapon. Given the fact that the RPK was not provided with a barrel-change capability, this adaptation of the AKM — basically just an AKM with a longer and heavier barrel — must be used for relatively

Two views of the Soviet Modernizirovanniyi Avtomat Kalashnikova skladyvayushchimsya prikladom (AKMS). This folding-stock version of the AKM is designed to be used in the BMP armored fighting vehicle as a firing-port weapon in addition to its basic role as an assault rifle. The bars of the folding stock were shortened slightly for the BMP role. Note that the stock bars are made from stamped-steel components instead of machined steel as in the AK47s.

Opposite page and above: **Three views of the Soviet fixed-buttstock Modernizirovanniyi Avtomat Kalashnikova. This is the same 1972 AKM illustrated on page 146. Its serial number is 171613. (NMAH 85-1312; 85-1309; 85-1310)**

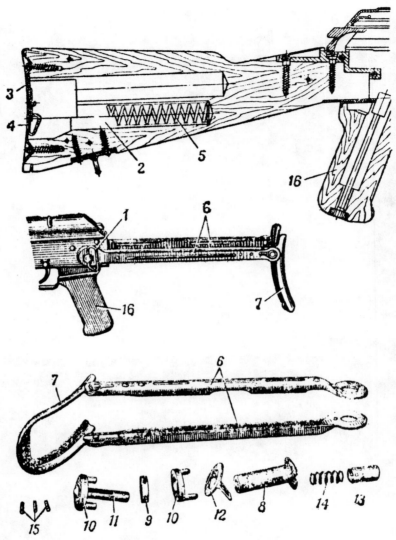

Рис. 30. Приклад и пистолетная рукоятка:

а — деревянный приклад; *б* — складывающийся приклад; *в* — складывающийся приклад в разобранном виде; *1* — антабка для ремня; *2* — гнездо для принадлежности; *3* — затыльник; *4* — крышка; *5* — пружина для выталкивания пенала с принадлежностью; *6* — тяги; *7* — плечевой упор; *8* — соединительная втулка; *9* — гайка; *10* — фиксаторы приклада; *11* — соединительный стержень; *12* — шайба с антабкой; *13* — колпачок; *14* — пружина; *15* — шпильки; *16* — пистолетная рукоятка

An illustration from the 1970 Soviet service manual showing the fixed and folding buttstocks for the AKM.

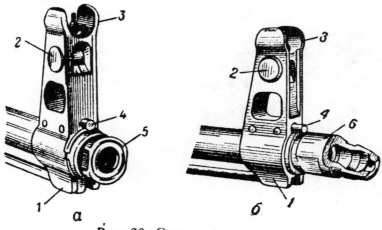

Рис. 26. Основание мушки:

а — с муфтой ствола; *б* — с компенсатором; *1* — упор для
шомпола и штыка-ножа; *2* — полозок с мушкой; *3* — предохра-
нитель мушки; *4* — фиксатор; *5* — муфта ствола; *6* — компен-
сатор

An illustration from the 1970 Soviet service manual showing the two basic types of muzzle attachments found on the AKM. *Left*, the basic muzzle nut, which serves to protect the muzzle threads that can accommodate a rifle grenade launcher or a silencer; *right*, the AKM muzzle compensator, which helps to keep the muzzle down during automatic fire.

short bursts of fire. Sustained shooting in excess of eighty shots per minute would likely lead to cook-offs (unwanted discharges due to cartridge detonation by an overheated barrel). The cook-off problem is exacerbated because the RPK is fired from a closed bolt, a feature that prevents the barrel from cooling between shots. Equipped with 40-shot box magazines and/or 75-shot drums, the RPK can provide good fire support within the limitations noted above. When necessary, the RPK can be fired with the standard AK47/AKM 30 cartridge box magazine because all of these feed devices are interchangeable.

Although an evolution of the basic Modernizirovanniy avtomat Kalashnikova, the RPK differs from the AKM in several ways: First, the barrel is heavier and longer, and it is fitted with a bipod; second, the receiver has been modified slightly to make it stronger; third, the rear sight is slightly different, having an adjustment for windage; fourth, the forestock and buttstock have been changed. Except for these details, tests indicate that all other parts of the RPK interchange with those of the AKM, a valuable feature when field repair is considered. Some RPKs are fitted with a mounting bracket to which an infrared night sight can be fitted. A more recent version, the RPKS, has a folding stock and is intended to be used by airborne troops. Its wood buttstock can be folded forward along the left side of the receiver to make it shorter to jump with.

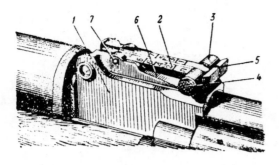

Рис. 29. Прицел:

1 — колодка прицела; *2* — прицельная планка; *3* — хомутик; *4* — защелка хомутика; *5* — гривка с прорезью; *6* — сектор; *7* — отверстия для цапф прицельной планки

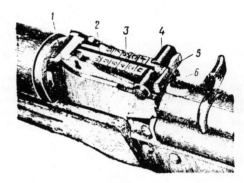

Рис. 28. Прицел:

1 — колодка прицела; *2* — сектор; *3* — прицельная планка; *4* — хомутик; *5* — гривка прицельной планки; *6* — защелка хомутика

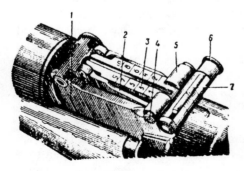

Рис. 31. Прицел:

1 — колодка прицела; *2* — сектор; *3* — прицельная планка; *4* — защелка хомутика; *5* — хомутик; *6* — маховичок винта целика; *7* — целик

Three Kalashnikov rear sights. *Top*, the AK47 sight, which is graduated to eight hundred meters; *middle*, the one thousand meter AKM sight; *bottom*, the one thousand meter RPK sight, with an adjustable windage setting.

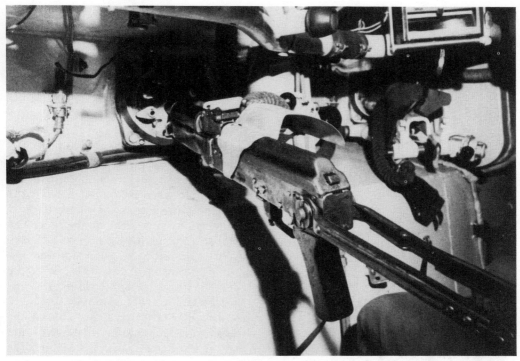

The Soviet Modernizirovanniyi Avtomat Kalashnikova skladyvayushchimsya prikladom (AKMS) mounted in the firing port of the BMP armored fighting vehicle.

Operation of the AK47/AKM/RPK Weapons

The operating mechanism for locking the Kalashnikov family of weapons is very similar to that of the US M1 and M14 rifles, and the M1/M2 carbines. In fact there is little new about the individual design elements of the Kalashnikov weapons. The inventor's accomplishment was the recombination of known design elements in a reliable and durable package. The bolt is very similar in design and size to that of the 7.62 x 33mm US M1 Carbine. Both weapons have turning bolts with two lugs, and both are unlocked by the rearward motion of the operating rod/

bolt carrier assembly. As the bolt carrier moves to the rear, the camming surfaces in the carrier rotate the bolt to the unlocked position.

The trigger/fire control mechanism of the Kalashnikov weapons is far more interesting from a design standpoint. This is especially true for the safety sear, which always holds back the hammer until the bolt carrier is fully forward and the bolt is completely locked. Again, there is little that is absolutely new; it is just the cleverness of the package that is fascinating. The trigger mechanism in principle is the same as that employed in the M1 and M14 rifles, and the AK47 and AKM/RPK mechanisms differ in some detail from one another. The description that follows is for the AKM. Additional details are presented in the illustrations that accompany this text.

When "single shot" is selected—the lowest position for the safety/fire selector lever, which is marked "OD" in Cyrillic letters—the hammer is held back only by the nose of the trigger. Rotation of the trigger to the rear moves the nose forward, the hammer hook is disengaged, and one shot is fired when the hammer strikes the firing pin. The hammer is rotated back by the rearward movement of the bolt. The "T" bar at the top of the bolt is held back by the spring-loaded secondary sear engaging the center of the cross bar of the "T". When the trigger is held back by the shooter, another shot cannot be fired until the trigger is released. The nose of the trigger moves up and holds the left-hand arm of the hammer head. Releasing the trigger moves the secondary sear clear, leaving the shooter free to pull the trigger again. Each time the hammer is propelled by a two-strand wrapped spring. The disconnector action takes place with each shot when the rifle is set on "single shot."

When "full automatic" is selected—this position is marked "AB" in Cyrillic letters (translated AV for *avtomatcheskiy* in Roman letters)—the spindle in the safety/fire selector lever is rotated upward. This action places an attachment on the spindle in a position where it forces the secondary sear back so it is no longer contacted by the hammer during its rearward rotation. The firing of the weapon is controlled entirely by the safety sear. When the bolt carrier has moved completely forward and the bolt is locked, the safety sear is rotated, thus releasing the hammer to fire another round. This firing process will

The 7.62 x 39mm Ruchnoi Pulemet Degtyareva (RPD) belt-fed light machine gun was replaced in the early 1960s by the magazine-fed 7.62 x 39mm Ruchnoi Pulemet Kalashnikova (RPK). The RPD shown here is the version made in the People's Republic of China.

Two views of the 7.62 x 39mm Ruchnoi Pulemet Kalashnikova. *Left*, the RPK has a 40-shot box magazine; *right*, an RPK with a 75-shot drum magazine.

continue until either the ammunition in the magazine is exhausted or the shooter releases his pressure on the trigger.

This trigger mechanism is based upon that of the AK47, but with the following changes. Instead of a double hook, as in the AK47, the nose of the trigger in the AKM/RPK has only one hook on its left side. Mounted in the trigger axis, on the right side of the receiver, is a spring-loaded pawl that is struck by the right arm of the "T" of the hammer crossbar every time the hammer rises. This pawl is linked to another hook, which moves over the hammer when the pawl is struck and holds the hammer down. The long curved face of the pawl causes the hook to hold the hammer for a few milliseconds. When the spring snaps the pawl back and releases the hook, the hammer is freed to hit the firing pin. This delay in the movement of the hammer does not significantly alter the rate of the weapon's fire, but it allows the bolt a little extra time to come to rest in the locked position before the weapon fires. This increases the safety of the weapon and also improves accuracy.

When the selector lever is raised to its highest or "safe" position this mechanism carries out two functions. The spindle has an arm that covers the trigger extension and prevents trigger movement. The selector also comes up to block the cocking lever and thus prevents the weapon from

Table 4-1
Comparative Technical Data for the AK47, AKM, and the RPK

	AK47	AKM	RPK
Caliber:	7.62 x 39mm	7.62 x 39mm	7.62 x 39mm
Overall length: (mm)	870	880	1040
Barrel length: (mm)	415	415	590
Weight, empty: (kg)	4.3	3.14	4.99
Magazine capacity:	30	30	40 or 75
Muzzle velocity: (m/s)	710	710	735
Practical rate of fire; semiautomatic (spm):	40	40	50
Practical rate of fire; automatic (spm):	100	100	150
Cyclic rate of fire; automatic (spm):	600	600	600
Practical range; semiautomatic (m):	300	300	400
Practical range; automatic (m):	200	200	300

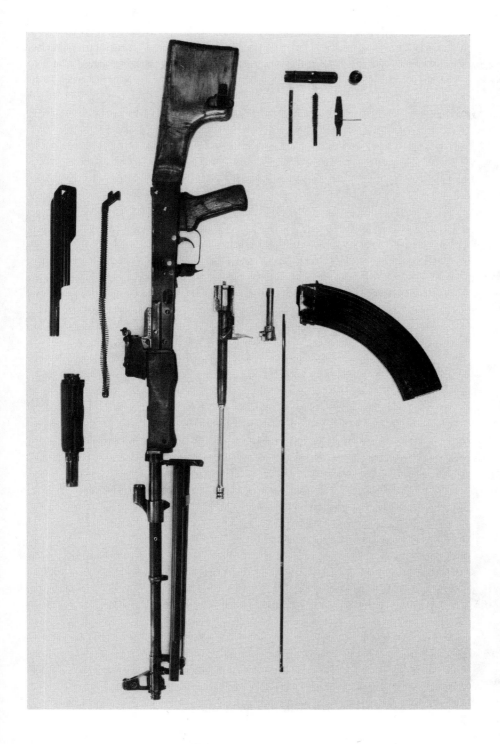

A disassembled view of the 7.62 x 39mm Ruchnoi Pulemet Kalashnikova. The 1964 RPK has the transliterated serial number "UM 0874" and is in the collection of the Royal Military College of Science, Swindon, Wiltshire, UK.

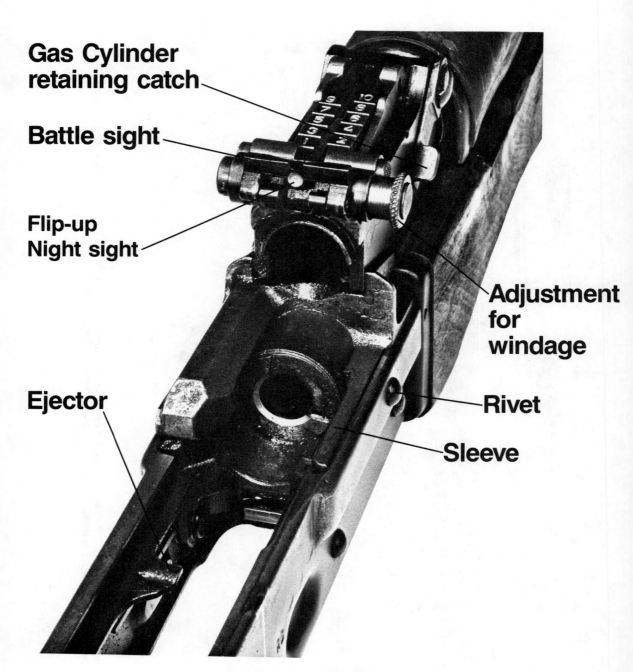

Gas Cylinder retaining catch

Battle sight

Flip-up Night sight

Ejector

Adjustment for windage

Rivet

Sleeve

A close-up view of the RPK lower receiver.

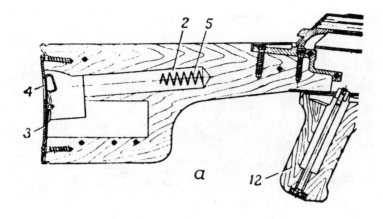

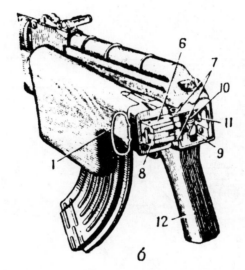

Рис. 33. Приклад и пистолетная рукоятка:

а — приклад РПК (разрез); *б* — приклад РПКС в сложенном положении; *1* — антабка для ремня; *2* — гнездо для принадлежности; *3* — затыльник; *4* — крышка; *5* — пружина для выталкивания пенала с принадлежностью; *6* — выступ приклада с ушками; *7* — проушина ствольной коробки; *8* — правая защелка приклада с пружиной; *9* — задняя часть левой защелки с насечкой; *10* — пружина защелки; *11* — вырез для правой защелки приклада; *12* — пистолетная рукоятка

An illustration from the 1970 Soviet service manual showing the fixed and folding buttstocks for the 7.62 x 39mm Ruchnoi Pulemet Kalashnikova.

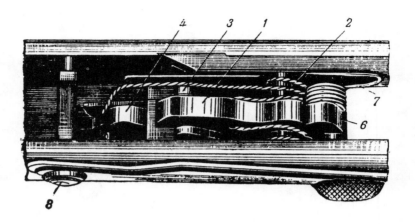

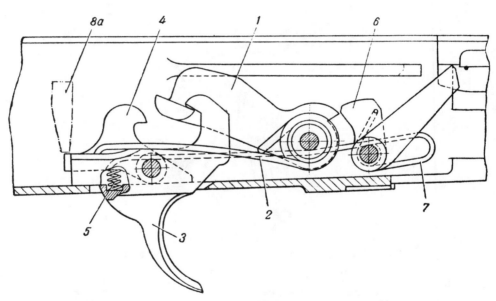

Рис. 32. Ударно-спусковой механизм (верхний — в собранном виде, нижний — разрез):

1 — курок (0-2); *2* — боевая пружина (0-3); *3* — спусковой крючок (0-8); *4* — шептало одиночного огня (0-9); *5* — пружина шептала; *6* — автоспуск; *7* — пружина автоспуска (0-6); *8* — переводчик (сб. 1-3); *8а* — рычаг переводчика

AK47 trigger mechanism.

1, hammer; *2*, hammer and trigger spring; *3*, trigger; *4*, disconnector; *5*, disconnector spring; *6*, full-auto sear; *7*, full-auto sear spring; *8*, selector; *8a*, selector-lever bar.

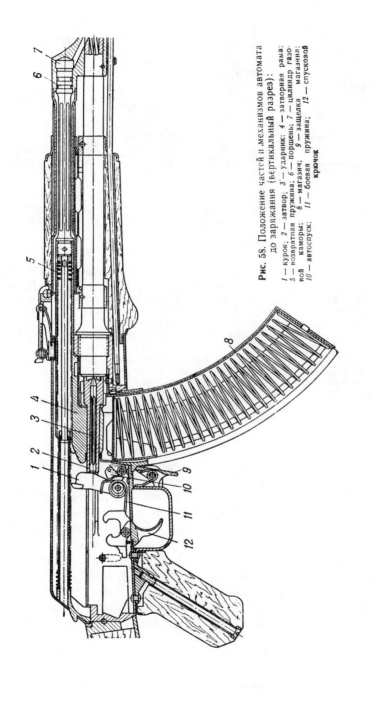

Рис. 58. Положение частей и механизмов автомата
до заряжания (вертикальный разрез):

1 — курок; *2* — затвор; *3* — ударник; *4* — затворная рама; *5* — возвратная пружина; *6* — поршень; *7* — цилиндр газовой камеры; *8* — магазин; *9* — защелка магазина; *10* — автоспуск; *11* — боевая пружина; *12* — спусковой крючок

Position of AK47 operational parts before loading in section view.

1, hammer; *2*, bolt; *3*, firing pin; *4*, operating rod; *5*, return spring; *6*, piston; *7*, gas cylinder; *8*, magazine; *9*, magazine catch; *10*, full-auto sear; *11*, hammer and trigger spring; *12*, trigger; *13*, loaded cartridges.

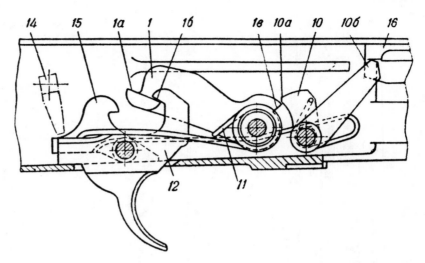

Рис. 59. Спусковой механизм автомата на предохранителе:

1 — курок; *1а* — взвод одиночного огня; *1б* — боевой взвод; *1в* — взвод автоспуска; *10* — автоспуск; *10а* — шептало автоспуска; *10б* — верхний конец рычага автоспуска; *11* — боевая пружина; *12* — спусковой крючок; *14* — рычаг переводчика; *15* — шептало одиночного огня; *16* — выключатель автоспуска

AK47 trigger mechanism with the safety/fire selector set on "safe."
1, hammer; *1a*, disconnector notch; *1b*, hammer cock notch; *1v*, full-auto sear notch; *4*, underside of bolt carrier; *10*, full-auto sear; *10a*, full-auto sear cock notch; *10b*, upper end of full-auto sear; *11*, hammer and trigger spring; *12*, trigger; *14*, selector lever; *15*, disconnector; *16*, full-auto disconnector.

being cocked while it is set on "safe."

There are a number of important human engineering touches in the design of the Kalashnikov weapons. One example: The safety/fire selector lever is designed so that it can be operated by a shooter wearing heavy arctic mittens. Another example is the rear sight used on the AKM and the RPK, which has a luminous dot that helps the shooter aim the weapon at night. This latter design feature is consistent with the Soviet emphasis on night-time operations.

These and other features attest that the Kalashnikov weapons have been adopted with the fighting man in mind. Another

example is that the Soviets decided to chromium-plate the barrels and chambers of all of their 7.62 x 39mm weapons. This extends barrel and chamber life expectancy, while allowing the Soviets to continue to use corrosive primer compounds that are hydroscopic—water attracting—in their cartridge primers. Without chrome-plated bores and chambers, the Soviets would have had severe problems with barrel corrosion and much more troop attention would have had to be given to routine cleaning of weapons. The essential ruggedness and durability of the Kalashnikov-designed weapons appear to answer a century-old Russian problem—the creation of

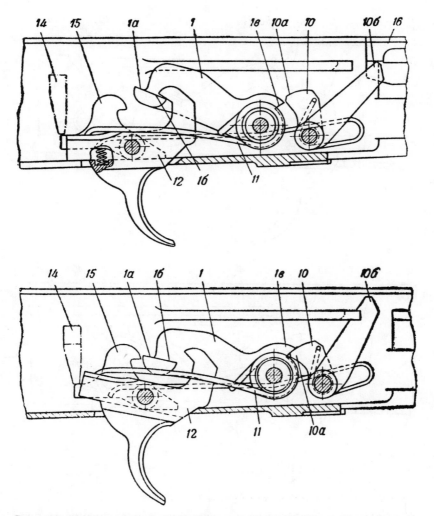

Рис. 60. Спусковой механизм автомата после установки переводчика для ведения автоматического огня (верхний — спусковой крючок отпущен, нижний — спусковой крючок нажат):

1 — курок; *1а* — взвод одиночного огня; *1б* — боевой взвод; *1в* — взвод автоспуска; *10* — автоспуск; *10а* — шептало автоспуска; *10б* — верхний конец рычага автоспуска; *11* — боевая пружина; *12* — спусковой крючок; *14* — рычаг переводчика; *15* — шептало одиночного огня; *16* — выключатель автоспуска

AK47 trigger mechanism with the safety/fire selector set on "full automatic." *Top*, ready to fire, forward trigger hooks engaged; *bottom*, during firing cycle with the trigger depressed, rear trigger hooks engaged awaiting release by full-auto sear.

1, hammer; 1a, disconnector notch; 1b, hammer cock notch; 1v, full-auto sear notch; 4, underside of bolt carrier; 10, full-auto sear; 10a, full-auto sear cock notch; 10b, upper end of full-auto sear; 11, hammer and trigger spring; 12, trigger; 14, selector lever; 15, disconnector; 16, full-auto disconnector.

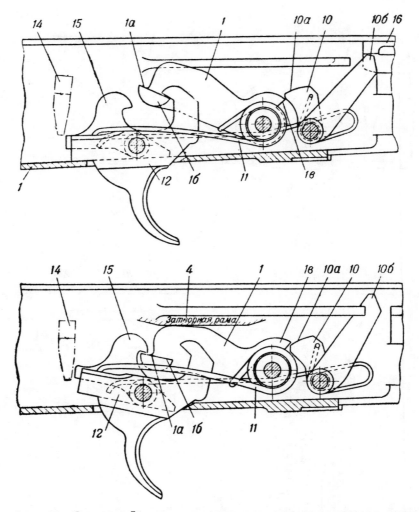

Рис. 61. Спусковой механизм автомата после установки переводчика для ведения одиночного огня (верхний — спусковой крючок отпущен, нижний — спусковой крючок нажат):

1 — **курок**; *1а* — **взвод одиночного огня**; *1б* — **боевой взвод**; *1в* — **взвод автоспуска**; *4* — **прилив затворной рамы**; *10* — **автоспуск**; *10а* — **шептало автоспуска**; *10б* — **верхний конец рычага автоспуска**; *11* — **боевая пружина**; *12* — **спусковой крючок**; *14* — **рычаг переводчика**; *15* — **шептало одиночного огня**; *16* — **выключатель автоспуска**

AK47 trigger mechanism with the safety/fire selector set on "semiautomatic." *Top*, ready to fire, forward trigger hooks engaged; *bottom*, during firing cycle with the trigger depressed, rear trigger hooks engaged to prevent the next shot.

1, hammer; *1a*, disconnector notch; *1b*, hammer cock notch; *1v*, full-auto sear notch; *4*, underside of bolt carrier; *10*, full-auto sear; *10a*, full-auto sear cock notch; *10b*, upper end of full-auto sear; *11*, hammer and trigger spring; *12*, trigger; *14*, selector lever; *15*, disconnector; *16*, full-auto disconnector.

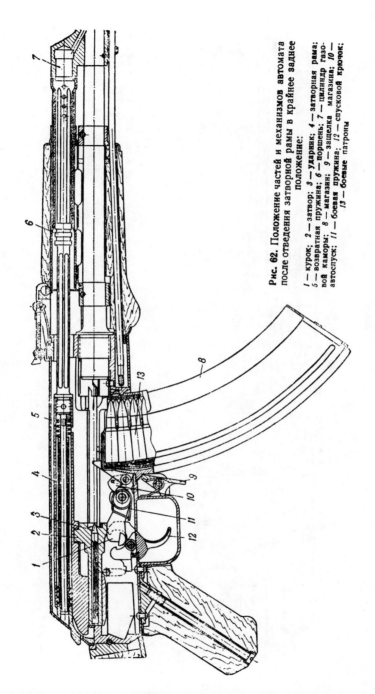

Рис. 62. Положение частей и механизмов автомата после отведения затворной рамы в крайнее заднее положение:

1 — курок; 2 — затвор; 3 — ударник; 4 — затворная рама; 5 — возвратная пружина; 6 — поршень; 7 — цилиндр газовой каморы; 8 — магазин; 9 — защелка магазина; 10 — автоспуск; 11 — боевая пружина; 12 — спусковой крючок; 13 — боевые патроны

Position of AK47 operational parts with operating rod in the extreme rear position.

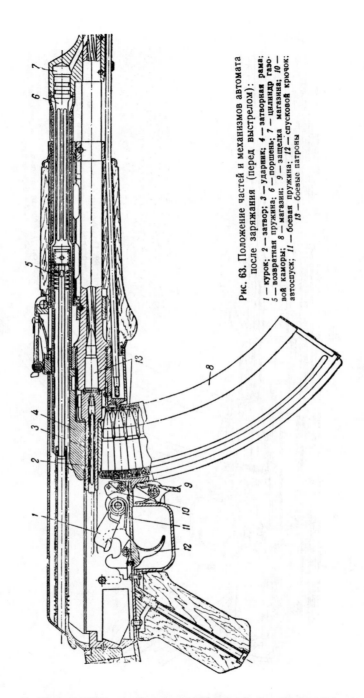

Рис. 63. Положение частей и механизмов автомата после заряжания (перед выстрелом):

1 — курок; 2 — затвор; 3 — ударник; 4 — затворная рама; 5 — возвратная пружина; 6 — поршень; 7 — цилиндр газовой камеры; 8 — магазин; 9 — защелка магазина; 10 — автоспуск; 11 — боевая пружина; 12 — спусковой крючок; 13 — боевые патроны

Position of AK47 operational parts after loading and before firing.

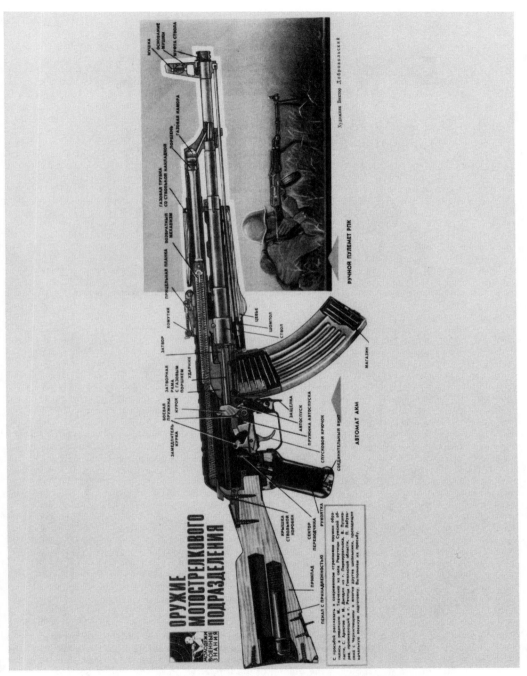

Section view of the Modernizirovanniyi Avtomat Kalashnikova.

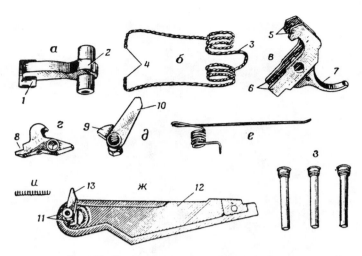

Рис. 37. Детали ударно-спускового механизма:

a — курок; *б* — боевая пружина; *в* — спусковой крючок; *г* — шептало одиночного огня; *д* — автоспуск; *е* — пружина автоспуска; *ж* — переводчик; *з* — оси; *и* — пружина шептала одиночного огня; *1* — боевой взвод; *2* — взвод автоспуска; *3* — петля; *4* — загнутые концы; *5* — фигурные выступы; *6* — прямоугольные выступы; *7* — хвост; *8* — вырез; *9* — выступ (шептало); *10* — рычаг; *11* — цапфы; *12* — щиток; *13* — сектор

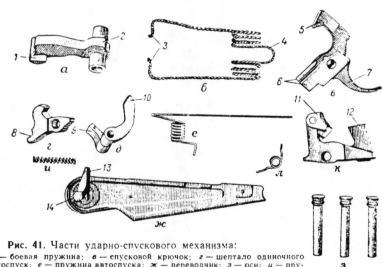

Рис. 41. Части ударно-спускового механизма:

a — курок; *б* — боевая пружина; *в* — спусковой крючок; *г* — шептало одиночного огня; *д* — автоспуск; *е* — пружина автоспуска; *ж* — переводчик; *з* — оси; *и* — пружина шептала одиночного огня; *к* — замедлитель курка; *л* — пружина замедлителя курка; *1* — боевой взвод; *2* — взвод автоспуска; *3* — загнутые концы; *4* — петля; *5* — фигурный выступ; *6* — прямоугольные выступы; *7* — хвост; *8* — вырез; *9* — шептало; *10* — рычаг; *11* — защелка; *12* — передний выступ; *13* — сектор; *14* — цапфа

Comparative views of the AK47 (top) and AKM (bottom) trigger assemblies. Note the differences in the full-auto sears (*center*) and the triggers (*upper right*). In the lower drawing, note the addition of the "hammer delay assembly" ("K") which fits along the right side of the modified trigger. Item 13 is the safety/fire selector bar, which blocks the pulling of the trigger when the safety/fire selector is set in the "safe" position.

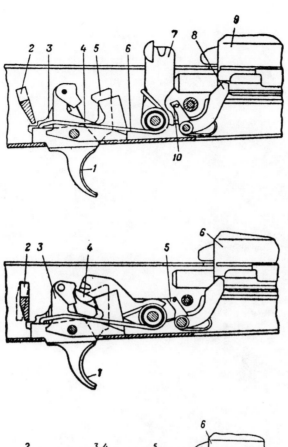

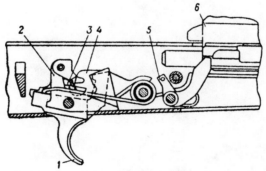

Three views of the AKM trigger mechanism: *top,* **position of the operating parts before loading with the safety engaged and the hammer released;** *middle,* **position of the operating parts with the hammer cocked and the safety off;** *bottom,* **position of the operating parts after firing with the selector set on "semiautomatic."**

Top: 1, trigger; *2,* selector bar; *3,* semi-auto sear; *4,* hammer delay; *5,* trigger hook; *6,* trigger/hammer spring; *7,* hammer; *8,* auto sear; *9,* bolt carrier; *10,* auto-sear pawl.

Middle: 1, trigger; *2,* selector bar; *3,* hammer delay; *4,* hammer; *5,* auto sear; *6,* bolt carrier.

Bottom: 1, trigger; *2,* hammer delay; *3,* semi-auto sear; *4,* hammer; *5,* auto sear; *6,* bolt carrier.

Soviet Army troops on winter exercise. Note that the soldier on the right has an AKM, while the other two infantrymen have RPKs.

Two frontier guards armed with AKMs watch the border somewhere in the Soviet Union.

infantry weapons that will withstand the abuse of the men and women who use them.

Once the Soviets had mastered production of the Kalashnikov avtomat at home they took steps to see that this weapon became the standard weapon within their political and military spheres of influence. With the exception of Czechoslovakia, all of the Warsaw Pact armies have adopted these weapons. The story of Kalashnikov-type assault rifles manufactured outside of the Soviet Union is told in photographs in the next chapter.

5

Design Variants of the Kalashnikov Avtomat
Proliferation of the AK Family

In addition to the Soviet Union, the People's Republic of China, the German Democratic Republic (East Germany), Poland, Romania, Bulgaria, North Korea, Hungary, and Yugoslavia have manufactured the AK47. The People's Republic of China, the German Democratic Republic, Poland, Romania, North Korea, Hungary, Yugoslavia, and Egypt have also manufactured the AKM-type assault rifle. Finland and Israel have produced their own variants of the Kalashnikov designs. While the safety/fire selector markings are one of the quickest ways of identifying the nation of origin, the accompanying photographs and drawings will help identify some of the different models. The word "some" is used because new models continue to appear with relative frequency. For additional illustrations of Kalashnikov weapons, see the 12th edition of *Small Arms of the World*. Additional information about countries and revolutionary/paramilitary

units using these weapons is presented in *Small Arms Today: Latest Reports on the World's Weapons and Ammunition.*

People's Republic of China

During the era in which the Soviets and the Chinese still cooperated politically, economically, and militarily, the Soviet Union provided considerable technical assistance to the People's Republic of China in the defense industry arena. Before 1958, a key element of that cooperation was the establishment of production facilities for the manufacture of Soviet-type weapons. In the mid-1950s the Chinese initiated production of both the SKS45 and the AK47; since that time they have progressed to the AKM design as well. In the case of the latter weapon it is not clear if there was Soviet technical assistance (unlikely due to the Sino-Soviet rift) in establishing the production of the AKM, or

This first model Chinese Type 56 "submachine gun" was a direct copy of the Soviet third model AK47.

This later model Chinese Type 56 "submachine gun" differs from its predecessor in having a permanently attached spike-type folding bayonet.

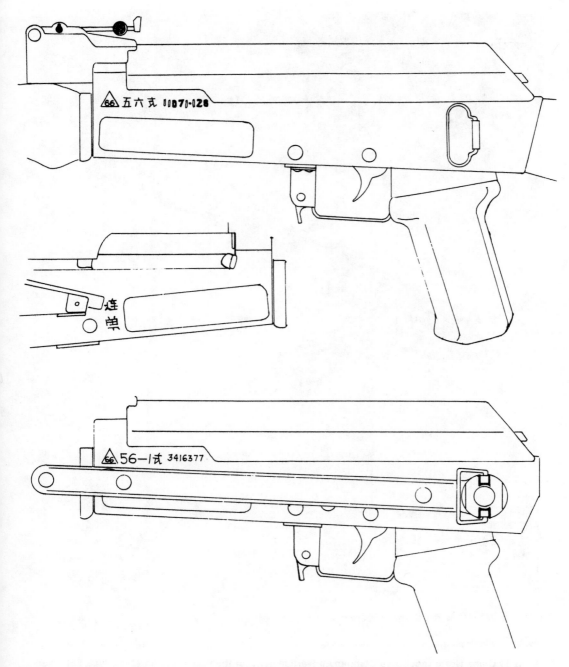

Chinese Type 56 "submachine gun" markings: *top*, early Type 56 with Chinese characters on the fire-selector markings; *bottom*, a Type 56-1, which had "L" and "D" on the fire-selector markings.

SUB-MACHINE GUN TYPE 56-2 *

Caliber	7.62 mm
Muzzle velocity	710 m/s
Effective range	400 m
Field condition rate of fire:	
single-shot	40 rds/min
burst	90-100 rds/min
Gun length:	
stock folded	654 mm
stock extended	874 mm
Weight	3.9 kg
Mag. capacity	30 rds

Other Small Arms Made by NORINCO

7.62 mm Pistol	Type 54	7.62 mm Light Sub-machine Gun	Type 79
26 mm Signal Pistol	Type 57	7.62 mm Light Machine Gun	Type 56-1
9 mm Pistol	Type 59	7.62 mm Light Machine Gun	Type 74
7.62 mm Pistol	Type 64	7.62 mm Light Machine Gun	Type 81
7.62 mm SD Pistol	Type 77	7.62 mm Heavy Machine Gun	Type 57
7.62 mm Automatic Pistol	Type 80	7.62 mm Heavy Machine Gun	Type 67-1
7.62 mm Sub-machine Gun *	Type 56	7.62 mm Heavy Machine Gun	Type 67-2
7.62 mm Sub-machine Gun *	Type 56-1	7.62 mm MP Machine Gun	Type 80

China North Industries Corporation

Add: 7A, Yuetan Nanjie, Beijing, China
Tel: 867019, 863398 Cable: NORINCO Telex: 22339 CNIC CN

Norinco of China

affordable innovations for today . . .

An 1985 China North Industries Company advertisement for their side-folding stock Type 56-2 sub-machine gun (AKM). Note the plastic cheek piece on the folding stock, and the new shape of the pistol grip.

whether the Chinese mastered production of the stamped-steel-receiver-type weapon on their own. As is typical with foreign adoptions of the Soviet weapons, the

basic design has further evolved over time. Most of these changes are minor, but they still merit brief note.

Chinese Model

1. Type 56 submachine gun, with Chinese characters for selector markings. Some of these Type 56 weapons are found with "M22" in place of the Chinese factory designator. These were intended for export sale.
2. Type 56 submachine gun, with Chinese characters for selector markings and permanently attached folding spike-type bayonet.
3. Type 56 submachine gun, with Roman "L" and "D" for selector markings and permanently attached folding spike-type bayonet. This weapon was made for export.
4. Type 56 submachine gun, with Chinese characters for selector markings and permanently attached folding spike-type bayonet.
5. Type 56-1 submachine gun, with folding stock. Chinese selector markings.
6. Type 56-1 submachine gun, with folding stock. Chinese selector markings and spike-type bayonet.
7. Type 56-1 submachine gun, with folding stock. Chinese selector markings and spike-type bayonet.
8. Type 56-1 submachine gun, with folding stock. Chinese selector markings, no bayonet.
9. Type 56-1 submachine gun with new-style side-folding stock, with plastic cheekpiece. Chinese selector markings and no bayonet.
10. Type 81 light machine gun with a 75-round drum. Both the weapon and the drum show uniquely Chinese features.

Soviet Model

1. Third model AK47, direct copy, with fixed wood buttstock.

2. Third model AK47, direct copy, with fixed wood buttstock.

3. Third model AK47, direct copy, with fixed wood buttstock.

4. AKM, direct copy, with fixed wood buttstock. Despite the change to the AKM-type receiver, the Chinese still call the gun the Type 56.
5. Third type AK47, with folding stock. Direct copy.
6. Third type AK47, with folding stock. Direct copy.

7. AKM, direct copy, with folding stock. They still call this the Type 56-1.

8. AKM, direct copy, with folding stock. They still call this the Type 56-1.

9. AKM-type receiver.

10. Copy of RPK.

There are certainly additional variants on these basic Chinese themes. Wood and plastic furniture (buttstock, forestock, and pistol grips) have been manufactured, and at least two different types of plastic pistol grips have been observed.

There are no known accurate estimates of the number of Kalashnikov-type weapons produced to date by the Chinese. With a regular army establishment of more than three million people and reserve forces numbering between five and seven million, it probably would not be unreasonable to project a production total somewhere between ten and twenty million. This estimate seems especially reasonable in view of the Chinese materiel support of North Vietnam in the 1960s and 1970s, and subsequent sales and gifts of such weapons. The People's Republic of China is currently very active in the international marketplace with export sales of their light infantry weapons being carried out by the China North Industries Corporation (NORINCO).

German Democratic Republic

The East Germans have also been a major manufacturer of Kalashnikov-type weapons, and they too have developed their own local variants.

German Model

1. MPiK—Maschinenpistole Kalashnikow, with the letter "D" (*dauerfeur*) for automatic fire and "E" (*einzelfeuer*) for semiautomatic fire.
2. MPiKS—Maschinenpistole Kalashnikow mit Schulterstutze.
3. MPiKM, with wood stocks and plastic stocks. The latter are distinctive because of their pattern of raised bumps.
4. MPiKMS72, with German side-folding stock. See accompanying figures.
5. KKMPi69. A .22 long-rifle-caliber training rifle configured to look like the MPiKM.
6. LMG-K.

Soviet Model

1. Third model AK47, direct copy with fixed wood buttstock.

2. Third model AK47, direct copy, with folding stock.
3. AKM, direct copy.

4. AKM, with new folding stock.

5. No comparable model known.

6. RPK.

Again, there are no reported estimates of the number of East German Kalashnikov-type weapons manufactured to date, but a reasonable guess would be between 1.5 and 2.0 million. The Germans have made substantial export sales of these weapons.

Poland

As with the East Germans, the Poles have been major manufacturers of the AK47- and AKM-type weapons. Among the unique local variants is the PMK-DGN-60 grenade-launching version of the

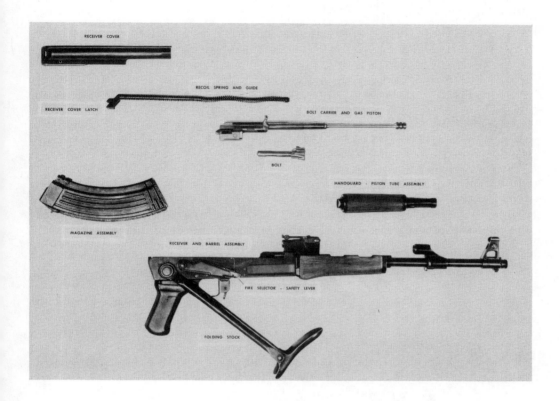

RECEIVER COVER

RECEIVER COVER LATCH

RECOIL SPRING AND GUIDE

BOLT CARRIER AND GAS PISTON

BOLT

HANDGUARD · PISTON TUBE ASSEMBLY

MAGAZINE ASSEMBLY

RECEIVER AND BARREL ASSEMBLY

FIRE SELECTOR · SAFETY LEVER

FOLDING STOCK

Top, a disassembled early East German MPiKs, which was a close copy of the standard Soviet AK47 with folding stock; *bottom*, the later version of the East German MPiKMS-72 with its side-swinging folding stock.

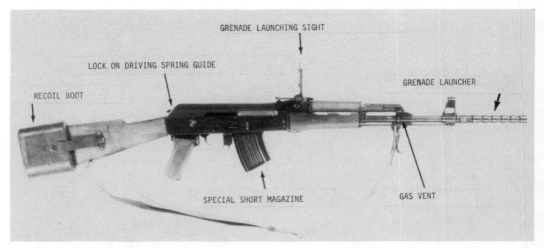

GRENADE LAUNCHING SIGHT

LOCK ON DRIVING SPRING GUIDE

GRENADE LAUNCHER

RECOIL BOOT

SPECIAL SHORT MAGAZINE

GAS VENT

The Polish PMK-DGN-60 grenade-launching rifle, a modified version of the standard Soviet AK47.

A Polish AKM made in 1980. This assault rifle, bearing the serial number "BA28233" and the Polish factory code, an "11" in an oval, was captured by Israeli Defense Forces from a PLO storage depot in 1982.

Two versions of the Romanian AKM with its distinctive laminated-wood forward hand grip.

standard Polish PMK (AK47). This weapon has the following special features: a recoil boot to protect the shooter and the buttstock (the latter when it is rested on the ground); a detachable grenade-launching sight; a detachable spigot-type grenade launcher with 20mm tube diameter which screws on the muzzle; and a special short magazine that will hold only grenade-launching blanks. The latter safety feature reduces the possibility of shooting a projectile into the rifle grenade. The LON-1 grenade launcher is used to launch either the F1/N60 antipersonnel grenade or the PGN antiarmor grenade. Both are launched by a special grenade-launching blank that is identified by its white tip.

The Polish small arms factories have also manufactured the AKM for domestic and export consumption. The earliest Bulgarian AK47s were manufactured in whole at first and then in component packages to be assembled before the Bulgarians established their own Kalashnikov production facilities. Recently, examples of Polish AKMs dated as late as 1980 have been observed in the Middle East and elsewhere. An estimated 1.5 to 2.0 million Polish Kalashnikovs have been manufactured to date. Polish Kalashnikovs have the letter "C" for the automatic-fire setting, and the letter "P" for the semiautomatic-fire setting.

Romania

Although the Romanians have one of the smaller armies in the Warsaw Pact, they have shown considerable enthusiasm for production of the Kalashnikov assault rifle. Their weapons are usually distinguished by their unique laminated-wood forestock with its integral pistol grip. The Romanians have manufactured the AKM since the late 1960s, but they only introduced a folding-stock version (AKMS) in the late 1970s. In the early 1980s, the Romanians began to manufacture their own version of the RPK squad automatic weapon, which differed from the Soviet RPK only in the manner in which the bipod was attached to the barrel. The Romanian version of the 7.62 x 54mmR Dragunov sniper rifle, based upon the AKM receiver assembly, is described in the next chapter.

During the past decade the Romanians and their neighbors the Bulgarians have been very active in the international arms market. The Kalashnikov assault rifles have been among their most popular products, and it is estimated that between them the arms factories of the two nations have made one million of these weapons. Romanian Kalashnikovs have the letters "FA" for the full-automatic-fire setting, and "FF" for the semiautomatic-fire setting. Bulgarian Kalashnikovs have the Cyrillic letters "AV" for the full-automatic-fire setting, and "ED" for the semiautomatic-fire setting.

Hungary

The Hungarian arms industry has produced some of the most distinctive Kalashnikov-type weapons. As with other Warsaw Pact countries, the Hungarians started out by manufacturing the AK47 in almost an exact copy of the Soviet weapon. When they got around to making the AKM in the early 1960s, the Hungari-

The paratrooper version of the Hungarian AKM. This weapon, the AMD, has grey/black synthetic pistol grips, a distinctive black exterior finish, and a large muzzle brake. This particular weapon bears serial number "D1 4208."

A comparative view of the Hungarian AMD-65 (Serial "KP3861") and the East German MPiKMS-72 (Serial obliterated). Note the differences in the location of the gas-port housings and the front sights. The Hungarian weapon has a special barrel attachment that permits the launching of grenades. The gas system has a valve that can be closed when grenades are being launched. When the gas port is closed, the rifle acts like a bolt-action weapon. By closing the gas port, damage to the operating parts of the rifle can be prevented. Both weapons are in the National Firearms Collection, SI. (NMAH 85-2728).

ans decided to make some substantial changes to their AKM-63. First, they developed a unique fore-end of stamped sheet metal to replace the standard wood forestock. Then they added a vertical pistol grip to that metal fore-end. In time they replaced the wood used for both the buttstock and pistol grips with a light grey-blue polypropylene material. With its synthetic stock, the AKM-63 weighed .25 kilogram (.50 pound) less than other standard AKMs. This first type of synthetic stock material gave way in the later 1960s to the dark grey-black material currently used on the AMD-65.

The AMD was a very interesting weapon because it had a much shorter barrel (318mm vs. 415mm) and a large muzzle device (that adds 60mm to the barrel length) that was supposed to make the weapon easier to control during automatic fire. While this device may work, it also increases the noise the weapon makes when it is fired. This short weapon, with its side-folding stock, was designed primarily for use by airborne troops. It is well suited to that tactical role. The AMD-65 is a more recent addition to the Hungarian Kalashnikov family, and is uniquely suited to its role of launching rifle grenades. This weapon is equipped with a shock absorber in the stock rod of the folding-stock assembly, a forestock that allows the shooter's off hand to remain stationary while the rifle reciprocates in his palm, and a detachable optical sight for aiming the rifle when grenades are being launched. Two grenades are currently used with the AMD-65: the fragmentation-type antipersonnel PGR, and the shaped-charge antiarmor PGK. Both are equipped with exhaust nozzles, indicating that they are rocket boosted for greater range.

The Hungarians may have built as many as half a million Kalashnikov-type rifles. They mark their selector settings with the infinity sign for full automatic fire, and 1 for semiautomatic fire.

Yugoslavia

Another active participant in the international arms trade, the Yugoslavian arms factory Zavodi Crvena Zastava, at Kragujevac, has produced a bewildering variety of Kalashnikov-type weapons. The following list should help sort out the types.

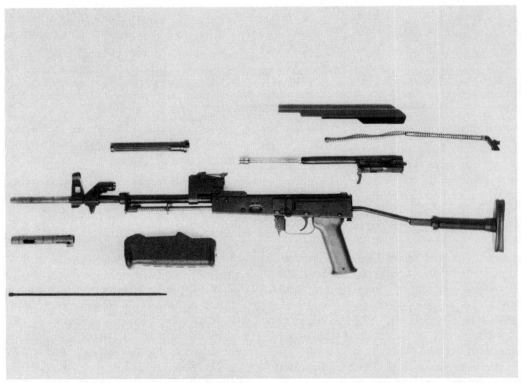

A view of the disassembled Hungarian AMD-65. Note the spring and guide-rod assembly below the barrel that allows the forestock to reciprocate during firing. (NMAH 85–2724)

Yugoslavian Model

1. Automat M64.

2. Automat M64A.

3. Automat M64B.

4. Automat M70.
5. Automat M70A.
6. Automat M70B1.
7. Automat M70AB2.
8. Automat M77B1 (NATO).

9. Automat M80.
10. Automat M80A.

11. M76.

12. Puskomitraljez M65A.

13. Puskomitraljez M65B.

14. Puskomitraljez M72.

15. Puskomitraljez M72B1.

16. Puskomitraljez M72AB1.

17. Puskomitraljez M77B1 (NATO)

Soviet Model

1. Standard third model AK47, with wood buttstock.

2. Same weapon with grenade-launching modifications.

3. Grenade-launching version, with folding buttstock.

4. Improved M64.
5. Improved M64, with folding stock.
6. AKM with wood buttstock.
7. AKM with folding stock.
8. M70-type in 7.62 x 51mm NATO. There are also folding-stock versions of this gun.

9. M70-type AKM in 5.56 x 45mm.
10. M80 5.56 x 45 mm with folding stock, as in M70AB2.

11. 7.92 x 57mm Mauser Sniper version of M70B1. This rifle is semiautomatic only.

12. Light machine gun version of M64, with fixed barrel. This is an RPK-type weapon.

13. Light machine gun version of M64, with quick-change barrel.

14. Light machine gun version of M64, with quick-change barrel. Variant of M70.

15. Light machine gun version of M70A, with fixed barrel. The Yugoslavs make a 75-shot RPK-type drum for this gun.

16. Light machine gun version of M70AB2, with fixed barrel and folding stock.

17. Light machine gun version of M70A, with fixed barrel. This weapon fires the 7.62 x 51mm NATO cartridge and is intended for export sales.

It is difficult to estimate the number of Kalashnikov weapons produced by the Yugoslavian arms factory Zavodi Crvena Zastava, but it is probably in the half-a-million to one million range. Many of these weapons have been exported. These

The Hungarian AMD-65 with optical sight in place. Note that the outer sleeve of the grenade-launcher assembly has been removed from the rifle. This part is normally disassembled only for cleaning.

A Yugoslavian 7.62 x 39mm Automat M70A, a close copy of the third model AK47, with special muzzle brake. This device can be removed, and a grenade launcher can be attached in its place. Note that the grenade-launching sight is an integral part of the rifle, and that when raised it closes off the gas port to the gas piston. When the gas port is closed, the rifle acts like a bolt-action weapon. By closing the gas port, damage to the operating parts of the rifle can be prevented.

A Yugoslavian 7.62 x 39mm Automat Model 70B1, a copy of the Soviet AKM. Note that in this weapon the grenade-launching sight is folded.

weapons have the letter "R" indicating full auto fire, and "J" indicating semiautomatic fire. In addition, the M64 series had the letter "U" to denote "safe."

Democratic People's Republic of Korea

The North Koreans have manufactured the third model AK47 as their Type 58, and the AKM as their Type 68. Both series have been produced in fixed wooden stock and folding-stock versions. The North Korean AKM does not have the hammer delay mechanism found in most other versions of the AKM. It has been estimated that the Korean small arms factories identified by the numbers 61 and 65 combined have been producing Kalashnikov weapons at an annual rate of about 150,000 units. It is not clear just how many years this rate has been in effect; if it has been in

effect for the past twenty years that would mean that the Koreans have manufactured in excess of three million guns. This may be the reason for the recent proliferation of North Korean assault rifles in the international arms trade. North Korean weapons of all types have been appearing in recent years in the Middle East and Africa in substantial numbers. All of their Kalashnikov-type weapons have the distinctive Korean characters on the fire-control selector.

Finland

Outside the Soviet Union, Warsaw Pact, and Asian communist powers, Finland has been the largest manufacturer of the Kalashnikov avtomat. The Finnish Defence Forces acquired their first weapons of this type—AK47s of the third model—

7.62 mm Automatic Rifle M70AB2

The 7.62 mm Automatic Rifle M70AB2 pertains to the family of automatic arms FAZ (Automatic Rifles M70B1 and M70AB2 and Light Machine Gun M72B1), designed on the basis of the 7.62 × 39 mm cartridge.

Arms of this family use the same magazine and have the same main components.

They are gas operated and can be fired in single shots or in automatic fire.

Automatic rifles contain within their set a knife which, combined with the scabbard, forms scissors for cutting of wire, telephone and radar cables.

The 7.62 mm Automatic Rifle M70AB2 represents a modern individual arm of a high fire power and light mass. It is a powerful offensive and defansive arm at any range to 400 m.

Unlike the M70B1 Rifle the M70AB2 7.62 mm Automatic Rifle has a metallic folding stock instead of a wooden one, thus reducing the arm length from 890 to 640 mm. The arm is suitable for use in limited space: for parachutists, armoured units, diversionists, senior staff etc.

This arm is used for launching of rifle grenades (antitank, fragmentation, smoke and illuminating) exclusively from hand. For firing of rifle grenades, the rifle has a launcher, carried extra. The rifle grenade launcher is fitted on the barrel muzzle, as necessary. For firing of rifle grenades, there is a rifle grenade sight which automatically shuts off the gas operation when lifted in position for sighting.

The night sight is marked by bright (tritium) spots.

General data

Calibre (7.62 × 39)	7.62 mm
Muzzle velocity of bullet	720 m/s
Rate of fire	600—650 rds/min
Practical rate of fire	100 rds/min
Efficient range	to 400 m
Length of arm	640/890 mm
Barrel length	415 mm
Length of line of sight	394 mm
Sight graduation	100/1000 m
Magazine capacity	30 rounds
Mass of arm	3.70 kg
Mass of empty magazine	360 g
Mass of loaded magazine	870 g

 FEDERAL DIRECTORATE OF SUPPLY AND PROCUREMENT
BEOGRAD — YUGOSLAVIA

Above and on following pages: **A four-page brochure from a Yugoslavian sales catalog for military weapons. Note the different types of ammunition illustrated and the knife-cutter bayonet, which is standard for all European AKMs.**

Ammunition

For 7.62 mm Automatic Rifle M70AB2 there are the following types of cartridges:

— 7.62 mm (7.62 × 39) Cartridge, Ball M67 is intended for annihilation of live force and light ordnance pieces.

— 7.62 mm (7.62 × 39) Cartridge, Ball with tracer M78. Dim trace to min 15 m from weapon, visible from max 115 m to min 800 m from weapon.

— 7.62 mm (7.62 × 39) Cartridge, Blank M68 (without bullet) is intended for training in sighting and opening of fire, imitating shots during maneuvers or tactical exercises. Used only with recoil booster.

— 7.62 mm (7.62 × 39) Ignition charge for rifle grenades is used to give the necessary muzzle velocity to the rifle grenade.

— 7.62 mm (7.62 × 39) Cartridge, Practice M76, max range 560 m.

— 7.62 m (7.62 × 39) Cartridge, Drill is intended for training of soldiers in loading and unloading of arms.

7.62 mm Cartridge, Ball M67

7.62 mm Cartridge, Ball with tracer M78

7.62 mm Ignition charge for rifle grenades

7.62 mm Cartridge, Blank M68

7.62 mm Cartridge, Practice M76

7.62 mm Cartridge, Drill

Detail of rifle with knife

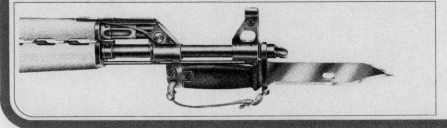

Rifle Grenades

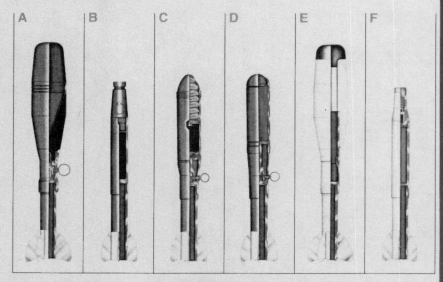

A   Antitank M60
B   Fragmentation M60
C   Illuminating M62
D   Smoke M62
E   Antitank, practice M68
F   Fragmentation, practice M66

Knife in scabbard

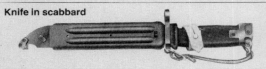

Combat knife
- scissors

The combat knife fitted to the rifle
and it is used as a bayonet. In
combination with the scabbard, it is
used as scissors to cut wire
obstacles, cables and the like.
Toothed part of the blade can be
used as a cutting saw. The handle
and scabbard are insulated.
The knife may be fitted to the rifle
cal 7.62 × 39 mm M70 and any
version utilising the cartridge
7.62 × 39 mm and and also to the
rifle based on the cartridge
7.62 × 51 mm (NATO), rifles based
on cartridge 5.56 mm and sniper
rifle 7.92 mm M76.

Knife as scissors

7.62 mm Automatic Rifle M70AB2

Ammunition data		Antitank	Fragmentation	Smoke	Illuminating
Length	[mm]	390	307	330	330
Mass	[g]	610	520	475	450
Muzzle velocity	[m/s]	61	67	74	78
Maximum range	[m]	330	410	430	450
Rate of fire with rifle grenades	[gren./min]	to 4	to 4	to 4	to 4
Sighting range	[m]	150	275	—	—
Smoke screen area	[sq. m]	—	—	350	—
Illuminating time	[s]	—	—	—	85—100

Launcher and Rifle Grenade Sight

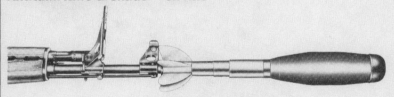

Antitank Rifle Grenade — on rifle

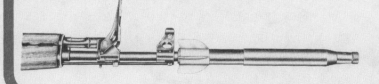

Fragmentation Rifle Grenade — on rifle

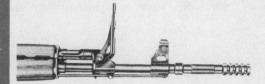

 SDPR

FEDERAL DIRECTORATE OF SUPPLY AND PROCUREMENT
1101 Beograd, 9 Nemanjina st. — Yugoslavia, Phone: 621-522, Telex: 11360, 11541 YU SDPR. Cables: DIRPROM, P.O.B. 308
Data contained herein are informative only and subject to amendment without previous notice
Issued by the Federal Directorate of Supply and Procurement

A semiautomatic 7.92 x 57mm M76 sniper rifle built on the standard Yugoslavian AKM assault rifle sheet-metal receiver.

A North Korean Type 58 rifle, which is a direct copy of the third model AK47.

NO RAILS

PERFORATIONS

A North Korean Type 68 rifle, a copy of the AKM with its distinctive perforated-metal folding buttstock.

A North Vietnamese TUL-1 light machine gun created out of a modified AK47 receiver and an RPK-type barrel and bipod assembly. This weapon represents depot-level work and should not be construed as reflecting small-arms manufacturing capacity.

Two views of the Finnish Ryannakkokivääri Malli 62 (Model 62 assault rifle), which was based upon the third model AK47. The weapon on the left has the early type buttplate, and no night sights. The rifle on the right has the stronger type buttplate and there is a flip-up night sight on the front sight. The rear sight is rotated 180 degrees to expose the night-sight elements.

Two views of the Ryannakkokivääri Malli 62-76 (Model 62-76 assault rifle). The weapon on the left is the standard M62-76, while the rifle on the right is the M62-76T folding-stock version.

A disassembled view of the Finnish Ryannakkokivääri Malli 62–76 (Model 62–76 assault rifle). Note the different type of gas-piston tube, the location of the rear sight, the forestock, and the flash suppressor as compared to the standard Soviet AK47.

from the Soviet Union in the late 1950s. This weapon was called the Ryannakko-kivääri Malli 54 (M54 assault rifle), and these were used only for troop testing of the weapon and later troop training with the Kalashnikov. Between 1958 and 1960, the state-controlled Valmet/Tourula small arms factory at Jyvaskyla experimented with several Finnish variants of the AK47 in a test program that led to the Ryan-nakkokivääri Malli 60 (M60 assault rifle). This weapon was field tested over the next two years by regular Finnish troops, and the results of these trials led to the adop-tion of a slightly modified gun that was called the Ryannakkokivääri Malli 62 (M62 assault rifle).

Large scale production of these Ryan-nakkokivääri Malli 62 for the Finnish Defence Forces started in 1965 at both the Valmet/Tourula small arms factory at Jyvaskyla, and the Sako factory in Riihi-

maki. These first weapons did not have luminous night sights and were designated the M62PT. From 1969 onward, Finnish assault rifles were fitted with night sights; i.e., two luminous dots on the rear sight and one on the front sight. Since 1972, the night sights have been illuminated by trit-ium capsules.

Over the years since its first introduc-tion, the exterior fittings of the M62 have been altered slightly. The buttplate assem-bly was modified to make it stronger, and the pistol grip was reshaped to make it easier to hold. All of these early models were fabricated by milling the receiver from steel-bar stock. In the mid-1970s, an AKM-type assault rifle was introduced, and it was designated the Ryannakko-kivääri Malli 62–76 (M62–76 assault rifle). The following models are or have been offered for sale by Valmet:

Model 255 470	5.56 x 45mm M82 Bullpup model.
Model 254 100	5.56 x 45mm M76F with side-folding stock.
Model 254 060	5.56 x 45mm M76T with tubular stock.
Model 254 080	5.56 x 45mm M76P with plastic stock.
Model 255 200	5.56 x 45mm M76W with wood stock.
Model 255 490	7.62 x 39mm M76 Bullpup model.
Model 254 090	7.62 x 39mm M76F with side-folding stock.
Model 253 810	7.62 x 39mm M76T with tubular stock.
Model 254 070	7.62 x 39mm M76P with plastic stock.
Model 255 460	7.62 x 39mm M76W with wood stock.
Model 255 170	5.56 x 45 mm M78 light machine gun.
Model 255 160	7.62 x 39mm M78 light machine gun.
Model 255 480	7.62 x 51mm NATO M78 light machine gun.

Valmet has also offered for sale in the United States semiautomatic versions of the M62 (called the M62S) and the M62-76 (called the M71). The latter series has been sold in both 7.62 x 39mm and 5.56 x 39mm. All of these weapons have a single dot on the safety/fire selector to indicate single-shot/semiautomatic fire, and three dots to indicate full automatic fire. There are no official estimates of the number of M62/M62-76 assault rifles made in Finland; however, the number probably exceeds seven hundred thousand, which is the number of troops available when the Finnish Defence Forces are fully mobilized.

The Valmet 5.56 x 45mm M82 Bullpup version of the M62-76 assault rifle. Intended for armored vehicle crews, this weapon has primarily been offered as an export-sale item.

Two models of the Israeli Military Industries 5.56 x 45mm Galil assault rifle. The top weapon is the 457mm barrel rifle version, with stock folded. The bottom weapon is the 330mm barrel carbine version, with the stock extended. Both weapons have the 35-shot magazine.

Israel

In the Middle East, both Israel and Egypt have manufactured versions of the Kalashnikov assault rifle. The Israeli Military Industries (IMI), at the urging of the Israeli Defense Forces (IDF), developed a 5.56 x 45mm version of the third model AK47. The IDF, following combat environment testing of the AK47 and the US M16A1 rifle, decided that they preferred the reliability of the AK47-type operating mechanism to that of the M16A1 rifle, and that they preferred the lethality of the United States 5.56 x 45mm cartridge to that of the Soviet M43 7.62 x 39mm cartridge. As a result, the IDF sought a weapon that would combine these two elements.

Creation of such a weapon was assigned to a team led by Israeli Galili (Balashnikov before he changed his name) at IMI. He worked up a 5.56mm version of the AK47 using a barrel, bolt face, parts, and 30-shot box magazines from the American Stoner 63 Weapons System. The resulting test weapon showed excellent promise. In their next step, preparation of a production model, IMI engineers purchased samples of the Valmet M62 from the European-American firm Interarms. Once a successful prototype version was built around these weapons, Yaacov Lior, head of the Small Arms Branch at IMI, arranged for the purchase of an undisclosed number of unmarked M62 receivers from Valmet. To these Finnish receivers, his

A view of the disassembled IMI 5.56 x 45mm Galil squad automatic weapon. Note the similarity between the components of this weapon and those of the Valmet M62 automatic rifle.

galil assault rifle

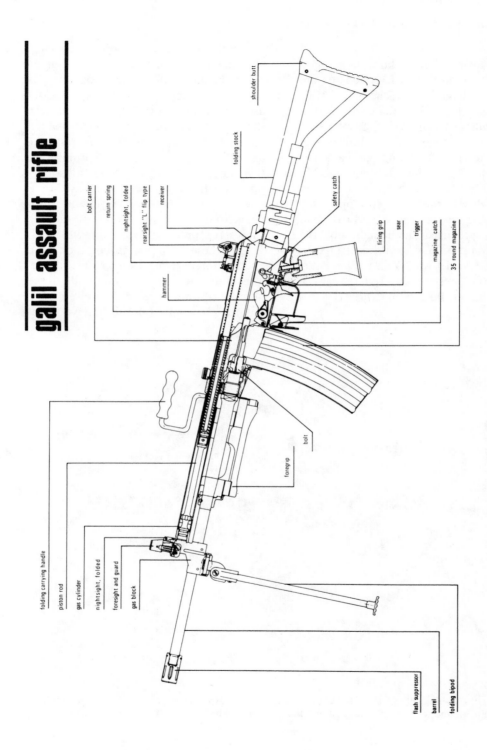

folding carrying handle

piston rod

gas cylinder

nightsight, folded

foresight and guard

gas block

bolt carrier

return spring

nightsight, folded

rearsight "L" flip type

receiver

hammer

foregrip

bolt

safety catch

folding stock

shoulder butt

firing grip

sear

trigger

magazine catch

35 round magazine

flash suppressor

barrel

folding bipod

A section view of the IMI 5.56 x 45mm Galil squad automatic weapon.

production people mounted barrels machined from Colt M16 barrel blanks. A modified Stoner 63 magazine was evolved for the rifle. In addition, the IMI team added a Fabrique Nationale FAL-type side-folding stock to the weapon, which was designated the Galil in recognition of the work done by the team leader Galili. Additional details concerning the features of the Galil are presented in the accompanying illustrations.

No production data is available for the number of Galil rifles manufactured by IMI for the IDF and for export sale. It is estimated that between one hundred thousand and three hundred thousand of these rifles have been made. IDF Galils have Hebrew markings on the safety/fire selector and Roman letters on the export models.

Arab Republic of Egypt

In the late 1950s, the Soviet Union as part of its military aid program assisted the Egyptians in the establishment of military production of Soviet-pattern small arms. This followed large purchases of similar weapons by the Egyptians from the USSR. Among the weapons that they have manufactured is an Egyptian version of the AKM at "Factory 54," a facility which is now part of the Maadi Military & Civil Industries Company, and which is in turn a subdivision of the state-owned enterprise called the Military Factories General Organization. Maadi-made AKMs are called the "Misr" in Egyptian sales catalogs, and significant quantities have been exported. A semiautomatic version of the "Misr" has been sold in the United States sporting market by the American branch of the Austrian firm Steyr-Daimler-Puch.

The Maadi "Misr" semiautomatic version of the 7.62 x 39mm AKM as imported for commercial sale in the United States by Steyr-Daimler-Puch.

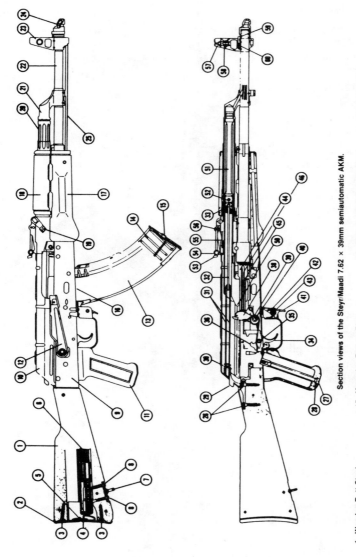

Section views of the Steyr/Maadi 7.62 × 39mm semiautomatic AKM.

1. Wooden Butt Stock
2. Butt Plate
3. Butt Plate Screws
4. Butt Plate Cover
5. Butt Plate Cover Spring
6. Oiler Trap Spring
7. Rear Sling Swivel
8. Rear Sling Swivel Screws
*9. Receiver Group
10. Receiver Cover
11. Pistol Grip
12. Safety Lever
13. Magazine
14. Magazine Spring

15. Magazine Bottom Plate
16. Cartridge Carrier (not shown)
17. Wooden Handguard, lower
18. Wooden Handguard, upper
19. Gas Cylinder Retaining Lock Lever
20. Gas Cylinder
21. Gas Block
22. Barrel
23. Front Sight Protector
24. Compensator
25. Cleaning Rod
26. Tang Screw (2)
27. Pistol Grip Screw
28. Pistol Grip Screw Washer

*Receiver Group consists of receiver and trigger guard.

29. Rear Guide Retaining Block
30. Recoil Return Spring
31. Rear Recoil Return Spring Guide
32. Front Recoil Return Spring Guide
33. Front Guide Retainer
34. Trigger
35. Trigger Pin
36. Sear
37. Sear Spring (not shown)
38. Hammer
39. Hammer Spring
40. Hammer Pin
41. Magazine Catch
42. Magazine Catch Spring
43. Magazine Catch Pin
44. Bolt

45. Firing Pin
46. Firing Pin Retaining Pin
47. Extractor (not shown)
48. Extractor Spring (not shown)
49. Extractor Plunger (not shown)
50. Bolt Carrier
51. Gas Piston
52. Gas Piston Retaining Pin
53. Leaf Rear Sight
54. Rear Sight Adjusting Slide
55. Rear Sight Spring
56. Rear Sight Pin
57. Front Sight Post
58. Front Sight Adjusting Block
59. Compensator Lock Pin
60. Compensator Lock Pin Spring

Section views of the Steyr/Maadi 7.62 x 39mm semiautomatic AKM.

Summary

Although not ubiquitous, the Kalashnikov assault rifles have enjoyed extraordinary success during the past four decades as a military tool and political currency. With some thirty to fifty million of them manufactured and untold millions still in service, these military weapons will be around for a long time. The durability of the basic design will help guarantee their survival. This fact is also confirmed by the Soviet decision in the early 1970s to develop yet another version of this weapon—the 5.45 x 45mm AK74. That newer weapon represents a new lease on life for Kalashnikov's basic design. But even without the AK74 series, Kalashnikov's design concepts have had a continuing impact on Soviet weapons design in other ways. Basic design elements taken from the Kalashnikov avtomat have been incorporated into the Dragunov sniping rifle and the Kalashnikov general purpose machine. Both of these weapons fire the old 7.62 x 54mmR cartridge. These adaptations—the AK74, SVD, and PK—are the subject of the next chapter in the Kalashnikov saga.

6

Design Evolution of Weapons Based on the Kalashnikov Avtomat, 1958–1985

Snaiperskaya vintovka Dragunova

The 7.62 x 54mmR Dragunov semiautomatic self-loading sniper rifle (Samozaryadnaya snaiperskaya vintovka Dragunova — SVD), adopted by the Soviet Army in 1963, is credited to the designer Yevgeniy Feodorovich Dragunov (1920–   ), a son in a family of gunsmiths. In the postwar years he worked at the Izhevsk Machine Factory designing sporting rifles. He began his work on the SVD sniper rifle in 1958, and the project lasted for four years. This project was designed to create a weapon that would replace all of the older 7.62 x 54mmR M1891/30 and SVT 40 sniper rifles, and at the same time be more accurate than those earlier weapons. As this 10-shot weapon evolved, it was essentially a scaled-up AK47 (the SVD had a machined-steel receiver) with a modified gas system and special mounting system for a PSO–1 telescopic sight.

Unlike other Kalashnikov-type weapons (AK47, AKM, and PK), the SVD employed a short-stroke piston system. This change was made to insure accurate fire from the rifle. In the long-stroke piston systems used with the earlier Kalashnikov designs, the operating rod assembly was rather heavy. When scaled up to the size necessary for the 7.62 x 54mmR cartridge, the operating rod was very heavy and tended to upset the center of gravity balance when it reciprocated during shooting. In the Dragunov variation of the Kalashnikov theme, the short-stroke piston delivered its impulse to the bolt carrier, which was a separate assembly. The remainder of the operation was essentially the same as that for the AK47, except that there was no full-automatic-fire cycle in the SVD design.

There is a 9 x 54mmR sporting rifle manufactured at Izhevsk called the Bear

The 7.62 x 54mmR Samozariyadnaya snaiperskaya vintovka Dragunova (SVD), with PSO-1 telescopic sight.

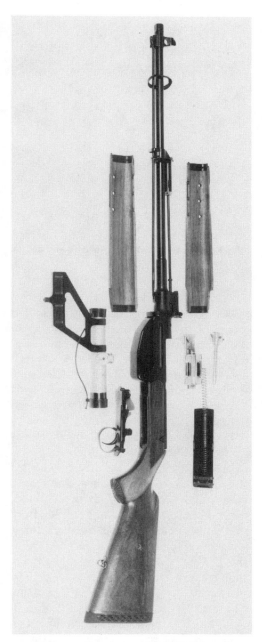

A view of the disassembled 9 x 54mmR Medved sporting rifle. Note the similarities and differences between this rifle and the SVD sniper rifle.

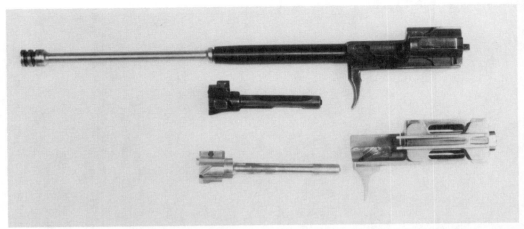

A comparative view of the AKM bolt and bolt carrier/piston rod assemblies (*top*) with the Medved bolt and bolt carrier.

(Medved), which is essentially a civilian model of the SVD (there are some detail differences in the trigger housing assembly, the receiver cover, and other components) with a less sophisticated telescopic sight. It is not certain which weapon came first, but a close look at both weapons in the accompanying photographs clearly indicates the debt of the designer to the work of Mikhail Timofeyevich Kalashnikov. Soviet sources have never indicated the extent to which Dragunov and Kalashnikov cooperated in the development of the SVD and the Medved. Both the Polish and Chinese arms factories have developed nearly exact copies of the 7.62 x 54mmR Samozaryadnaya snaiperskaya vintovka Dragunova. The official designations for these Polish and Chinese rifles are not known.

In the early 1980s, the Romanians introduced a sniper rifle based directly on the AKM. Because the bolt and bolt carrier assembly of the AKM travels 30mm farther to the rear than is necessary to feed the 7.62 x 39mm cartridge, the receiver

mechanism can be made to fire such diverse cartridges as the 7.62 x 51mm NATO, the 7.62 x 54mmR, and the 7.92 x 57mm Mauser. The Romanians decided to take advantage of this design opportunity to create a sniper rifle. First, the Romanian designers altered the bolt face to accommodate the larger rimmed base of the M1891 cartridge case. Then they added a new and longer rifle barrel and lengthened the RPK-type bolt carrier/piston rod assembly. Note that they did not make provision for a short-stroke piston. They just stayed with the existing long-stroke assembly.

The Romanians developed several unique elements for their sniper rifle. They created their own 10-shot magazine for their rifle. They also fabricated a skeleton buttstock assembly from laminated wood (plywood) much like the Dragunov stock, but slightly different in execution. Finally, the Romanians riveted two steel reinforcing plates to the rear end of the receiver to help absorb and spread the increased recoil of the more powerful 7.62 x 54mmR car-

The Romanian 7.62 x 54mmR FPK sniper rifle, which is built upon the standard AKM receiver mechanism.

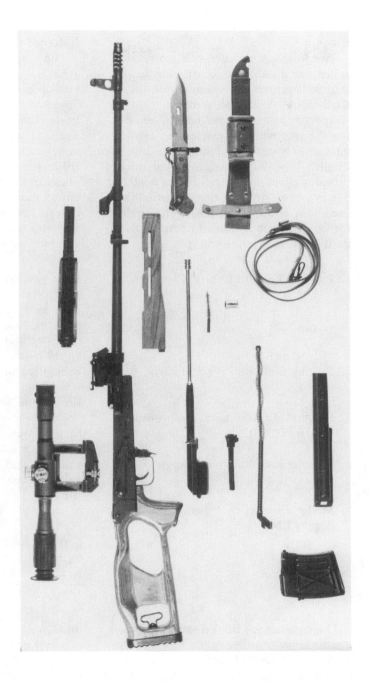

View of the disassembled Romanian 7.62 x 54mmR FPK sniper rifle. Note the AKM-type knife-cutter bayonet, which is standard issue with the FPK.

tridge.

The Romanian sniper rifle, sometimes called the FPK, has its own distinctive muzzle brake, which will mount the standard AKM knife-cutter bayonet. This weapon appears to have been developed for the international market, as existing telescopes have their windage markings in English. The Yugoslavs, as noted in the previous chapter, have developed a 7.92 x 57mm sniper rifle for their own military use and a 7.62 x 51mm NATO sniper rifle for export. Both are based upon the standard AKM receiver assembly.

Pulemet Kalashnikova

The family of general purpose machine guns first came to the attention of Western intelligence specialists in 1964. Recent Soviet sources indicate, however, that the basic general purpose model of this weapon came into service in 1961. This new weapon, the Pulemet Kalashnikova (PK), was then believed to be just a replacement for the RP45 Company machine gun. But Kalashnikov's design bureau has shown considerable ingenuity and flexibility. Several different models currently exist.

1. Pulemet Kalashnikova (PK)

Basic general purpose machine gun with stamped sheet metal receiver; feed mechanism with stamped and sheet-metal components; heavy fluted barrel; plain buttplate without shoulder rest. Weight: 8.9 kg (19.8 pounds).

2. Pulemet Kalashnikova Stankoviy (PKS)

Basic PK gun mounted on ground tripod, which can be converted for antiaircraft fire. Tripod weight: 7.4 kg (16.5 pounds)

3. Pulemet Kalashnikova na bronetransportere (PKB)

Basic PK gun mounted flexibly on military vehicles. This model had rear-mounted spade grips.

4. Pulemet Kalashnikova tankoviy (PKT)

Basic PK gun mounted coaxially on tanks and armored personnel carriers. Solenoid fired.

5. Modernizirovanniy Pulemet Kalashnikova (PKM)

Modernized or product-improved PK. Feed cover made entirely from stamped parts. A folding shoulder rest was added to the buttstock assembly. Weight reduced by about .6 kg (1.3 pounds). All models of PK are made in PKM series.

The significance of the series of Pulemet Kalashnikova lies in the fact that the Kalashnikov design bureau learned major lessons from the development and manufacture of the AKM and was able to transfer those lessons to the creation and production of a family of general purpose machine guns. These PKs borrow a number of component concepts from Kalashnikov's earlier weapons. The bolt/bolt carrier/piston rod assembly was simply a redesign of the assembly used in the Kalashnikov avtomat. For purposes of the machine gun the bolt carrier/piston rod assembly is located beneath the barrel. And thus the bolt is above the bolt carrier/piston rod assembly in the PK machine gun.

The Kalashnikov team borrowed design elements from other machine guns as well. For the feeding mechanism, the Kalashnikov team chose the cartridge gripper from the Goryunov series of machine guns. They also used the Goryunov quick-change barrel mechanism in the PK design—not unlikely choices since Kalashnikov had worked on those weapons during his time at the Ensk Proving Ground. In the feed mechanism, the idea of using the piston to power the feed pawls was evolved from the Czechoslovakian vz.52 light machine gun. And finally, the trigger mechanism was an adaptation of the one used in the Ruchnoi Pulemet Degtyareva.

Perhaps the single most interesting feature of the Pulemet Kalashnikova is the extensive use made of sheet-metal stampings throughout the weapon. This allowed the Soviets to build a machine gun that took advantage of the lessons learned while mastering production of the Modernizirovanniy Avtomat Kalashnikova. By using the steel metal production technology, the Soviets were able to extend the utilization of their technology base, and at the same time manufacture a modern machine gun in an economical manner. Even though the PK fires an antiquated rimmed cartridge (7.62 x 54mmR), all of these design elements, when combined together, yielded a very reliable and rugged general purpose machine gun. Introduction of the Pulemet Kalashnikova family gave the Kalashnikov-designed shoulder weapons a virtual monopoly in the Soviet arsenal.

The 7.62 x 54mmR Modernizirovanniyi Pulemet Kalashnikova (PKM). Note the sheet-metal construction of the receiver, top cover, feed housing, and bipod.

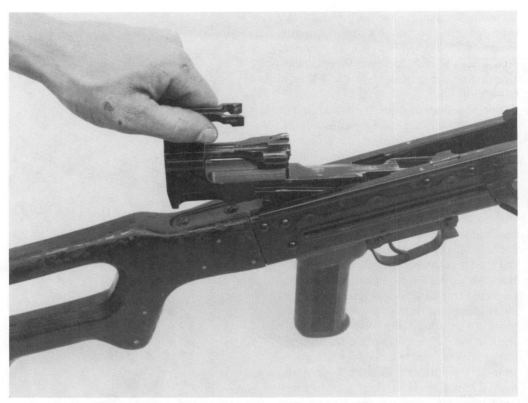

The Kalashnikov-type bolt mechanism of the 7.62 x 54mmR Modernizirovanniyi Pulemet Kalashnikova (PKM). Note the sheet-metal and riveted construction of the receiver.

5.45 x 39mm Avtomat Kalashnikova obrazets 1974g

The introduction of the 5.45 x 39mm Avtomat Kalashnikova obrazets 1974g into the front line units of the Soviet Army was of singular importance to the European military scene. First, the appearance of the AK74 will permit the Soviets and their Warsaw Pact allies to improve their basic infantry weapons without discarding the technological base upon which the older generation was founded. Second, after a quarter of a century of cartridge standardization at the squad level within the War-

saw Pact armies, the Soviets made the decision in the early 1970s to replace their 7.62 x 39mm family of weapons — AKM assault rifles and RPK light machine guns — with new versions of those weapons firing 5.45 x 39mm cartridges.

When the first reports (circa 1978) of this new cartridge and weapon family reached western technical intelligence analysts, those specialists assumed that these rifles and machine guns would be used only by specialized units. The western analysts could not believe that the changeover would be for all rifles and light squad auto-

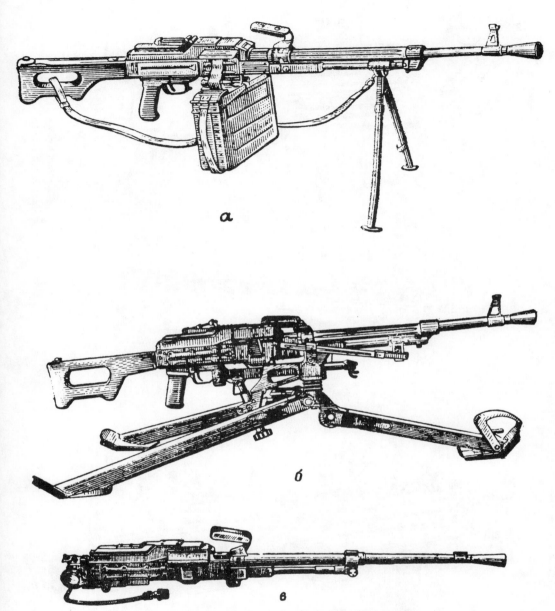

Рис. 1. Общий вид пулемета Калашникова:
а — пулемет на сошке (ПК); *б* — пулемет на станке (ПКС); *в* — пулемет танковый (ПКТ)

Three models of the 7.62 x 54mmR Modernizirovanniyi Pulemet Kalashnikova: *top*, the PK; *center*, the PKS; *bottom*, the PKT.

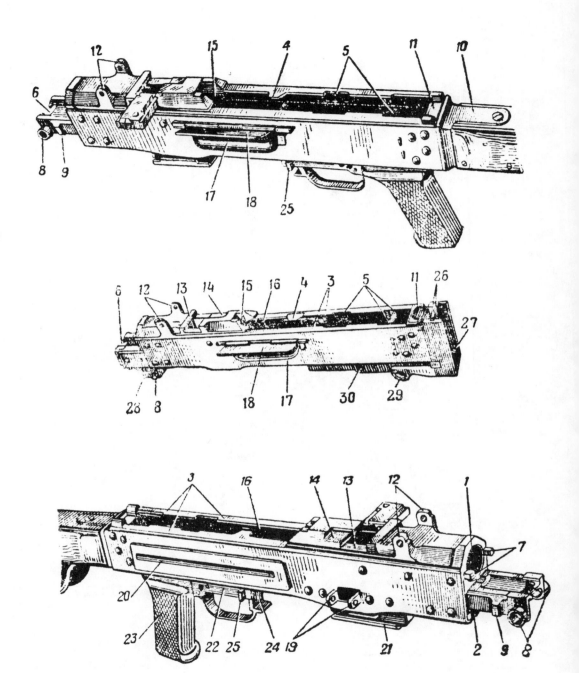

Three views of the stamped-sheet-metal receiver of the 7.62 x 54mmR Modernizirovanniyi Pulemet Kalashnikova.

Two of the newer 5.45 x 39mm Kalashnikov-type weapons: *left*, the Avtomat Kalashnikova obrazets 1974g (AK74) with fixed-wood buttstock; *right*, the Ruchnoi Pulemet Kalashnikova skladyvayushchim-sya prikladom obrazets 1974g (RPKS74), folding stock extended. Note the different-style muzzle devices used on these two weapons, and the 30- and 40-shot steel-reinforced fiberglass magazines. Magazines of this type construction have been issued with recent AKMs, but the design of the AKM and AK74 magazines is different due to the different dimensions of the cartridges employed in those weapons.

A close-up view of a Soviet mechanized infantryman holding his 5.45 x 39mm Avtomat Kalashnikova skladyvayushchimsya prikladom obrazets 1974g (AKS74), with its stock folded.

matics because of the logistical problems and production costs involved in switching calibers and retiring the 7.62 x 39mm weapons. Subsequent observations indicate that the Soviets plan a complete changeover to the smaller caliber. The fact that the Soviets are updating their arsenal with the 5.45mm weapons indicates that their industrial sector is advanced enough to support such a massive undertaking. In addition, the change keeps Soviet small arms factories busy, and Soviet arms makers employed.

Still more recent reports that the Hungarian and East German arms factories are manufacturing their own 5.45 x 39mm versions of the AK74 indicate that the Warsaw Pact armies will follow this Soviet

shift in caliber. It would appear that the Polish arms factories are tooling up to produce the 5.45mm rifles as this book goes to press. Thus one can expect to see client countries currently using the 7.62mm Kalashnikovs to make the switch also to the 5.45mm weapons.

Soviet change to the 5.45 x 39mm cartridge has caused considerable speculation in the West as to the possible tactical implications of the shift to the new ammunition. The 5.45 x 39mm cartridge is the least powerful military rifle cartridge currently used. The muzzle velocity of the Soviet 5.45mm projectile is 900 meters per second, compared to 947.5 meters per second for the SS109 bullet standardized in the NATO 5.56 x 45mm cartridge. Muzzle energy for the Soviet projectile is 1,365 joules versus 1,796 joules for the SS109. The Soviet 5.45mm cartridge case has 15 percent less volume than the 5.56mm NATO cartridge case, and 29 percent less volume than the 7.62 x 39mm M1943 cartridge case.

The new Soviet 5.45mm cartridge makes up for its small powder volume in three ways. First, the bullet is not seated as deeply as in the western 5.56 x 45mm cartridges. Second, through the use of a shorter and larger diameter case than the 5.56 x 45mm case, the Soviet bullet design could be modified in such a fashion that their bullet is still efficient, but short in length. Otherwise, this new cartridge is basically standard with the thick rim being its best design feature. That rim assures that the strong extractor forces of the AK-type operating will not tear through the rim.

Third, the Soviets have developed a very good propellant. The new Soviet propellant has an almost ideal burning rate for this type of cartridge. Composition of this powder is reported to be 81 percent virgin nitrocellulose base material, 11.6 percent nitroglycerine, 5.3 percent ethyl centralite, 0.9 percent dinitrotoluene, a stabilizer, and 0.4 percent undefined organics.

The limited energy level of the Soviet 5.45mm projectile has raised some yet to be answered questions about the lethality

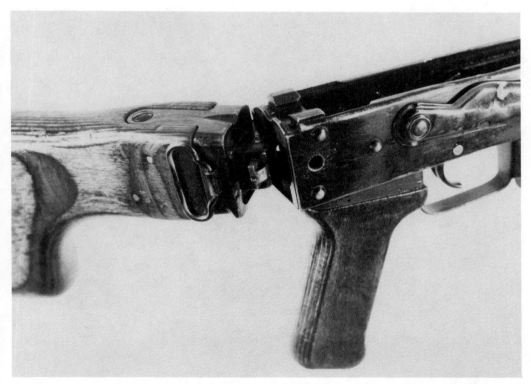

Illustrated here is the Ruchnoi Pulemet Kalashnikova skladyvayushchimsya prikladom obrazets 1974g (RPKS74), folding stock unlatched.

The armored vehicle crewman's 5.45 x 39mm "AKSU." Notable features of this weapon include the side-folding stock, altered sights, gas system, and the new-style muzzle brake.

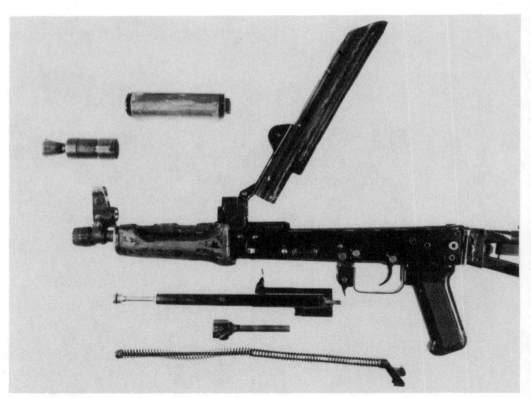

View of the disassembled 5.45 x 39mm "AKSU" Note the new way of retaining the receiver cover and the shortened gas-piston/bolt-carrier assembly.

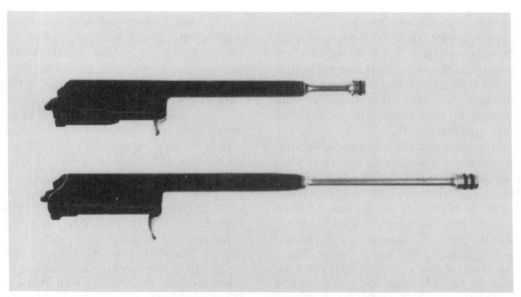

A comparative view of the piston-rod/bolt-carrier assemblies: *top*, the "AKSU"; *bottom*, the AK74.

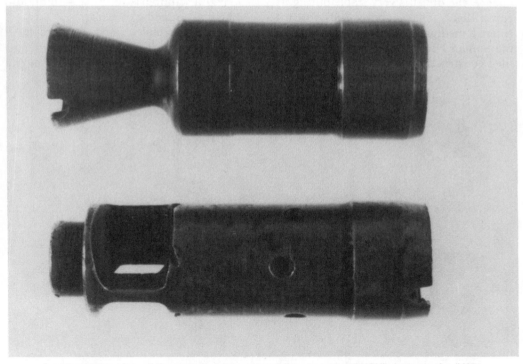

A comparative view of the muzzle-brake assemblies: *top*, the "AKSU"; *bottom*, the AK74.

of this projectile, and just what the tactical goals were when the Soviets adopted this new cartridge. Some Western technical experts thought at first that the Soviets might have a much higher velocity projectile held in reserve for wartime. To date there is no data to support or to refute that hypothesis.

It is clear that the 5.45mm Soviet projectile has a much flatter trajectory than any of their earlier 7.62 x 39mm projectiles. This change alone should make it easier to hit targets out to four hundred meters. But, the question remains: What will the projectile do when it hits the target? The AK74 rifle has a 414mm barrel with tight rifling (1 turn in 235) twist, so that the bullet is spun very rapidly (4,600 revolutions per second). As a consequence, the bullet is very stable during its entire flight. That stability ends when it enters a medium denser than air—such as the human body—because of the projectile's construction.

The basic 5.45mm ball projectile has a gilding metal-plated mild-steel jacket. Inside that jacket is a lead sheath, which surrounds a 15mm long mild-steel core. That core is mounted with its base at the base of the bullet jacket. At the nose of the steel core is a 3mm-long lead plug, which is actually an extension of the lead sheath. In front of the lead plug is an air space about 0.5mm long. By having placed the center of gravity of the projectile toward its rear, the bullet's designer virtually ensured that the projectile would flip when it hit a human body, especially when the lead plug moves forward upon impact. The shift in center of gravity that occurs at impact almost guarantees that the bullet will tumble. See COL Martin Fackler's wound cavity profiles in chapter 7 for a comparison of 5.45mm and 5.56mm wounding effects.

When the bullet begins to tumble, it rapidly dumps its kinetic energy into the target, thus bringing maximum wounding

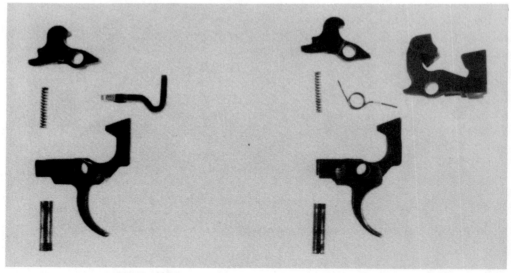

A comparative view of the trigger assemblies: *left*, the "AKSU"; *right*, the AK74.

force to the target. This is important when one remembers that lethality is the product of the amount of energy deposited into the target over time. Bullets such as the full power 7.62 x 51mm NATO tend to be less lethal than smaller higher-velocity projectiles, because bullets such as the NATO one tend to go all the way through the target. As they pass through the target they do not deposit as much energy as would a projectile that stops in the target.

As further evidence of the Soviet philosophy of improving basically sound weapons — product-improvement — the 5.45 x 39mm Avtomat Kalashnikova obrazetsa 1974g, or AK74 assault rifle, is basically a modified Modernizirovanniy Avtomat Kalashnikova, or AKM. Basic parts changed are the bolt head, which accommodates the smaller-diameter 5.45mm cartridge case; the new and improved extractor; and the new composite-steel and fiberglass box magazine. A good deal of the Kalashnikov's reputation for reliability is a result of the favorable weight relationship between the bolt carrier and piston assembly and the bolt. In the AK47 and AKM, that ratio is nearly 5:1, and in the AK74 series it is 6:1. In addition to providing adequate energy for extracting fired cartridge cases, it ensures continued operation when the weapon is dirty.

The most interesting new element of the AK74 design is its very effective muzzle device, which is based upon fluidic principles of gas flow. Apparently it is designed primarily to benefit right-handed shooters. This muzzle device not only reduces the blast and noise levels produced when the rifle is fired, but it also reduces recoil by counteracting the recoil with a forward and downward movement. When fired with an empty magazine in place, the AK74 produces a recoil energy (kick) of

about 3.39 joules compared to the 6.44 of the M16A1 rifle and 7.19 joules for the AKM. As a consequence, this Soviet muzzle device is probably one of the more effective small-caliber recoil reducers deployed on a standard issue weapon.

The combined change in ammunition and the addition of the muzzle device lead to the AK74 being a better shooting weapon. Limited test firing indicates that the AK74 has two to two and a half times greater effective range than the AKM. When this is coupled with the fact that the 5.45 x 39mm ammunition is lighter than the 7.62 x 39mm ammunition (50 percent more cartridges can be carried for the same basic weight), then it is clear to see that the AK74 will be a more effective combat weapon than its predecessor Kalashnikovs. (For more performance data on the AK74 see Andrew C. Tillman, "IDR Test-Fires the AK-74," *International Defense Review* (October 1983): 1427–30).

The AK74 is currently issued in four rifle versions. The first and earliest model was the AK74 with fixed plywood buttstock. The second was the Avtomat Kalashnikova skladyvayushchimsya prikladom obrazetsa 1974g (AKS74), with a side folding plywood buttstock. The third was the Avtomat Kalashnikova skladyvayushchimsya prikladom obrazetsa 1974g (AK574), with a side-folding triangular metal buttstock. And the final version identified to date is the AKSU, a much shortened avtomat believed to have been designed for armored vehicle crews. This latter weapon, which has the same type of side-folding metal buttstock as the AKS74 noted above, probably dates from 1975, since that was the year that S. G. Simonov's design bureau created a similar weapon in the 5.45mm caliber.

In addition to the AK74 models listed

above, there have been two RPK light machine gun versions developed. These were the 5.45 x 39mm Ruchnoi Pulemet Kalashnikova obrazetsa 1974g (RPK74), and the 5.45 x 39mm Ruchnoi Pulemet skladyvayushchimsya prikladom Kalashnikova obrazetsa 1974g (RPKS74). The first of these light machine guns has a fixed plywood buttstock, while the latter weapon has the plywood side-folding stock of the first model AKS74 assault rifle. The photographs in this section illustrate the basic features of the 1974 series of Kalashnikov avtomats and light machine guns.

Conclusions

By the mid-1980s, the Soviet defense industry had grown to be one of the largest in the world. And according to some American studies it is the biggest. But the debate about size aside, there are some important things to remember about this part of the Soviet economy. First, the Soviet leadership has always given a special high priority to the creation of military power. And they interpret military power largely in terms of weapons and the capability to manufacture such weapons. To create this type of military power, the Soviet government throughout the years has established special means for extracting the resources — manpower, financial, and raw materials — from the overall economy in order to provide support for their defense industrial complex. Since military power is equated with national survival, the defense sector of the Soviet economy receives substantial support, sometimes at the expense of the civilian sector. The small arms industry can be viewed as a good example of the manner in which they built an independent and self-sustaining industry.

Second, foreign technologies have played an important part in building the Imperial Russian and Soviet defense industries. Much of what the Soviets possess in the realm of defense manufacturing technology can trace its beginnings to the creation of the Imperial Russian small arms industry in the nineteenth century. And as pointed out earlier in this volume, that Imperial weapons-making system was based largely upon Western European manufacturing technology before 1870, and upon the American System of interchangeable manufacture after that date. Whereas, the Russians were borrowers of production techniques and weapon mechanisms before the First World War, they have become creators of their own technology in these areas in the post-revolutionary period.

In the post-1945 period, the technical and materiel assistance the Soviets received from their allies during World War II disappeared. But in the area of small arms they were already capable of meeting their military requirements by 1945. Although the West has made a concerted effort to prevent the transfer of new technology to the Soviet Union, some of that effort has been wasted because the Soviets are now launched on their own technological path. Within the context of their own military needs, the Soviets are clearly independent from the West in small arms. In fact, small arms manufacture and design was one of the first areas in which the Soviets gained their independence from and equality with the rest of Europe and the United States.

Today, the Soviet Union possesses some of the world's best infantry, armor, air force, and other military equipment. Much of this materiel has originated from their own domestic strength and vigorous defense industrial structure, which now also possesses a viable and effective research and development complex. In the small arms field, the current generation of infantry small arms are all of post-1945 design, with many being second and third generation evolutions of basic designs. And nearly all of the basic designs either are the result of the work of Mikhail Timofeyevich Kalashnikov or of his design bureau at the Izhevsk Mashinostroitel'ny Zavod (Izhevsk Machine Factory). The belief in gradual product improvement of weapons illustrated by their small arms can also be seen in their motor vehicles and armored fighting vehicles. Proven weapons are abandoned only when a clearly improved alternative is matured.

One of the consequences of this concurrence of manufacturing capacity and development capability is the almost ubiquitous nature of Kalashnikov's weapons. As noted at the outset, at least 55 nations use the AK47, AKM, and the Kalashnikov machine guns on a regular basis. These weapons are seen in the hands of little children in Lebanon and Afghanistan. They are used by government and antigovernment forces from Indochina to Central America and Africa.

And now that the Warsaw Pact countries are beginning to manufacture the AK74, it is expected that there will be renewed enthusiasm for the Kalashnikov rifles. There will be enthusiasm on the part of the consuming countries who can update their weapons and improve performance, without having to introduce a completely new weapon that will require training troops with an entirely new design. There will be enthusiasm on the part

of the Soviet military and foreign affairs people because the AK74 and the RPK74 will allow them to continue their military aid programs, and hence military and political influence in customer countries.

Therefore, as with the American series of M16 rifles, old and new models of Kalashnikov assault rifles will be around for a long time. Even if the Soviets should suddenly make a major breakthrough in small arms design, and eliminate the Kalashnikovs from their own arsenal of weapons, one can reasonably expect these weapons to be around in the year 2025 or later. Since a major technological breakthrough in small arms design is not all that likely, the Kalashnikov weapons old and new will probably be around for a much longer time. After all, some military and paramilitary forces still use bolt-action rifles introduced at the turn of the century.

It should be no wonder then that Mikhail Timofeyevich Kalashnikov is a social and economic hero in his native land. In a land that honors its technological elite, Kalashnikov stands out because his family of successful weapons have given reliable firepower to his nation's infantrymen, and full employment to his weapons factory's employees. And beyond that the name Kalashnikov is known worldwide. In backwater regions, where a Russian has never been seen, men and women equipped with AKs know that Russians make good reliable weapons. It was once noted, only half in jest, the Americans export Coke, the Japanese export Sonys, and the Soviets export Kalashnikovs.

7

Ammunition Data

As additional background for the readers of this study of the Kalashnikov-designed small arms, we are including the following illustrative material and data relating to some of the cartridges used with Kalashnikov's weapons.

As noted in chapter 3, Soviet historians state that work was begun on the development of a new intermediate-power rifle cartridge in 1938–1939. As is so often the case, the coming of the Second World War interrupted the preparations for that conflict. Thus during the 1939–1945 conflict, the basic Soviet rifle and machine gun cartridge continued to be the Model 1891 7.62 x 54mm rimmed cartridge with updated projectiles. Soviet records go on to state

that work on the intermediate-type ammunition was restarted in 1943 and led to the Model 1943 7.62 x 39mm cartridge. This new round has been attributed to the designers N. M. Elizarov and B. V. Semin, but very little additional information regarding these individuals or their design projects has been presented in Soviet histories.

The accompanying illustrations are designed to present more information about several of the basic Soviet cartridges that have been used in recent years for rifles and general purpose machine guns. We start with the oldest cartridges first and come forward in time to the present.

Table 7-1
Comparative Technical Data for Soviet and NATO Cartridges

	5.45 x 39 M74 Ball	5.56 x 45 NATO Ball (SS109)	7.62 x 39 M43 Ball (Type PS)	7.62 x 51 NATO Ball (SS77)	7.62 x 54R Type L Ball
Cartridge length:	39.5mm	45mm	38.6mm	51mm	54mm
Cartridge weight:	10.75g	12.50g	18.20g	23.95g	22.55g
Projectile weight:	3.42g	4.0g	7.91g	9.30g	9.65g
Muzzle velocity:	900 m/s	915 m/s	710 m/s	837 m/s	853 m/s
Muzzle energy:	1,385j	1,700j	2,970j	3,180j	3,945j

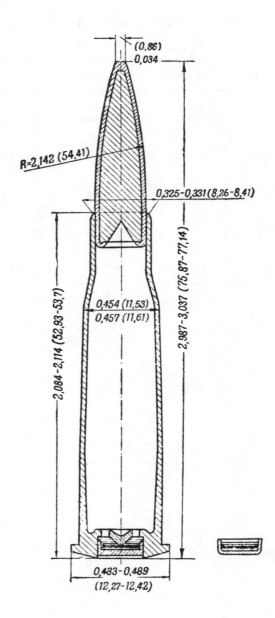

A dimensioned section view of the 7.62 x 54mm rimmed Model 1891 cartridge, with the 9.65 gram Model 1908 bullet, which is called the Type L by the Soviets. From Federov's 1938 book *Evolyutsiya strelkogo oruzhiya*, with English dimensions given first and metric dimensions in parentheses.

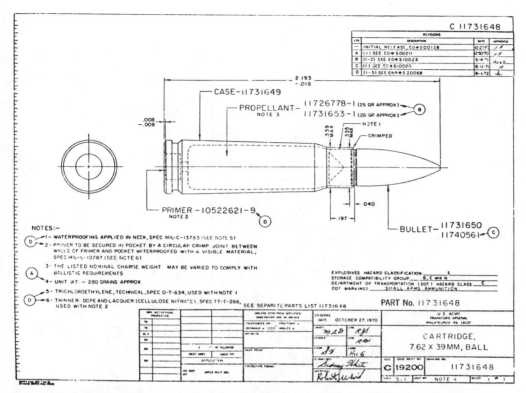

A dimensioned production drawing for the Soviet M43 7.62 x 39mm cartridge as manufactured by the US Army Lake City Army Ammunition Plant during the Vietnam War. The dimensions in this drawing are in English units.

The standard 7.62 x 39mm Ball projectile cartridge Type "PS".

PACKAGING

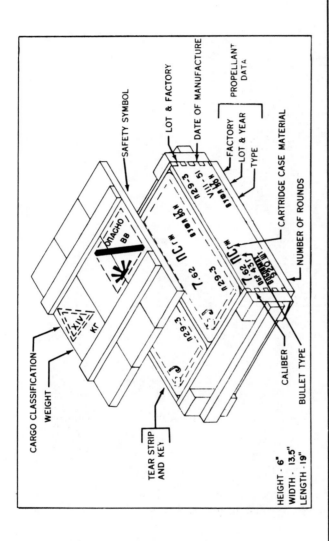

This round is packed either in clips or without clips. In clips, 20 rounds (two 10-round clips) are packed to a cardboard box, 23 cardboard boxes to a hermetically sealed zinc-plated metal case. Without clips, 20 rounds are packed to a cardboard box, 33 cardboard boxes to a metal case. Two metal cases are packed to a wooden box, making a total of 1,320 rounds without clips, or 920 rounds in clips. When the rounds are packed in clips, the Russian words B ОБОЙМАХ (in clips) are stenciled on the wooden box, which bears no identifying stripe.

CHARACTERISTICS

Caliber	7.62 mm (cal. .30)
Weight of cartridge	16.4 gm (253 gr)
Weight of case	6.8 gm (106 gr)
Weight of bullet	7.95 gm (123 gr)
Weight of propellant	1.62 gm (25 gr)
Weight of core (mild steel w/lead sleeve)	3.56 gm (55 gr)
Length of cartridge	55.9 mm (2.20 in.)
Length of case	38.7 mm (1.52 in.)
Length of bullet	26.6 mm (1.05 in.)

Packaging details for the standard 7.62 x 39mm Ball projectile cartridge Type "PS".

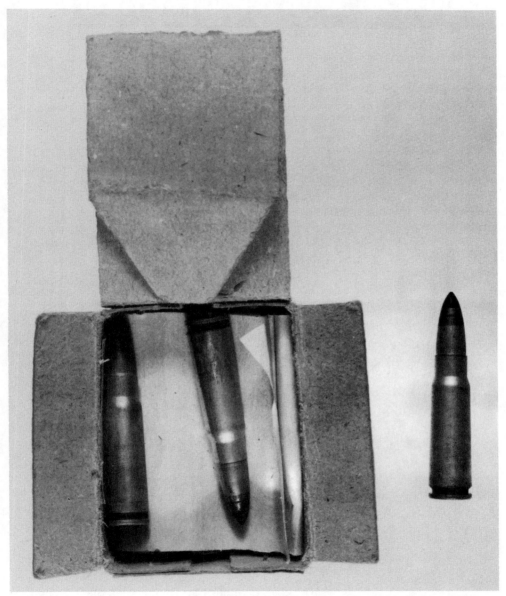

(7.62-мм ПАТРОНЫ обр. 1943 г. С БРОНЕБОЙНО-ЗАЖИГАТЕЛБНОЙ ПУЛЕЙ "БЗ")

A box of twenty 7.62 x 39mm armor-piercing incendiary cartridges with the Type "BZ" bullet. These bullets are marked with a black-over-red paint on the tip.

CARTOUCHE DE 7.62 mm POUR LE FUSIL

Type 56 et mitrailleuse

Tracer bullet
balle traçante

Incendiary bullet
balle incendiaire

Armor-piercing incendiary bullet
balle perforante incendiaire

Ball cartridge
cartouche ordinaire

 SOCIETE INDUSTRIELLE DU NORD DE LA CHINE

A page from a China North Industries catalog illustrating (*from left to right*) the tracer, incendiary, and armor-piercing incendiary projectiles.

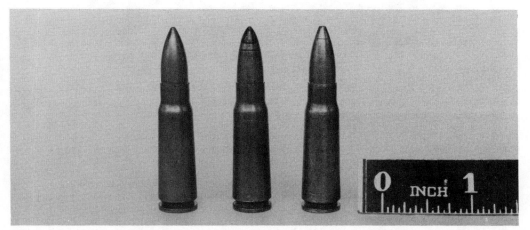

Three different 7.62 x 39mm cartridges. *From left to right:* tracer-type "T45"; armor-piercing incendiary-type "BZ"; and incendiary-type "Z".

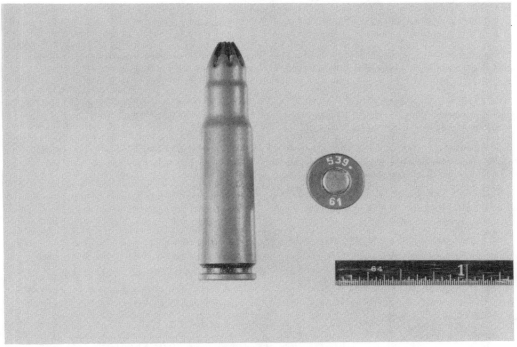

(7.62-ММ ХОЛОСТОЙ ПАТРОН обр. 1943 г.)

The 7.62 x 39mm Soviet M43 blank used for field-training exercises involving blank firing attachments on the AK47/AKM/RPK and RPD.

7.62 mm (7.62x39) Cartridge, Blank M68

FOR SEMI–AUTOMATIC RIFLE M59/66, AUTOMATIC RIFLES M70 AND M70A, LIGHT MACHINE GUN M72 AND SUB–MACHINE GUN KALASHNIKOV

BULLET

Caliber [mm]	7.62
Type	Blank

CARTRIDGE

Length [mm]	49.0
Weight [g]	8.8

Length, cartridge case 49.0 mm
Weight, propelling charge 0.76 g

NOTE: When firing this cartridge from semi–automatic rifle M59/66 a special recoil booster is used. The recoil booster is the same for automatic rifles M70 and M70A and light machine gun.

PACKING

40 rds in carton

48 cartons in sheet metal box

1 sheet metal box with 1920 rds in wooden case

Wooden case dimensions [cm]	58 x 34 x 20	
Case gross weight [kg]	24	
Case volume [m³]	0.036	

SDPR

FEDERAL DIRECTORATE OF SUPPLY AND PROCUREMENT BEOGRAD–YUGOSLAVIA

The 7.62 x 39mm Yugoslavian M68 blank used for field-training exercises involving blank firing attachments on the AK47/AKM/RPK and RPD.

7.62 mm Cartridge, Drill

FOR SEMI–AUTOMATIC RIFLE M59/66, AUTOMATIC RIFLES M70 AND M70A, LIGHT MACHINE GUN M72 AND SUB–MACHINE GUN KALASHNIKOV

7.62 mm drill cartridge is intended for training of soldiers in loading and unloading of arms.

BULLET
Caliber [mm]   7.62
Type   drill

CARTRIDGE
Length [mm]   55.8
Weight [g]   17

TECHNICAL DATA

ELEMENT		MATERIAL	Weight [g]	Length [mm]
BULLET	Jacket	Gilding metal	8.50	34.50
	Core	Lead-antimony		
	Tracer	Tracer composition		
CARTRIDGE CASE		Brass Steel	11.50	51.18
PROPELLING CHARGE		NCD powder	–	–
PERCUSSION PRIMER		Sinoxide	–	–

INERT

PACKING

15 rds in carton

60 cartons in sheet metal box

1 sheet metal box with 900 rds in wooden case

Wooden case dimensions	[cm]	47 x 33 x 17		
Case gross weight	[kg]			27
Case volume	[m³]			0.026

FEDERAL DIRECTORATE OF SUPPLY AND PROCUREMENT BEOGRAD–YUGOSLAVIA

The 7.62 x 39mm Yugoslavian M68 drill cartridge used for field-training exercises.

7.62 mm Cartridge, practice M76

FOR SEMI–AUTOMATIC RIFLE 7.62 mm M59, M59/66 AND M59/66A1, AUTOMATIC RIFLE 7.62 mm M70, M70A, M70AB and M70B LIGHT MACHINE GUN 7.62 mm M72, M72B

BALLISTIC DATA

V_{25} [m/sec]	Bullet range	*Accuracy
700	max 560m	R_s at 100 m < 6 cm

TECHNICAL DATA

ELEMENT		MATERIAL	Weight [g]	Length [mm]
BULLET	Jacket	Gilding metal	1.70	15
	Core	Aluminium		
CARTRIDGE CASE		Brass	7.5	38.5
PROPELLING CHARGE		NC powder	1.7	–
PERCUSSION PRIMER		Fulminate	0.7	2.5

*from heavy barrel

BULLET
Caliber [mm]   7.62
Type   practice

CARTRIDGE
Length [mm]   49
Weight [g]   11.5

PACKING

15 rds in carton

84 cartons in sheet metal box

1 sheet metal box with 1260 rds in wooden case

Wooden case dimensions	[cm]	51 x 31 x 15
Case gross weight	[kg]	21
Case volume	[m³]	0.024

FEDERAL DIRECTORATE OF SUPPLY AND PROCUREMENT
BEOGRAD–YUGOSLAVIA

The 7.62 x 39mm Yugoslavian M68 short-range practice cartridge used for gallery-training exercises.

A comparative photograph of the 5.45 x 39mm; 5.6 x 39mm (hunting); 7.62 x 39mm M43; and US 5.56 x 45mm M193 cartridges.

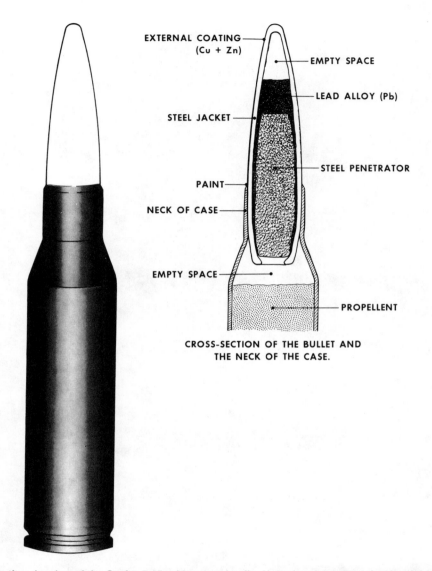

EXTERNAL COATING (Cu + Zn)

EMPTY SPACE

LEAD ALLOY (Pb)

STEEL JACKET

STEEL PENETRATOR

PAINT

NECK OF CASE

EMPTY SPACE

PROPELLENT

CROSS-SECTION OF THE BULLET AND
THE NECK OF THE CASE.

Cross-section drawing of the Soviet 5.45 x 39mm projectile. Note the airspace at the tip of the bullet. As the result of test firings of the 5.45 x 39mm cartridge by Colonel Martin L. Fackler, M.D., at the Wound Ballistics Laboratory, US Army Letterman Institute of Research, Presidio of San Francisco, California, it has been postulated that the rapid deceleration of the bullet upon hitting tissue-replicating gelatin causes the lead element behind the air space to flow forward into the tip of the bullet envelope. If it moves forward asymmetrically, it could unbalance the projectile. Dr. Fackler's experiments are described in Martin L. Fackler, M.D., John S. Surinchak, M.A., John A. Malinowski, B.S., and Robert E. Brown, "Wounding Potential of the Russian AK-74 Assault Rifle," *The Journal of Trauma*, Vol. 24, No. 3 (March, 1984): 263–66, and Martin L. Fackler, M.D., and John A. Malinowski, B.S., "Internal Deformation of the AK-74 Bullet; A Possible Cause for its Erratic Path in Tissue," an eight-page typescript to be published.

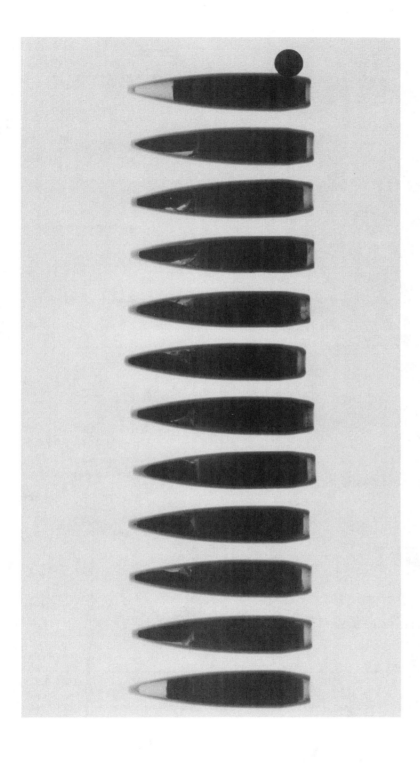

A roentgenogram showing ten consecutive fired bullets (flanked by two unfired ones for comparison) to illustrate that the postulated shift in the portion of the Soviet 5.45mm bullet did occur in every case, and that it produced an unequivocally asymmetrical bullet in each firing. Fackler and his associates suggest that this "internal deformation" of the AK74 bullet is a possible cause for its curved course in tissue. See Martin L. Fackler, M.D., and John A. Malinowski, B.S., "Internal Deformation of the AK-74 Bullet; A Possible Cause for its Erratic Path in Tissue," an eight-page typescript to be published.

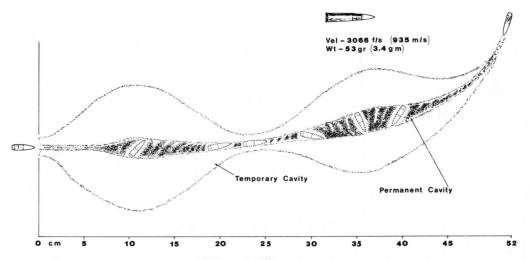

Vel – 3066 f/s (935 m/s)
Wt – 53 gr (3.4 g m)

Temporary Cavity

Permanent Cavity

0 cm   5   10   15   20   25   30   35   40   45   52

The wound profile of the 5.45 x 39mm AK74 bullet when fired in 10 percent ballistic gelatin blocks 20 x 22 x 47cm at four degrees Celsius.

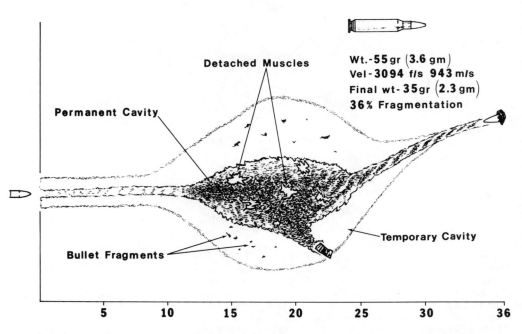

Detached Muscles

Permanent Cavity

Wt.-**55** gr (**3.6** g m)
Vel-**3094** f/s **943** m/s
Final wt-**35** gr (**2.3** g m)
36% Fragmentation

Temporary Cavity

Bullet Fragments

5   10   15   20   25   30   36

The wound profile of the 5.56 x 45mm M16A1 bullet when fired in 10 percent ballistic gelatin blocks 20 x 22 x 47cm at four degrees Celsius.

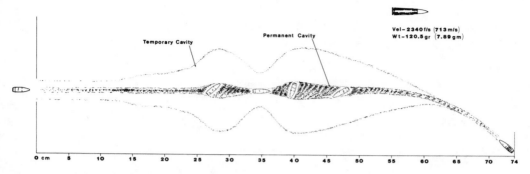

Vel–2340 f/s (713 m/s)
Wt–120.5 gr (7.89 gm)

Temporary Cavity

Permanent Cavity

0 cm   5   10   15   20   25   30   35   40   45   50   55   60   65   70   74

The wound profile of the 7.62 x 39mm AK47 bullet when fired in 10 percent ballistic gelatin blocks 20 x 22 x 47cm at four degrees Celsius.

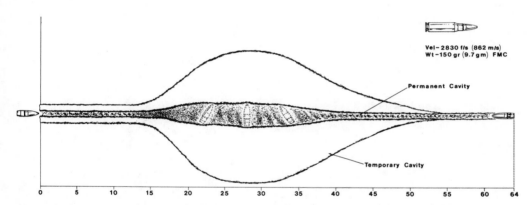

Vel – 2830 f/s (862 m/s)
Wt – 150 gr (9.7 gm) FMC

Permanent Cavity

Temporary Cavity

0   5   10   15   20   25   30   35   40   45   50   55   60   64

The wound profile of the 7.62 x 51mm NATO bullet when fired in 10 percent ballistic gelatin blocks 20 x 22 x 47cm at four degrees Celsius.

The accompanying four "wound profiles" show the respective paths for the bullets fired from the 5.45 x 39mm AK74, the 5.56 x 45mm M16A1, the 7.62 x 39mm AK47, and the 7.62 x 51mm NATO M14. These wound profiles were taken from studies conducted by Colonel Martin L. Fackler and associates at the U.S. Army Letterman Institute of Research. Some of this work is described in Martin L. Fackler, M.D., John S. Surinchak, M.A., John A. Malinowski, B.S., and Robert E. Brown, "Bullet Fragmentation: A Major Cause of Tissue Disruption," *The Journal of Trauma*, Vol. 24, No. 1 (January, 1984): 35–39, and Martin L. Fackler, M.D., and John A. Malinowski, B.S., "The Wound Profile: A Visual Method for Quantifying Gunshot Wounds Components," *The Journal of Trauma*, Vol. 25, No. 6 (June, 1985): in press.

Notes

Introduction: Who Is Kalashnikov?

1. Colonel M. Novikov, "Designer of Submachine Guns," *Soviet Military Review*, English ed., no. 6 (1972): 44.

2. M. Novikov, "Wo ist Kalashnikow," [This is Kalashnikov], *Volksarmee* (January 1968): 9.

3. In addition to Novikov, see D. N. Bolotin, "Talantlivuy konstruktor strelkovogo oruzhiya (K 50-letyiyu so dnya rozhdeniya M. T. Kalashnikova)" [Talented designer of infantry weapons (The 50th anniversary of M. T. Kalashnikov's birthday)], US Army Foreign Science and Technology Center translation J-7899 of an article that appeared in *Voyenniy Vestnik*, no. 11 (1969), 117–19; D. N. Bolotin, "Sovetskoe strelkovoe oruzhie za 50 let" [Fifty years of Soviet infantry weapons] (Leningrad: Izdanie Voenno-Istoricheskogo Muzeya Artillerii, Inzhenernik voisk i voisk Sbyazi [Military Historical Museum of the Artillery, Engineer and Signal Services Press], 1967, translated by the US Army Foreign Science and Technology

Center in 1976 as their document FSTC 1870–75); and *Bol'shaya sovetskaya entsiklopediya* [Great Soviet encyclopedia], XI, s.v. "Mikhail Timofeyevich Kalashnikov," (Moscow, 1972), 195. A more recent version of D. N. Bolotin's study was published in 1983 as *Sovetskoe strelkovoe oruzhie* [Soviet infantry weapons] (Moscow: Voennoe Izdatel'stvo, 1983).

Chapter 1.
Imperial Russian Arms Manufacture: The Patriotic War to World War I, 1812–1917

1. Unless otherwise noted, this chapter is drawn heavily from L. G. Beskrovniy, *Russkaya Armiya i flot v XIX veke: Voenno-ekonomichesky potentsial Rossi* [The Russian army and navy in the 19th century: The military-economic potential of Russia] (Moscow: Izdatel'stvo Nauka, 1973). Chapter 2 is especially significant for this study—"Proizvodstvo i obespechenie voisk strelkovium oruzhiem"

[The manufacture and supply of army infantry weapons], pp. 277–329 — because it is based upon archival materials contained in the *Tsentral'nyi Gosudarstvenniy Voenno-Istorichesky Arkiv SSR* [State Central Military-Historical Archives of the Soviet Union], and contemporary nineteenth-century Russian military journals and publications.

2. A. S. Britkin, *The Craftsmen of Tula; Pioneer Builders of Water-Driven Machinery* (Jerusalem, 1967), 10. This translation of *Pervye tul'skie stroiteli slozhnykh vododeistvuyusshchikh mashin* (Moscow, 1950) was prepared by the Israel Program for Scientific Translations for the Smithsonian Institution and the National Science Foundation.

3. Merritt Roe Smith, *Harpers Ferry and the New Technology: The Challenge of Change* (Ithaca and London: Cornell University Press, 1977); Felicia J. Deyrup, *Arms Making in the Connecticut Valley* (York, Pa.: George Shumway, 1970), 233; and Colonel Lord Cottesloe [T. E. Fremantle], "Notes on the Royal Small Arms Factory, Enfield Lock," (unpublished typescript in the RSAF, Enfield Library).

4. Beskrovniy, *Russkaya armiya i flot*, 277.

5. Ibid., 278–80.

6. Edwin A. Battison, "Eli Whitney and the Milling Machine," *The Smithsonian Journal of History*, I (Summer 1966): 9–34.

7. Britkin, *The Craftsmen of Tula*, 39. See also United Kingdom, *Report from the Select Committee on Small Arms; Together with Proceedings of the Committee, Minutes of Evidence* (Commons), and Appendix (12 May 1854); and Jeannette Mirsky and Allan Nevins, *The World of Eli Whitney* (New York: Macmillan, 1952).

8. Beskrovniy, *Russkaya armiya i flot*, 281–82.

9. Ibid., 283–84. See also United Kingdom, *Report from the Select Committee on Small Arms* (Commons, 1856), 334, which identifies David William Witton, a military gunmaker of London ca. 1830–1870, as one of the contractors to the Russian government in 1831.

10. *Report from the Select Committee on Small Arms* (Commons, 1856): 109, 111, and 116.

11. Beskrovniy, *Russkaya armiya i flot*, 290.

12. C. H. Roads, *The British Soldier's Firearm, 1850–1864* (London: Herbert Jenkins, 1964), 83–91.

13. Beskrovniy, *Russkaya armiya i flot*, 293.

14. W. H. Russell, *The British Expedition to the Crimea* (London: G. Routledge & Co., 1858), 207, 212, and 215; and Roads, *The British Soldier's Firearm*, 40.

15. Beskrovniy, *Russkaya armiya i flot*, 293–94. Beskrovniy cites *"Otchet za trekletnee upravlenie artilleriei General-Fel'dtseikhmeistera"* [Quartermaster-General's report on three years of artillery operations], *Artilleriisky Zhurnal*, no. 1 (1860): 3; and F. I. Surota, *Perevooruzhenie russkoi armii vo vtoroi polovine XIX veke* [Rearmament of the Russian army in the second half of the 19th century] (Leningrad, 1950).

16. Edward Ralph Goldstein, "Military Aspects of Russian Industry: The Defense Industries, 1890–1917," (unpublished doctoral dissertation, Case Western Reserve University, 1971), 47–52; and Beskrovniy, *Russkaya armiya i flot*, 294–96. The latter draws heavily on two works by V. N. Ashurkov, "Russkie oruzheinye zavody vo vtoroi polovine XIX veke" [Russian arms factories in the second half of the 19th century], (doctoral dissertation, Moscow State University, 1962), and "Russkie oruzheinye zavody v 40-50-kh godakh XIX v" [Russian arms factories in the 1840s and 1850s] in *Voprosy voennoi istorii Rossii: XVIII i pervaia polovina XIX vekoy* [Questions in Russian military history: 18th and first half of the 19th centuries] (Moscow: Izdatel'stvo Nauka, 1969).

17. Ashurkov, "Russkie oruzheinye zavody v 40-50-kh godakh XIX v," 267.

18. Goldstein, "Military Aspects of Russian Industry," 52–53; and Beskrovniy, *Russkaya armiya i flot*, 296.

19. V. G. Federov, "Vooruzhenie russkoi armii v XIX stoletii" [Armaments of the Rus-

sian army in the 19th century], *Oruzheiny Sbornik* (1901): 237.

20. *Russkii Invalid* (No. 267, 1873).

21. Beskrovniy, *Russkaya armiya i flot*, 297–98.

22. Ibid., 300.

23. V. G. Federov, *Evolyutsiya strelkovogo oruzhiya* [Evolution of Infantry Weapons], Part I (Moscow: Gosudatstvennoe Voennoe Izdatel'stvo Narkomata Obornyi Soyuza SSR, 1938), 115–16 cites the text of Gorlov's report. See also Richard Irving Wolf, "Arms and Innovation: The United States Army and the Repeating Rifle, 1865–1900," (unpublished doctoral dissertation, Boston University, 1981).

24. Beskrovniy, *Russkaya armiya i flot*, 301; and Federov, *Evolyutsiya strelkovogo oruzhiya*, 105.

25. Beskrovniy, *Russkaya armiya i flot*, 303.

26. F. V. Greene, *The Russian Army and its Campaign in Turkey in 1877–1878* (London: W. H. Allen & Co., ca. 1979), 52.

27. Beskrovniy, *Russkaya armiya i flot*, 303.

28. Federov, *Evolyutsiya strelkovogo oruzhiya*, 116–17.

29. Ibid., 119.

30. Ibid., 121.

31. Birmingham Small Arms Company, "Extracts from the BSA Records for the Period 1861–1900," 27: 35–39, and 43–51. These extracts can be found in the Library of the Royal Small Arms Factory, Enfield Lock.

32. This section is based upon manuscript notes about the history of Greenwood & Batley, which are in the possession of Geoffrey H. Brown, Patley Bridge, Yorkshire, England. This specific quotation is taken from a letter from T. Greenwood to J. H. Burton, 19 March 1871, James Henry Burton Papers, Yale University Archives.

33. Greenwood & Batley MS notes, 7.

34. A. Krell, Tula Weapons Factory, to Messrs Greenwood & Batley, 29 May 1874, Greenwood & Batley Papers, 11/3/53A, Archives Department, Leeds Public Library, Leeds, England.

35. Beskrovniy, *Russkaya armiya i flot*, 314.

36. Claude Feys and Rene Smeets, *Les Revolvers et Les Fusils Nagant* (Paris: Jacques Grancher, 1982), 96.

37. Beskrovniy, *Russkaya armiya i flot*, 313–15.

38. G. N. Danilov, *Rossiya v Mirovoi, 1914–1918* [Russia in the World War, 1914–1918] (Berlin: *"Slove,"* 1924), 246 and 249.

39. A. A. Manikovskyi, *Boevoe snabzhenie russkoi armii v mirovuiu voinu* [The armament and ammunition supply of the Russian army in the first world war], vol. I (Moscow: *Gosudarstvennoe Izdatel'stvo otdel voennoi literatury*, 1930), 119–23.

40. Ibid., 86.

41. Danilov, *Rossiya v Mirovoi, 1914–1918*, 283.

42. Nicholas N. Golovine, *The Russian Army in the World War* (New Haven: Yale University Press, 1931), 128.

43. Manikovskyi, *Boevoe snabzhenie russkoi armii v mirovuiu voinu*, 39.

Chapter 2.
The First Generation of Soviet Infantry Rifles, 1917–1945

Unless otherwise noted this chapter is based on D. N. Bolotin, "Sovetskoe strelkovoe oruzhie za 50 let."

1. Jan M. Meijer, ed., *The Trotsky Papers, 1917–1922* (London et al.: Mouton & Co., 1964), 1:615.

2. Ibid., 651–53.

3. Bolotin, "Sovetskoe strelkovoe oruzhie za 50 let," 96–97.

4. Ibid., 100–103.

5. Julian S. Hatcher, *The Book of the Garand* (Washington: Infantry Journal Press, 1948), 13.

6. D. N. Bolotin, "Development of Soviet Automatic Weapons" (in Russian), *Krasnaya Zvezda* (21 May 1950).

7. Ibid.

8. F. V. Greene, *The Russian Army and its Campaigns in Turkey in 1877-1878* (London: W. H. Allen & Co., ca. 1879), 118-22.

9. D. N. Bolotin, "Stareishy sovetsky oruzheinik (K 75-letiyu so onya rozhdeniya S. G. Simonova)" [A senior Soviet small arms technician (The 75th Anniversary of S. G. Simonov)], *Voenniy Vestnik*, no. 10, (1969): 117.

10. O. Valentinov, "Oruzheinoe delo zapolnyalo vsyu moyu zhizn" [Firearms have been my whole life], *Yuni Tekhnik* (August 1975): 36.

11. Bolotin, "Sovetskoe strelkovoe oruzhie za 50 let," 32-33; and V. G. Federov, *Oruzheinoe delo na grani dvukh epokh: rabot' oruzheinika, 1900-1935* [Weapon work on the boundary between two epochs: A designer's work, 1900-1935] (Moscow: Izdatel'stvo Artilleriskoi Akademii RKKA im Dzershinskogo, 1939), 15-16.

17. Bolotin, "Sovetskoe strelkovoe oruzhie za 50 let," 35.

13. Ibid., 111.

14. Ibid., 119.

15. Federov, *Oruzheinoe delo na grani dvukh epokh*, 106.

16. F. V. Tokarev, "Soviet Small Arms," translation of an article that appeared in *Starshina-Serzhant* (No. 1, 1968), 1-2. FSTC-HT-23-249-68.

17. These quotes are drawn from three articles written by B. L. Vannikov. One appeared in the *Voyenno-Istoricheskiy Zhurnal* (February, 1962), 78-88; and the other two appeared in *Voprosy Istorii* (October, 1968), 116-23 and (January 1969), 122-35. Colonel General of the Engineer-Technical Services (retired), Vannikov was the Commissar of the People's Armament Commissariat during World War II. The quotes used are based upon an unnumbered translation prepared for the US Army Foreign Science and Technology Center.

18. Ibid.

19. Bolotin, "Sovetskoe strelkovoe oruzhie za 50 let," 139-49. Note that the production figures presented here differ from those given previously in *Small Arms of the World*, 11th and 12th editions. As presented here they are believed to be correct.

Chapter 3.
Evolution of the First Kalashnikov Assault Rifles, 1943-1953

Unless otherwise noted this chapter is based on D. N. Bolotin, "Sovetskoe strelkovoe oruzhie za 50 let." For additional comments on weapons production see also B. L. Vannikov. One appeared in the *Voyenno-Istoricheskiy Zhurnal* (February, 1962): 78-88; and the other two appeared in *Voprosy Istorii* (October 1968): 116-23 and (January 1969): 122-35.

1. Vannikov, *Voprosy Istorii* (January 1969): 123-24.

2. Typical of the articles promoting the German origin of the 7.62 x 39mm M43 cartridge are the following: William B. Edwards, "Russia's Secret All-Purpose Cartridge," *Guns* (September, 1956): 17-19, and 70-72; Peter Labbett, "New Range of Russian Small Arms," *Guns Review* (November, 1963): 24-25; George C. Nonte, "The Mysterious AK-47," *Guns* (July 1968): 18-19, and 56-59;, and George C. Nonte, "World's Most Popular Cartridge," *The Rifle Magazine* (January-February, 1971): 24-25, and 52.

3. Hans-Dieter Götz, *Die deutschen Militärgewehre und Maschinenpistole 1871-1945* (Stuttgart: Motorbuch Verlag, 1974), 208.

4. Bolotin, "Sovetskoe strelkovoe oruzhie za 50 let," 180.

5. M. Novikov, "Wo ist Kalashnikow," 9; and D. N. Bolotin, "Talantlivuy konstruktor strelkovogo oruzhiya (K 50-letyiyu so dnya rozhdeniya M. T. Kalashnikova)," 117-19.

6. Novikov, "Wo ist Kalashnikow," 9.

7. Bolotin, "Talantlivuy konstruktor strelkovogo oruzhiya (K 50-letyiyu so dnya rozhdeniya M. T. Kalashnikova)," 117.

8. Colonel M. Novikov, "Designer of Sub-machine Guns," 44.

9. Ibid., 45.

10. Bolotin, "Sovetskoe strelkovoe oruzhie za 50 let," 182–237.

11. Bolotin, "Talantlivuy konstruktor strel-kovogo oruzhiya (K 50-letyiyu so dnya rozhde-niya M. T. Kalashnikova)," 116–17.

12. Bolotin, "Sovetskoe strelkovoe oruzhie za 50 let," 182–237.

13. Novikov, "Designer of Submachine Guns," 45; and Bolotin, "Talantlivuy kon-struktor strelkovogo oruzhiya (K 50-letyiyu so dnya rozhdeniya M. T. Kalashnikova)," 118.

14. Ibid.

15. Ibid.

Chapter 4.
Design Evolution of the Kalashnikov Avtomat, 1948–1959

This chapter is based on examination of Ka-lashnikov assault rifles and data contained in Soviet service manuals for these weapons. For additional comments on weapons production, machine tool technology, and related aspects of the Soviet defense industry, see B. L. Vanni-kov, *Voprosy Istorii* and *Voyenno-Istoricheskiy Zhurnal*.

Index